UNIX System Administrator's Companion

Michael R. Ault

John Wiley & Sons, Inc.
New York • Chichester • Brisbane • Toronto • Singapore

Publisher: Katherine Schowalter

Editor: Robert Elliott

Managing Editor: Susan Curtin

Text Design & Composition: Publishers' Design and Production Services, Inc.

Designations used by companies to distinguish their products are often claimed as trademarks. In all instances where John Wiley & Sons, Inc., is aware of a claim, the product names appear in initial capital or all capital letters. Readers, however, should contact the appropriate companies for more complete information regarding trademarks and registration.

This text is printed on acid-free paper.

This publication is designed to provide accurate and authoritative information in regard to the subject matter covered. It is sold with the understanding that the publisher is not engaged in rendering legal, accounting, or other professional service. If legal advice or other expert assistance is required, the services of a competent professional person should be sought.

Library of Congress Cataloging-in-Publication Data

Ault, Michael R.
    UNIX System Administrator's companion / Michael Ault.
      p. cm.
    Includes Index.
    ISBN 0-474-11144-9 (pbk. : alk. paper)
    1. (Computer file) 2. Operating systems (Computers)
I. Title.
QA76.76.063A89 1995
005.4'3—dc20
                                       95-37073
                                         CIP

Printed in the United States of America

10 9 8 7 6 5 4 3 2 1

This book is dedicated to my wife Susan and my daughters Marie and Michelle. They have had to put up with me missing school functions, not always being there, being late for dinner, grumpy, and basically unfit to live with for the year-plus it has taken to write this book. (My wife says this book should be called *My Wife Hates UNIX*, and I don't blame her.) Without their support, I couldn't have done it.

Contents

Preface

You are probably standing in a bookstore right now thinking, "I've been given a UNIX system to administer and I can't even spell UNIX . . ." Don't despair. This somewhat irreverent and definitely enlightening book will provide many of the answers for which you are searching.

I have attempted to provide an accurate look at UNIX system administration for the beginning administrator, and I hope I have provided some food for thought for experienced administrators as well. Progressing from UNIX history to setup, reconfiguration, files and users, communications, backup and restoration, terminals and peripherals, and auditing and tuning, the *UNIX System Administrator's Companion* is designed to provide all of the information you will need in your job. Security, definitely an issue with UNIX, is covered throughout the text. Many security features are discussed in the chapters on user and network administration, and the methods for monitoring the success or failure of your security plans are covered in the chapter on auditing.

In short, I have tried to pull together the many resources on UNIX and take from each the important aspects of UNIX administration. I hope I have succeeded.

ACKNOWLEDGMENTS

Behind each book on a shelf there are many more people than just those whose names appear as the authors. Behind this book stand family, friends, co-workers, editors, and editorial assistants. I wish I knew of all of the people who have had a hand in its creation all along the way so I could thank them, but it would probably take a book just to do that.

I want to thank Michael L. Thomas for encouraging me and allowing some work to be done "on company time," and for the loan of the AIX workstation upon which I proved out some of the commands and scripts. I also want to thank Bob Elliott at John Wiley & Sons. As my editor he knew when to push and when to keep quiet, as well as when to allow some dates to stretch. Terry Canela at John Wiley also deserves thanks for helping me when no one else could.

I wish to thank Douglas G. Conorich for a very lucid review of the initial manuscript. Finally, I want to thank all of those who have taken the time to write other books on UNIX. If I see far it is only because I stand on the shoulders of giants.

Introduction

If anyone had told me five years ago that I would be writing a book on UNIX system administration, I probably would have laughed out loud. At that time I was a confirmed VAX/VMS bigot who felt that UNIX, while an interesting first-timer's operating system, wasn't friendly or full-featured enough to be a real contender in the computer arena. Well, I was wrong. I freely admit it—UNIX has shown itself to be a survivor. Indeed, it has gone on to become one of the major players in the world of computer operating systems. I was fond of saying that if Henry Ford had given away the Edsel, it would have been the most popular car of its time. While UNIX owes some of its early popularity to having been so freely and widely distributed to universities and research centers, this can't completely explain its phenomenal success.

So, to what does UNIX owe it success? This is a good question and a difficult one to answer. UNIX adherents tend to be fiercely loyal. At first glance one wonders why. UNIX commands, which usually bear no obvious relationship to their function, appear complex and convoluted because of their many options. It is this very complexity that leads to UNIX's flexibility. Once the operator learns a few basic commands and their options, he or she can usually get around in UNIX pretty well. Most of the options to the commands are little used, but when you need them, it is nice to have them around. The other item that makes UNIX seemingly hard to grasp for many is its ability to allow redirection. Redirection permits the output from one command to be ported directly to another, ad infinitum. This can lead to huge commands that do quite complex operations. However, it is also one of UNIX's strengths. One of the frustrations in other operating systems is that the output from one command is usually placed in an intermediate file before it can be operated on by another command. While this leads to better internal documentation of scripts, it also causes frustration due to the added complications in file input and output.

Another factor in UNIX's favor is that for most versions the source code is readily available and is written in C. This means that if you don't like the way a function does its job, you can rebuild it. While this flexibility helps make UNIX easily reconfigurable, it has also led to the many flavors of UNIX that are currently available. In most cases commands operate the same in different UNIX versions. Sometimes they do not. One hopes the new effort toward UNIX standards will help make UNIX more monolithic in nature and function.

In this book I will try to provide both first-time UNIX administrators and old hands with some useful insights into making UNIX administration easier. I am lucky in that I have access to several versions of UNIX and also have access to several UNIX administrators. I will also be using input garnered from the CompuServe UNIX forum (UNIXFORUM), the Sun OS forum (SUNFORUM), and other diverse sources.

So, why did I write this book? It began with a question related to the ORACLE database system and its need for contiguous disk space. It seemed that no one knew how to figure out if the disks on the UNIX system were fragmented (this is covered in the book, by the way), and this then led to the question: Why are answers so hard to find in UNIX documentation? Eventually I found the answer, but it left me with frustration over the cryptic nature of most UNIX references. Either they were written on too high a level or at so low a level as to be useless. I hoped to write this book as a middle ground. I want it to answer the questions that the others either assume you know already or that they answer in such a way that you are left more confused than when you started.

The book will begin with a review of the history of UNIX and go on to discuss the duties and responsibilities of the UNIX system administrator (Chapter 1). The Appendix covers the use of various system editors. For the beginner these chapters are a must read; the old hand can skip right to the chapters in between. In addition, there is a chapter on kernel configuration right at the start. I laid it out this way to proceed logically from installation to configuration to management of various UNIX areas. If you are terrified of even saying the word *kernel*, skip Chapter 2.

You might be asking who I am right now. This is another valid question. I am currently a consultant for MIACO Sqlware, a database systems consulting and training firm. I got my start with UNIX on XENIX on an Altos 586T system back in 1985. I have also used IBM-RISC using AIX, and HP using HP-UX, and I am an expert with the ORACLE database system. Perhaps you've seen my other book, *ORACLE7.0 Administration and Management* or some of my numerous articles.

Well, enough introduction. Let's start our journey into UNIX administration with a little history lesson.

1.1   UNIX HISTORY

In the beginning was MULTICS. MULTICS ran on the General Electric GE645 computer and was used by a joint project of the computer research group of MIT and General Electric (Bell Labs). The major part of the research that involved UNIX was a program called Space Travel, which simulated the movement of the planets in the solar system. The use of the GE645 and MULTICS proved costly, with a per-run cost of $70 (1966 dollars) and numerous runs required per test. In addition, use of MULTICS was reported to be awkward, which led to frustration on the part of the operating staff. In 1969 Bell Labs pulled their support from the MULTICS project.

1.1.1 UNIX Is Born

The removal of support for the MULTICS system and operating budget considerations resulted in the question of how to continue the Space Travel program. The answer was to move it to a smaller, less expensive system. Remember, this was 1969 and there weren't that many small systems or that many (read *none*) small-system multiuser operating systems. This lack of multiuser operating systems led Ken Thompson, Dennis Ritchie, and Rudd Canaday of Bell Labs to develop a cut-down version of MULTICS that would run on a Digital Equipment PDP-7 computer. This original system was jokingly referred to as UNICS (perhaps a reference to how much functionality was cut off of MULTICS? We may never know . . .) It eventually became the first version of UNIX.

1.1.2 UNIX Grows Up

The first version of UNIX on the PDP-7 wasn't user friendly, nor was it very functional. Since it was a pared-down version of MULTICS, many functions were reduced or eliminated altogether. The operating system quickly outgrew the PDP-7 and was moved to a PDP-11/20, and the first real user application was added, a text processor. This first UNIX was functional enough to be chosen over available commercial systems for use by the Bell patent offices in 1971. This first production version took up 16K of core memory, with another 8K taken by the text processing system. By 1972 UNIX had ten users.

At first UNIX wasn't portable. Like all other operating systems it had been written in the host processor's assembler language. Perhaps the most important event in UNIX history happened in 1973 when it was converted to a new language. This new language was written in the late 1960s and reached its first stable configuration in its third major revision. The first revision was language A; the final revision, as you have guessed by now, was C. With this final growing pain, UNIX became portable, and Dennis Ritchie was quoted as saying, "It is easier to port UNIX to a new machine than an application [UNIX-based] to a new operating system."

The second most important milestone in the history of UNIX was the decision by Bell (AT&T) to provide this new portable operating system to universities and research centers free of charge. This led to its explosive growth as it was ported to new systems and new users got "UNIXed." Until that point operating systems had been the purview of the white-coated elite inside [the glass house]. Now came UNIX, an operating system whose source code was readily accessible and thus hackable. This low (or no) cost and hackability caused UNIX to be the operating system of choice for new hardware platforms—after all, why write a brand-new operating system each time when, with minor alterations and a C compiler port, you could use UNIX? The system provided was known as system IV. Later, an update now known as system V was provided at a nominal fee.

The 1970s saw the release and proliferation of microchips, which led to the micro- and minicomputer explosion and the need for operating systems. Release of version 6 of the original UNIX took place in 1975, and licensing to business users (for a substantially higher rate) began. This was also when the Defense Advanced Research Project Agency (DARPA) became interested in UNIX. DARPA hired the University of California, Berkeley, to do further research for them with UNIX. This also led to the Internet, but that is another story. The final release of the original UNIX was Release 7, and it was at this point (in the early 1980s) that the UNIX clones started to be produced.

The Berkeley research–DARPA project resulted in the creation of a new UNIX variant that took advantage of the virtual memory systems being provided by Digital Equipment Corporation (DEC) on its new VAX line of computers. This variant was called BSD (Berkeley Standard Distribution). The research was spearheaded by Bill Joy. The first production release of BSD UNIX was in 1977.

Other sections of the industry weren't silent. In 1980 Microsoft developed a UNIX variant known as XENIX (Released at Version 2.3) that would run on the new ALTOS and other 32-bit machines. By the mid-1980s it was the most popular UNIX clone. Eventually XENIX was sold to Microsoft's competitor, Santa Cruz Operation (SCO). SCO sought and received permission from AT&T to use the UNIX name, and so XENIX became SCO-UNIX. XENIX and its brother (or sister, if you prefer) SCO-UNIX became the two most popular personal computer versions of UNIX in the world.

With the creation and release of the Motorola 68000 series of CPUs, a group of students at Stanford University ported UNIX to these CPUs. Thus was born another variant. These students, headed by Bill Joy, eventually formed the Stanford University Network— SUN for short. Whether or not they sought to use the name UNIX for their version hasn't been reported. They called their clone SunOS, and it was, of course, based on BSD. One of the unique features of the SunOS was that it was the first UNIX variant to allow use of network file systems (NFS).

In 1982 Western Electric (Bell's manufacturing and supply arm) released SYSTEM III, which was actually an improved release of Version 7 of UNIX. The next Bell release was an internal one (SYSTEM IV), and the final Bell release, in 1983, was SYSTEM V. Remember, AT&T owns Bell, which uses Western Electric to distribute its products (my, what a tangled web . . .).

From 1987 to 1988 AT&T acquired a substantial portion of SUN. This led to the cross-breeding of SunOS and Release V, and the new hybrid became SYSTEM V Release 4. In May 1988 the Open System Foundation (OSF) was formed, consisting of players from Apollo, DEC, Groupe Bull, HP, IBM, NixDorf, and Siemens. The foundation's purpose was to promote an open (and standard) version of UNIX called OSF/1. Its members pledged that future releases of their UNIX clones would be OSF/1 compliant. Of course, anyone who follows the computer industry has seen this commitment waver and strength-en depending on industry winds and trends. In response to OSF the AT&T–Sun group formed the UNIX International (UI) group, with Unisys Data General and several other players, to develop a set of standards. Now there are two sets of standards for UNIX, each look-ing to be the one standard. Both have many of the features of BSD 4.3 as a basis.

One ray of hope is that both OSF and UI support the X-Win-dows consortium, X/Open, that is developing and supporting X-Windows standards. This support allows developers to use a standard Graphics User Interface (GUI) tool to develop user inter-faces—a large step towards true open systems.

AT&T's final (perhaps) move in the growth of UNIX was to pass complete ownership of SYSTEM V Release 4 to UNIX System Labo-ratories (USL.) In 1993 USL was bought by Novell. According to USL, the minimum UNIX configuration now stands at a 16 MHz 386SX with a minimum of 4 megabytes of random access memory (RAM) and a 60-megabyte hard drive. For a multiuser environment a mini-mum of 6 megabytes of RAM and an 80- to 120-megabyte hard drive is strongly suggested. A far cry from the original 16K UNICS.

1.2   SYSTEM ADMINISTRATOR DUTIES AND RESPONSIBILITIES

The job of system administrator in any system is probably one of the toughest anyone can undertake. To be totally honest, it is thankless, the hours are long, and generally, unless you are very lucky or very talented, the pay is not good. So, why do people do it? Probably a majority of system administrators got there by inheritance. In most cases of job inheritance the original system administrator, if there was one, quit, got fired, or decided to get a real life selling Volkswa-gens, and the person inheriting the job was just in the wrong place at the wrong time.

What are the requirements for a good system manager/administrator? The person must be a self-starter who thrives on adversity. He or she must be tenacious, refusing to let go of a problem until it is licked. The person must be proactive, which means anticipating any and all possible failures and having procedures and contingencies in place for them. The person must also be highly motivated to do a good job regardless of whether or not he or she is noticed for doing so. Remember, you generally won't be remembered for doing 100 great days of system management in a row, where nothing bad happened to any user and you were proactive enough to see just far enough into the future to avoid the many pitfalls that litter the landscape of system administration. You will, however, be reminded at all group functions and in all evaluations of the one time you weren't able to pull the rabbit out of the hat or the bacon from the fire, or take the moon from the sky and hand it to your users.

In the Navy we had a saying: "One screw-up wipes out all previous atta-boys." Nowhere is this more true than in system administration. You won't be able to make a correct decision. Either your decisions will be too draconian or they will be too lenient; I'm afraid you won't find a middle ground. However, you must be consistent and choose an administration style that suits you and gives you the inner feeling that you are doing your best to serve the interests of the users first and of the system last.

Wait a moment, users first? system last? aren't you supposed to be a system administrator? Yes, you are a system administrator; however, the purpose of the system is to serve the users. Whether they are a small group of secretaries doing word processing or a multimillion-dollar corporation doing key research into the workings of the cosmos, the users are the most important piece of the administration puzzle. You keep them happy, you keep your job. Of course, happy users are happy because the system stays up, the resources are available when required, and files aren't lost. It sounds like keeping the users happy means doing excellent system administration, doesn't it?

The odd thing about system administration is that if you do it correctly, nobody notices. The entire idea behind this book is to make you invisible to the users. Ideally, the system administrator should be able to anticipate needs before they occur, fulfill them without being asked, and continue to maintain the system. This is a tall order, and no one can fill it. If you are lucky, your boss will understand; if not, you are in for a rough ride. If your feelings are easily hurt or you take everything anybody says about your work to heart, get out of system administration. You won't be happy and neither will your users.

Users will ask for everything. You, as system administrator, will have the unpleasant job of explaining why they can't have it. They will want your $20,000 platform to respond like the computer from the fictional star ship *Enterprise*. They will want Cray performance from a Pentium-based (insert whatever the new, hot chip is by the time this gets to print) PC. They will want you to restore a file that they erased—two months ago. Sometimes you will be able to work miracles, and they will be convinced you can walk on water; sometimes you won't. I don't have mention what they will think of you then.

So, why be a system administrator if the working conditions are so poor, the hours are lousy, and everyone will think you are stupid or lazy or both (just because you can't restore their 5-gigabyte disk farm from a crash they caused, and in less than 10 minutes). System administration is its own reward. You must derive satisfaction from solving tough problems, from going were no one has gone before. Besides, you get to play with neat toys and be paid for it.

What are the tasks that a system administrator should perform? What are the duties and responsibilities? They will depend entirely on where you work and how much of the elephant you desire to eat. Some system administrators do nothing but work with the system itself. Some do everything from specifying new equipment to climbing into the ceiling to string cable. I've tried to put together a list of duties; however, this list isn't complete, and I don't have the space to make it so. Besides, I detest lists because eventually someone will use them to justify not doing something and quote me as saying they didn't need to. To them I say in advance: Hogwash, your job is what you (primarily) and your boss (secondarily) make it, no more and no less. Enough said. Here is the list:

■ Adding and removing user accounts.

■ Communicating with users.

■ Backing up and restoring files.

■ Starting up and shutting down the system.

■ Changing the hardware configuration.

■ Communicating with other systems.

■ Security management.

■ Administrating the X-Windows system.

■ Monitoring and tuning.

■ Queue monitoring.

■ Program installation and operating system updates.

■ Monitoring and freeing disk space.

■ Hardware reconfiguration (moving equipment).

■ System troubleshooting (why program X doesn't work today when it worked yesterday).

■ Attending meetings.

■ Data file repair.

■ Script generation for system management functions.

Looks pretty formidable doesn't it? As I said before, your duties may be fewer, or they may be more than are listed here.

There is no room for the weak in system administration. When I did system administration full-time I did whatever was required to get the job done. Sometimes, this got me into trouble (usually because of the outmoded concept of my turf versus your turf. The truth is, it is all our turf—you help me do my job and I'll help you do yours, and anything else is spitting into the wind). Even in situations where "policy" sets rigid lines of responsibility (also read "blame"), it is generally easier to get forgiveness for getting the job done than it is to get permission to step over the boundary. The only thing that can't be forgiven is failing to deliver, no matter whether it was your fault or not. Nothing is worse than talking a good game but not being able to play it.

Let's examine the duties of a system administrator and get a better perspective on what is required for each.

1.2.1 Adding and Removing User Accounts

As you can imagine, this duty involves adding users to the system and, when they no longer require access, removing them as well. Adding users consists of setting the user environment (directories, setup files, profiles), setting the user security (system and file level), and also some amount of training: How do they log on? How do they log off? What printer do they use? How do you use this damn thing?

On the other side of the coin is the removal of users. Do you transfer their files to archive, to another user, or just delete them? What about any special operations they performed—who takes them over? As system administrator you may be responsible for all or (if you are lucky) none of these duties.

1.2.2 Communicating with Users

Yes, I know. It's a dirty job but someone has to do it. Someone has to tell the users the system won't be available, someone has to tell user X that his runaway process has to be terminated or user Y that her hogging of disk space with redundant files isn't appreciated.

That someone is you. With system tools such as "mail," "talk," and "wall," as well as startup messaging using /user/motd, you will be responsible for communicating with your users.

One thing to remember is that communication is never one way, it has to go two ways to be truly effective. Establish a communication path with your users. Let them know that you appreciate being notified when the system acts oddly (to them), get them used to writing you a note with any error messages they encounter. These pesky users can be your most valuable resource when you are troubleshooting problems. Nothing is more frustrating than hearing "Oh, that? It's been happening for a couple of days . . ."

1.2.3 Backing up and Restoring Files

This is probably one of the more tedious, and most important, duties of the system administrator. Your ability to recover a crashed system is only as good as your last backup. With some installations this may be a simple tar backup to a single tape; in others it may be a several-hour babysitting job while the multigigabyte disk farm is backed up. Nothing is more important to your long-term job picture than the ability to recover the system.

You don't want to take the time to keep a current backup? Better have your resumé updated. Backups aren't just important for crash recovery; they also enable you to fix your, and your users', OOPS. OOPS are situations where you suffer cerebral flatulence. There is no better way to put it I'm afraid. What else do you call doing a wildcard delete on your top-level directory? It happens, and it will happen to you.

My bacon has been saved by having a good backup. Probably at least once during the writing of this book I'll lose an entire chapter because of a cerebral incident of the aforementioned type. If I follow my own advice, I'll pull my backup out and at least get some of the chapter back.

Backup and recovery are more than just physical acts. A good system administrator will develop policies and procedures that give detailed instructions for each type of anticipated system crash, from loss of a single disk to complete site loss. Remember, crashes won't happen while you are there; they will happen while you are on the first vacation you've had in five years. It is much easier to guide a panicking assistant through a detailed procedure than to attempt to tell him or her every little step.

You must also test your backup and recovery procedures. A wonderful bound set of procedures with gilt edges, neatly lined up in a row on a shelf over the system administrator's desk, is worthless if it hasn't been tested. Backup and recovery procedures should be living documents that grow and change as your system does. This isn't a one-time deal. I worked at a shop once that had procedures for everything, but nobody read them. In reality they were quite useless because they hadn't been revised since the time they were originally written for a computer system that had been replaced a year before. Documentation is the programmer's and system administrator's bane—a necessary evil that can, and will, save your life.

1.2.4   Starting up and Shutting down the System

I was once called down to the laboratory of a nuclear power plant where I worked because the computer system had stopped working. I attempted a startup and then attempted a shutdown, but nothing happened. I did a standalone boot and discovered that several key files had become corrupted.

After fixing the problem I did a little investigation into its cause. It turned out that the users had bought the system and, without reading a manual and flying completely by the seat of their pants, had been operating it for several weeks. I asked about their startup and shutdown routines. Their answer was to shrug and show me the on–off switch. Yes, you experienced managers have permission to shudder. This wasn't even a UNIX machine; in fact, it was a VAX-VMS computer that, generally speaking, is more tolerant of such abuse than most (read *all*) UNIX computers.

My point is that you must have well-documented startup and shutdown procedures. UNIX must be started and shut down properly. On large installations the file system rebuilds required by a bad shutdown can cost you hours of time. A bad startup will generally result in a poorly operating system, if it functions at all.

1.2.5 Changing the Hardware Configuration

This should be an infrequent duty. Once you reach a stable configuration you should leave it alone. With the new tools available on most UNIX systems, configuring a new terminal, printer, or other piece of hardware into the system is much less tedious than when you had to do everything by hand. However, just because reconfiguration is an infrequent task, this doesn't mean you can neglect your hardware. You should have good diagrams showing how each of your systems is configured and how it fits into the general scheme of things. Hardware reconfiguration may also involve upgrades to CPUs, memory, or peripheral interfaces. You should schedule these events well in advance and warn users (remember the section on user communications?). Each proposed change should be accomplished in a timely manner and should be thoroughly tested. It is very embarrassing to brag about how a new piece of gear is going to be so wonderful, only to have it fail in front of the big brass because you didn't test it properly.

1.2.6 Communicating with Other Systems

In the parlance of the computer world this is called "Network Management." If you are lucky, you have a person called the network manager who handles this. If you are with a small shop, look in the mirror because this person is most likely you. Generally speaking, if you do networking under UNIX, you do it in TCP/IP network protocol. The systems you communicate with may be down the hall—or somewhere in the Antarctic. The actual physical location of the equipment isn't important to your users. The only thing that matters to them is whether or not they can get data file X from node Y for the report that was due yesterday. If they can't, it is your fault (regardless of the fact that the biggest solar flare ever recorded just fried the communication satellite and the network rerouted through Auckland via Cleveland, London, and Houston). It is strongly suggested that you become familiar with whatever flavor of TCP/IP your system is using. I'm afraid that there are as many different implementations of TCP/IP as there are of UNIX—probably more—and they are just enough alike that the differences will kill you.

You will also be responsible for maintaining the IP address network. Each piece of your network will have an IP address. If you give the same address to two different pieces of equipment, the odds are that neither will function. Keep a detailed network map with addresses and equipment types. Keeping track of who uses the equipment is also valuable. It is better to eject Smith the clerk from the network than Smith the vice president of information services.

This part of system administration may also find you crawling into cable runs, snaking under raised floors, and carefully negotiating your way through dropped ceiling warrens. You should also be able to discourse at the drop of a hat on the benefits of optical versus coax, the best router to use for long versus short hauls, and so on. And you will have to explain, probably several times, why you can't switch to the latest protocol/router/cable type to come along, to every executive who has just read about it.

1.2.7 Security Management

Security administration is the biggest headache that you will experience in the entire system administration game. In this area you will never be able to satisfy all of your users, so don't try. You will run into executives who want to be able to look at "everything" all of the time and office workers who get cold sweats every time someone mentions computers. You have to gently steer the executives away from what they want; the office workers you have to force to use the system. You must have policies and procedures that implement your security plan. Make them big enough and they are very handy for swatting recalcitrant users, and terminals, with.

A good security plan is worth its weight in gold. It delineates who gets what access, how they can get more access, and how to give it to them. A security plan should also tell how to monitor for security breaches and what should be done to prevent them. Security is more than locking the doors to the computer room.

Unfortunately, UNIX isn't the most secure system to come down the pike. You must be the first line of defense. You need to understand usage patterns for the users. You need to be alert for unusual usage and monitor for attempts at break-ins, both external (a modem line that tried to log in for three hours) and internal (file surfing by inquisitive employees). If the tools don't exist (usually the case), you will have to improvise and create your own. You have to understand your system so that you can tell when it is being threatened.

1.2.8   Administrating the X-Windows System

As a user, I love the X-Windows system. As an administrator, I find it can be a pain. X-Windows is a standard graphic user interface (GUI) package. The entire X-Windows movement was generated from such platforms as the Macintosh from Apple. The point-and-click icon environment is X-Windows', and singlehandedly it has brought computing into the lives of thousands of people who thought they could never use computers. This is the up side. The down side is that X-Windows systems tend to be resource hogs unless they are closely monitored and administered. This task falls to you, the system administrator. With character-mode terminals, you specified baud rate, parity, stop bits, and so on, to configure the system. In X-Windows an entire layer of additional drivers and interfaces is required that you have to administer (can you say fonts? Sure ya can . . .) X-Windows is the wave of the future. The days of the VT100 are over.

Why is X-Windows so popular? It provides the programmer with a standard methodology for interacting with the user in his or her program. If the system is X-Windows-compliant, the developer knows he or she can write an application using standard X-Windows calls, and the system will handle the rest. Of course, you need to be aware of what drivers, font libraries, and interfaces your system has to have (generally, several sets depending on the types of X-Windows-compatible terminals you have). Welcome to the future.

1.2.9   Monitoring and Tuning

I don't care what machine you are on (with the possible exception of Macintosh), you have to tune the environment for your operating system. On DOS you tune shared memory, extended memory, buffers, and so on. On VMS there are literally dozens of parameters used to tune the system for proper performance. UNIX is no exception. As system administrator, you must monitor the system performance and adjust (tune) the kernel parameters to ensure optimal efficiency. Thus you must become proficient at monitoring and tuning. As you add more users and applications to your system, the entire operating substrate has to be adjusted. You will have to allocate more buffer space, increase shared memory, increase semaphores, alter the number of files allowed to be open by one process—the list goes on and on. This is one of the tasks that no one will notice if you do it right but that everyone will notice if you do it wrong.

UNIX systems aren't static entities; they are constantly growing and changing. As system administrator, you are the midwife to this process. You must ensure that there is order to this change and that it is accomplished via the monitoring and tuning aspects of your job.

1.2.10   Queue Monitoring

Queue: A line in which one waits for something. Under UNIX you have printer queues, where print jobs wait to be serviced by the printer, and batch queues, where jobs wait to be executed. It will fall on your shoulders, as system administrator, to monitor and administer these queues. You need to monitor for stalled or stopped queues (What do you mean, I can't print out an executable image file?). You must also be alert to when new queues are needed and when old queues can be removed. Currently batch queues aren't implemented in many UNIX environments; instead, the cron process and cron job handle what are traditionally known as batch processes. Some flavors provide limited batching through use of the **at** and **batch** commands, and AIX offers some limited batch queue processing. Therefore, the major part of queue monitoring is watching print queues.

1.2.11   Program Installation and Operating System Updates

This is going to be your major headache. In the current software environment it seems that just as the latest release of an application becomes stable, a new and improved version is released. Unfortunately, this new and improved version generally has new and improved bugs as well. As system administrator, you must install this new and improved software. If you have a test environment, this job will be easier to bear since if a new installation fails, it doesn't affect your production installation. Unfortunately, most of us don't have that luxury and we have to cross our fingers, install, and pray that we can catch and correct any problems. The only solution is to test, test, and test again before turning over new and improved versions of applications and operating systems to users.

Read your documentation. I realize most of it is about as exciting as watching paint dry, but it might just prevent errors during installation. When I worked as a product support engineer more than half of the service calls, and charges, could have been avoided had the users read the manuals. Look for readme files on install media. Read the readmes first because they can save a lot of headaches. Always cut a backup before doing an upgrade install—it gives you a fallback point.

1.2.12 Monitoring and Freeing Disk Space

One rule is that users never clean up after themselves. Luckily, UNIX does this for them by restricting the number of file versions (usually to one). Under VMS, unless the system administrator specifically sets a file version limit, there is none. One time I purged over one hundred versions of a file from a user's directory. However, even though this usually isn't a problem on UNIX, you do have to watch for it. Editors and other file-handling programs sometimes leave log and journal files strewn about your disk farm. Users may need that 1-megabyte file now, but six months from now it is so much trash. Don't depend on them to clean it out.

UNIX is also a dynamic disk system. This means that as files expand their pieces aren't contiguous but are placed wherever there is room. While this is wonderful for the user, it can result in fragmentation of disk resources. This fragmentation has to be monitored for and corrected if it becomes excessive. You also need to watch for disk hogs. Disk hogs waste disk space because they just can't bear to part with old files—you never know when you might need those six-month old mail files . . .

1.2.13 Hardware Reconfiguration (Moving Equipment)

I wish I had a dollar for every piece of equipment I have lugged from point A to point B. Perhaps heavy lifting wasn't part of the job description, but it had to be done. You, too, will know this joy. Sometimes it's wait for three days or do it yourself. I usually choose to do it myself. In some companies unions will prohibit you from doing equipment moves. I know of one shop where a system manager was nearly fired for picking up a screwdriver (no, this time it wasn't me, but it could have been). If you work in one of these shops, it's a mixed blessing I guess. You may be spared physical labor, but you are at the mercy of folks who don't always operate on your timetable.

Moving equipment, cables, monitors, and printers can be part of the job. Remember, lift with your legs, not your back. Better yet, lift with junior personnel.

1.2.14 System Troubleshooting (Why doesn't program X work today when it worked yesterday?)

This duty is almost as much trouble as doing installs and upgrades. A user moves a critical file or changes a protection, and suddenly an application stops working; a piece of hardware is reconfigured, and now all it will display or print is Japanese; a print queue keeps stopping for no apparent reason. You can come up with an almost endless list of examples. This is the true test of a system administrator's mettle. If you can hone your troubleshooting skills to a fine edge, you won't have any problems. I generally follow this basic set of guides. For hardware:

1. Check power supplies (is it plugged in, turned on).

2. Check network connections (check both ends and anything in between).

3. Check the equipment (bad board, broken connector, a switch up when it should be down, etc.).

4. Check the configuration.

For software:

1. Who used it last?
2. What did they change?
3. What has changed between the last successful run and now?
4. Has anyone tampered with privileges or protections?
5. Can root run it (if so, it is a protection problem)?

And never overlook operator or user stupidity.

1.2.15   Attending Meetings

Management by meeting is probably the least productive method I can think of. "Something is wrong . . . oh, let's have a meeting!" "Meetings will continue until productivity improves." "The project is behind so let's have daily status meetings." "Sorry, can't fix that, I've got to prepare for a meeting." Tell me when to stop. I believe that the efficiency of management is directly related to its ability to communicate without the use of meetings. If you must have a meeting, have an agenda, stick to it, and when you've covered all of it, finish the meeting. Document action items and take good notes. After the meeting send out a list of action items with names responsible and delivery dates.

Meetings are a necessary evil; whenever possible avoid them. If you can't, the best meeting is a short one. Since you are the technical expert on the system (you can stop cringing), you will be called upon to attend numerous meetings. You will have to be ready to explain to computer illiterates why you can't give them full multimedia capabilities at a moment's notice. Remember to breath deeply, think each answer through, and never promise anything you haven't already delivered.

1.2.16 Data File Repair

Users and data don't mix. I can say without fear of contradiction that you will have to repair a corrupted data file sometime in your career—probably several times, if not several times this week. Users discover break keys, Ctl-C, and many other ways of being stupid ("Well, it didn't look like anything was happening, so I shut off my terminal . . .") All of these can result in corrupted files that you will have to repair if you can. I wish I could tell you a tried and true method, but each case will be different. Good luck.

1.2.17 Script Generation for System Management Functions

If you do this task right, it will make the rest of your job much easier. Scripts can be used to automate repetitive tasks so that they are done uniformly and correctly each time. You need to become proficient in scripting. Do the task several times manually; then automate it. Test scripts thoroughly. There is nothing as bad as doing something wrong quicker. Once you build a toolset (hopefully with the help of this book), system administration should be much easier.

1.3 SYSTEM ADMINISTRATOR GOALS

What should your goals be as a UNIX system administrator? As a system administrator, you answer to the users. I know, on your admin chart it shows you reporting to some manager or director, but remember, the purpose of management is to carry water to the team. Your managers should supply you with the tools and the horsepower to provide services to your users. Responsibility without authority is useless. Given the above truths, your goals should revolve around keeping the users happy. For instance:

1. I will keep the UNIX systems up and available for use.

2. I will ensure that, should there be a system crash, I can restore the system to a viable state in as short a time as possible.

3. I will minimize the impact on the users of all system upgrades and modifications.

4. I will respond to user requests in a way that is both proper and timely.

5. When downtime is required, I will notify users in advance.

6. I will maintain security at an appropriate level to ensure that business needs are balanced against ease of user access to the system.

These are just a few example goals. Your list may be longer than this, or it may be much shorter. If you only follow the number-one goal listed above, you will be doing the others (more or less.)

UNIX Kernel Reconfiguration

2

This chapter deals with the heart of any UNIX system, the kernel. Like the kernel of a seed, the UNIX kernel is the center of the system, from which everything is controlled. Just as without the kernel the seed will not grow and develop, without the UNIX kernel the system will not function. In view of its importance, you need to be very careful when doing any work that affects the kernel. Since kernel configuration and reconfiguration directly alter the very heart of your UNIX system, review all pertinent documents before attempting it. This chapter isn't intended to be the last word on kernel configuration; it is only intended to give you an overview of the files and processes involved for the major releases of the UNIX software. As with everything else associated with this standard operating system, there are numerous differences between various releases and flavors.

Essentially, kernel reconfiguration is a three-step process:

1. Alter the kernel configuration file or parameters.
2. Relink the kernel using **conf**, **make**, and other UNIX commands.
3. Install and test the kernel.

How these three steps (sometimes broken into more) are implemented depends on the version of UNIX you are maintaining. Some versions, such as HP-UX and AIX, provide automated interfaces that take a majority of the pain out of this operation (SAM and SMIT), while others' reconfiguration procedures have remained virtually unchanged since their original release.

For most UNIX releases and installations, the default setup is enough, and sometimes too much. The smaller you can make your kernel file, the better off you are, especially in memory-poor systems. The kernel is loaded into real memory whenever the system is booted. As you will recall if you read Chapter 1, one of the first items on startup is to load the kernel into memory. This memory-resident executable and its tables stay loaded until shutdown.

Even though the kernel exists in memory, a **ps** command won't show it; it exists outside the normal user environment. The kernel directs all traffic and operations throughout the system. Generally speaking, it consists of the executable section that contains all code for memory-resident commands, code for all loaded drivers, and the kernel-specific tables (buffers) that contain system information used by the kernel in its functions.

Unless you are using some of the home-grown UNIX clones such as LINUX, you probably will have only the UNIX kernel object modules. This means that you can't alter the core of the kernel—that part that is actually UNIX—but only add drivers on top of it and bundle in parameters that control the size of its internal tables. This object-code-only distribution is required because of the way ATT license agreements work. In almost all cases you are required to have an ATT source code license before you can obtain the source code for any version of UNIX.

As with most other software packages, you shouldn't apply "wild" patches to your kernel. A wild patch is one not provided by the supplier of your kernel code—for example, an open download off of a user-group bulletin board. Some wild patches may be quite benign, or even very useful, but all it takes is one bad patch to ruin your whole day.

In this section we will discuss SVR4, BSD, and HP-UX kernel reconfiguration.

2.1   SYSTEM V RELEASE 4 (SVR4) KERNEL RECONFIGURATION

For most generic installs of SVR4 you will have to reconfigure the kernel to include system-specific drivers. Unfortunately, even though your kernel may state that it is SVR4, depending on the platform this procedure will probably differ. Therefore, check your system documentation for the proper procedure. For most SVR4 implementations the procedure for reconfiguring the kernel breaks into five parts:

1. Edit the kernel Makefile.
2. Create or modify a description file.
3. Run config to create the compile code from the description file.
4. Use make to build the new kernel.
5. Install and test the new kernel.

In the next sections we will take a look at what is required in each of these steps. Before you start, make a hard copy and backup copy of the existing description and Makefiles. This gives you a fallback position should you make a mistake.

2.1.1 Editing the SVR4 Makefile

The Makefile for the current kernel should be located in either /usr/src/uts/cf or /usr/src/uts/machine/cf, where the machine specification is the current type of computer platform upon which the kernel is running. Use the **cd** command to move your work directory to this location. There should be a file called Makefile in this directory, which is the file to edit. Generally, there are several variables in this file that can (but probably shouldn't) be altered. These are

SYS   The hostname of the machine you are running on.

NODE   The uucp name of the machine (it should be same as hostname unless you just like to be obtuse).

REL   The release number of the operating system. You shouldn't change this.

VER   The version of the kernel. This should be reset to the date on which you rebuild the kernel or to something that will uniquely identify this kernel to you.

MACH   The hardware name of your machine. This shouldn't be altered.

Once the Makefile is altered, proceed to editing the description file.

2.1.2 Modifying the SVR4 Description File

Unfortunately, there is no standard naming convention for the description file. It may be named for the creator, the machine it is supposed to reside on, or simply UNIX or VMUNIX. The name will probably be in uppercase; look around the configuration directory and you will probably find it. If there is no file to be found, you can create one based on the installed kernel by using the **sysdef** command. Check your man pages for the exact syntax of this command. I suggest calling your new description file whatever your system name is, or name it for the changes added so that it tells you why the kernel was created. For example, if you reconfigure a kernel to add a tape drive, you might call the new description file TAUNIX or TPUNIX. Remember, simpler is better. You should document the name you use in the system log.

The first section of the description file will contain the device driver specifications. Your new device may include a file section to be included here, or you may have to glean the required information from the system documentation. In any case, the general format for these device lines is

```
devname vector address bus number nexus
```

where

> **devname** is the name of the device as it appears in the **/etc/master** device table.
>
> **vector** is the octal address of the device's interrupt vector.
>
> **address** is the octal address of the device.
>
> **bus** is the priority or bus request level for the device.
>
> **number** is the number of devices connected to the controller.
>
> **nexus** is the number of the unibus adapter connected to the device.

The first four parameters are required for all systems. The last two are generally used only on DEC/VAX systems. If **nexus** is present, both **nexus** and **number** must be specified. If they are not specified, both will default on VAX systems. The other parameters can be specified with a question mark (?) and the system will interrogate the controller on startup. The line for an rp06 disk controller with three drives will look like:

```
rp06      254     776700 5       3
```

The rest of the description file contains parameters that describe the internal kernel specifications. Examples of these parameters follow.

root   This specifies the root file system device, for example: **root**   **rp06**   **0**.

pipe   This specifies the location for the interprocess communications channel file system.

swap   This specifies the location for the system swap areas. The format of this argument is

```
swap devname minor_dev_num swaplow numswap
```

where

devname is the disk device where the swap partition should reside.

minor_dev_num is the minor device number for the disk drive to be used.

swaplow is the block where the swap section should start (for example, if you have a 15,000-block file system and want the last 5,000 blocks as a swap area, **swaplow** is 10,000).

numswap is the number of blocks for the swap area (using the same example, this is 5,000).

dump is the directory where any dump files of the kernel's address space should be placed.

procs is the number of process slots. As a base, there should be 25 slots for the system and an additional 5 for each interactive user. If your system uses X-Windows, there may be more allocated.

maxproc is the maximum number of processes each user may run concurrently, usually set between four and eight.

file is the maximum number of files that can be opened at one time. If this is set too low, there won't be enough space set up in the kernel's internal tables and an attempt to open a file will result in a "no file" error.

There may be additional parameters in your configuration file. If you aren't sure what they are for, check your system documentation or man pages. Once your description file is altered, you can run the conf process against it.

2.1.3   Running the conf Process for SVR4

The conf process reads your description file, gathers the appropriate device drivers and configuration files, and creates two or more object modules. These object modules are then used by the make process to actually create the kernel. To run conf, you should be in the appropriate configuration directory and the description file should also be there. If your configuration file is called TPUNIX, the command to run the conf process is

```
$ /etc/conf TPUNIX >&CONFERR
```

If you get any errors, you will need to correct them before proceeding. Errors will be spooled into the CONFERR file for your review. Once you get a clean conf run, you can then execute make on the resultant files and build your kernel.

2.1.4   Running the make Process for SVR4

Like the conf process, the make process requires you to be residing in the configuration directory before you can run it. If for some reason you left the directory after the conf process, return there with the **cd** command. The Makefile has been updated and modified by the conf process. The format for using the make process is

```
$make VER=ver >& MAKEERRS
```

if you want to override the **VER** specification in the Makefile; if not, this format should be used:

```
$make >$ MAKEERRS
```

You must check the MAKEERRS file before ascertaining if errors occurred. Generally, errors at this stage will be due to devices not yet specified that other devices may depend upon. The make process will create a SYSVER executable file; this file is the new kernel.

The make process may take several minutes to run and probably won't tell you what is going on. Be patient. While the actual UNIX code is quite small, the drives layered on top of it may take a while to load and link.

Once you get a clean make process, you are ready to install and test the new kernel.

2.1.5   Installation and Testing of the New SVR4 Kernel

In most cases, a clean make process means that the kernel will be bootable; however, after that all bets are off. In view of this unpredictability of results, I suggest that you make a copy of the existing kernel as a fallback.

To test the kernel, consult your documentation to see how to boot from an alternate kernel file. Once you have the directions at hand, simply boot from the SYSVER file in the configuration directory.

Testing the New Kernel   Testing can be as simple as checking that a new device such as a disk or tape is usable, or as complex as a full system ring-out. I suggest modifying the kernel in a stepwise fashion and testing each change as you proceed. This allows an easier fallback if trouble occurs. If you decide to do all the changes in one fell swoop, testing is made more difficult because you must back out the changes one at a time until you discover the problem. Why not start out in a more logical way and do the changes incrementally instead of all at once? Once the kernel functions to your expectations, you are ready to replace the existing kernel file.

Installing the New Kernel Most systems will use a link file to point to the location of the actual kernel. The actual kernel may reside in the / directory as the unix file, or this unix file may be a link pointing to the actual location. To see if the unix file is a link, use the **ls -l** command to show the linked file location if it exists. The size of the file is also a dead giveaway. A mere link file will be much smaller than an actual kernel.

If the /unix file is just a link file, then all you must do is remove the existing link file and recreate it pointing to the new kernel executable. This is accomplished via the commands (using our TPUNIX kernel file)

```
$ rm /unix
$ ln -s /usr/src/uts/cf/SYSVER /unix
```

If, instead, the /unix file is the actual kernel file, then copy or move the existing file and replace it with the new file:

```
$mv /unix /oldunix
$mv /usr/src/uts/cf/SYSVER /unix
```

Once the new kernel is in place, be sure to notify users via the motd file that there is a new UNIX kernel installed and that they should notify you of any problems that result. Once the kernel is operating, document the description file by using comment lines. Comment lines are preceded by an asterisk (*). Err on the side of overexplanation in your documentation efforts. Will you remember every nuance of the process a year from now? I guarantee that your replacement won't should you decide to seek greener pastures, like selling Volkswagens.

2.2   RECONFIGURATION OF THE BSD KERNEL

In some ways the BSD kernel is easier to configure than the SVR4 kernel. The BSD kernel depends on one file for the arguments it uses to build the kernel. This file will usually reside in the SYS top-level directory under a subdirectory named for the kernel. BSD usually provides a GENERIC example configuration file that configures into the kernel every device known to the BSD world. For most situations you will alter a copy of the GENERIC file to remove the drivers that you don't need.

The SYS top-level directory contains numerous subdirectories holding perhaps hundreds of different files used to configure the kernel. You usually won't get involved with these files or at most will have to install a new subdirectory containing the drivers for a new type of device (perhaps a holographic memory device? Fascinating!) or update an existing driver to a newer version. In any case, these operations will be delineated by a procedure supplied for the device installation. If not, look to the SYS directory and its subs for device-specific drivers.

The procedure for reconfiguring the BSD kernel is as follows.

1. If needed, perform a hardware audit (include internal hardware) to determine actual driver requirements.

2. Copy and alter the GENERIC or existing configuration file.

3. Create a new subdirectory under SYS that is named for the new kernel, and copy the new configuration file into it. Run the **config** command on the new kernel configuration file.

4. Run the **make depend** command on the new kernel Makefile (this step was probably already done by the **conf** command).

5. Run the make process on the new kernel.

6. Test and install the new kernel.

The next few sections discuss these steps.

2.2.1   Performing a Hardware Audit

This step is required only if you are doing an initial configuration to reduce the size of the kernel. In most BSD implementations the GENERIC configuration is used to build the initial kernel, which, while it can probably handle any device you throw at it, is also a memory hog. After you get a new system up and operating it is advisable to do an audit of all devices that the system needs (be sure to look internally; some are even on the CPU board!) and then edit out the unneeded ones from the configuration file and rebuild it. If you are already sure that the kernel has been optimized for your configuration and are just adding a new device or modifying BSD kernel setup parameters, skip this step.

2.2.2   Modifying the BSD Configuration File

The configuration file has a few conventions that most if not all BSD implementations will follow:

■ "#" denotes a comment line.

■ Blank lines are ignored.

■ A tab at the start of a line denotes a continuation line.

■ Keywords are surrounded by whitespace.

- Other than with keywords and beginnings of lines, all other spaces and tabs are ignored.

- There is one keyword per line.

- Arguments are generally one per line. If multiple arguments are specified for the keyword in your documentation, they will be a comma-separated list.

- Arguments may be decimal, octal, or hexadecimal. Octal arguments are preceded by a leading zero; hexadecimal arguments, by a leading "zero-x" ("0x").

- If an argument contains both text and numbers, it must be surrounded by double quotes.

The format of a keyword in a configuration file is

```
keyword    argument(,argument...)
```

Some examples of keywords are shown in Figure 2.1.

The keyword maxusers is of particular importance because it is used to calculate the size of several of the internal kernel tables. Figure 2.2 shows how maxusers is used in calculating file sizes.

The maxusers calculations for your system are documented in the SYS/conf/param.c file. To find your maximum sizes, use the **pstat -T** command.

The options keyword can have hundreds of arguments depending upon the specific BSD implementation you have. Check your documentation for a complete list. Some of the major arguments are shown in Figure 2.3.

The config keyword specifies the location of the root partition, the crash dump area, and the swapping/paging areas on the system disks. Since the system at startup has no idea where these items exist, this information is linked into the kernel. Only swap areas that have been configured into the kernel in this fashion can be used. This keyword can be specified several times in the same configura-

Keyword	Argument	Meaning
machine	vax, sun, etc.	The machine type the kernel is for.
cpu	numeric or text	The cpu type for the kernel.
ident	numeric or text	The unique identifier for this version.
timezone	numeric or text	The time zone as specified relative to GMT.
maxusers	numeric	The maximum number of expected users (interactive users, not a hard limit); sets up internal file sizes.
options	numeric or text	Used to set compilation options.
config	text	Location of root and swap areas.
controllers	text	Specifies controller file.
disk	text	Specifies disk controller file.
tape	text	Specifies tape controller file.
device	text	Declares devices without controllers.
pseudo-devices	text	Declares pseudo-devices.

FIGURE 2.1 Keywords used in the BSD configuration file.

File Variable	Definition
Maximum number of processes	20+(8*MAXUSERS)
Maximum number of active shared texts	36+MAXUSERS
Maximum number of active files	68+(9*MAXUSERS)
Number of system file table entries	32+((8/5)*(36+(9*MAXUSERS)))
Number of callout structures	36+(8*MAXUSERS)
Number of clist structures	60+(12*MAXUSERS)
Number of quota structures	3+((9/7)*MAXUSERS)
System page table size (in pages)	20+MAXUSERS

FIGURE 2.2 How maxusers is used to calculate internal table sizes.

Argument	Use
QUOTA	Sets up code for handling user disk quotas.
MAXDSIZE	Sets the maximum data area size for users; an argument expressed as a double quoted equation—"64*1024*1024"—would set limit to 64 meg.
MAXTSIZE	Sets up the maximum text working area. Can be up to MAXDSIZE and is set the same way.
INET	Used for environments where Ethernet protocol will be used for networks. You will also need to set up pseudo-devices "loop" and "ether." Sets up standard Internet networking protocols inside kernel.
NS	Includes the Xerox NS (XNS) protocols for networking into the kernel.
COMPAT	Provides compatibility for executables compiled under BSD 4.1, 4.2, and 4.3.
CMASK	Sets up a universal umask value for users of the system. Their individually set umask will override. The most secure is 077, the least is 000.
GATEWAY	Used if you have more than one network interface for Internet routing and forwarding; obsolete in some systems.
NSIP	Only used if **INET** and **NS** are used. Encapsulates XNS packets inside IP for transmission through gateways.
TCP_COMPAT_42	4.3BSD only with **INET** installed. Used to compensate for problems when a 4.2BSD tries to do a TCP connect to a 4.3BSD. Tells the 4.3BSD to ignore checksums when packets originate at 4.2 hosts.
IPFORWARDING	Disables the packet-forwarding functions of IP if set to 0 instead of the default 1. Not normally used.
IPSENDREDIRECTS	Instructs the IP software to correct other machines' notions of the network's connectivity if **IPFORWARDING** is set to 0. Not normally used.
THREEWAYSHAKE	Used for the XNS protocol; sets up a more secure handshake protocol. Normally not used.

FIGURE 2.3 The options keyword example arguments.

tion file so that you can create alternate kernels that look to different disks for these critical files. Some examples of the use of this keyword are

```
config  vmunix root on ra swap on ra0b and ra1b dumps on
   ra0b
config  hpvmunix     root on major 0 minor 0 swap on major
   0 minor 1
```

The config keyword will also accept **swap generic** to allow a nonspecific swap space configuration. In a nonspecific swap configuration the kernel asks for the location of a swap space on startup. Another option is **args on *disk***, where *disk* is the location for enhanced swapping (in some special cases).

The keywords controller, device, tape, and disk all have the same general format. The controller keyword specifies a device controller; the device keyword specifies a terminal interface, network interface, frame buffer, or graphics accelerators; and the tape and disk keywords specify tapes and disks attached through specific tape and disk controllers. The general format for these keywords is

```
keyword  device_name at connection_info csr address
         drive drive_number flags flags
         priority priority_level vector vector_info
```

The data for the ***device_name, connection_info, address, drive_number, flags, priority_level,*** and ***vector_info*** arguments can usually be found in the GENERIC configuration file or in the manufacturer's documentation. If all else fails, most of the arguments can be replaced by a question mark (?), and the kernel will interrogate the device at startup for the information.

The pseudo-device keyword is used to specify drivers that act like regular devices but don't have physical devices connected to them. An example would be the X-Windows pseudo-devices that allow keyboard definitions and multiple sessions per terminal. The general format of the pseudo-device keyword is

```
pseudo-device    device_name    number-of-instances
```

The **number-of-instances** argument is optional and used only on rare occasions. In most cases the smart way to handle pseudo-devices is to leave all of those in the GENERIC file configured. Some example pseudo-devices are shown in Figure 2.4.

Once you have altered the configuration file, you are ready to proceed with the conf process.

2.2.3 Running the conf Process for BSD

The first step in running conf on the BSD configuration file is to establish a working directory in which to gather the required files and build the new kernel object modules and executable. It is required that you name this directory after the kernel you are compiling to allow the conf process to find it, not to mention making finding it easier a couple of months or years down the road. This

Device	Purpose
pty	Mimics a terminal and is used by the rsh and rlogin processes.
loop	Used to force a loopback during Ethernet testing.
ether	Must be present on systems using Ethernet. Forces inclusion of Ethernet-related material in the kernel.
imp	Stands for "intelligent message processor" and is used to talk with ARPANET.
ns	Does for the XNS network what ether does for Ethernet.

FIGURE 2.4 Example BSD pseudo-devices.

subdirectory will be placed under the SYS upper-level directory. To create this subdirectory, use the following commands:

```
$ cd SYS
$ mkdir kernel_name
```

Once the directory exists, it will be used by conf as the location in which to place the Makefile it creates.

The next step is to **cd** to the SYS/conf directory and run conf against the configuration file that was created or modified as detailed in Section 2.2.2. The commands to perform this action on our example kernel, TPUNIX, are

```
$ cd SYS/conf
$ conf TPUNIX |& CONFERR.LOG
```

As with other steps, should any errors result from this command, they will show up in the specified file—in this case CONFERR.LOG. Once you get a clean conf run, you can proceed to the next step, running the make depend process. On some systems, such as SunOS, this step is automatic. Even so, rerunning the process does no harm.

2.2.4 Running the make depend Process for BSD Kernels

The next step is to run the make depend process. As I said in the previous section, some operating systems, such as SunOS, will run the make depend process automatically. If you aren't sure that your system has run it or not, it doesn't hurt to run it again. The process gathers all of the dependent files in one place so the make process doesn't have to work so hard. Naturally, this process is run from the new kernel's configuration directory—in our example SYS/TPUNIX.

The command to run the make depend process is

```
$ cd SYS/TPUNIX
$ make depend tpunix |& tee MDEPERR.LOG
```

Once this process completes, your configuration directory will contain numerous files, which will be used in making the kernel. Believe it or not, all of these files will be compressed into one or two object modules that will be used to actually generate the kernel executable. This is done in the next step using the **make** command. Once you can execute the **make depend** command with no resultant errors in the MDEPERR.LOG file, you are ready to proceed to the next phase, the make process.

2.2.5   Using the make Process on the BSD Kernel

The make process actually creates an executable image of your kernel. Remember the config keyword and how it can have multiple occurrences in the same configuration file? This is where this feature becomes important. You can tell the make process which version of the kernel is to be built by specifying the config kernel variant you wish to link. With the other commands we have been specifying a kernel configuration file name as our argument; make assumes that you are in the proper subdirectory and that you have created a proper Makefile and collected the proper files with the **conf** and **make depend** commands. If this is the case, you only specify the name of the kernel variant, as it is given in the configuration file config keyword line, to the **make** command and it will locate that variant definition in the Makefile and build the kernel according to its specification for root, swap, and dump locations.

If you get errors during the kernel make process, they will probably be due to a missing line in your configuration file. This missing line will probably relate to a driver file that is required by one of the other drivers. Try doing man -k requests against the driver types (such as disk, tape, etc.) and see what dependencies exist. Once you get a clean make your kernel is ready for testing.

2.2.6 Testing and Installation of the New BSD Kernel

Never directly replace the existing kernel with a just-made one. Always allow yourself a place to which you can step back from the install if there is a problem. This means that you will need to first determine if the /vmunix file is a link or actually the kernel by using the **ls -l** command on it to see if it points to another file. If it does, then it can be safely deleted and a new link file called /vmunix can be created to point to your new kernel. Essentially, there are two paths available to you to install the kernel for testing:

Path 1—the /vmunix file is a link file:

```
$ rm /vmunix
$ ln -s SYS/TPUNIX/tpunix /vmunix
```

Shut down to maintenance mode and do a **fsck -p**.
Reboot.

Path 2:

```
$ mv /vmunix /vmunix.works
$ cp SYS/TPUNIX/vmunix /vmunix
```

Shut down to maintenance mode and do a **fsck -p**.
Reboot.

If the kernel boots, you are probably going to be okay. If it doesn't, you will have to go into maintenance mode and undo the link to the new kernel or replace the copy of the new kernel with the one that works. Then it is time to review the processes outlined here and see what mistake you have made. If it appears that you haven't made any mistakes, it may be time to call in the experts from the vendor.

Once you get a successful boot, you can test the basic system functionality by issuing a few commands that use the kernel. These commands are **ps** and **w**. Another test to do is **ls** on the file systems attached to the system. If you get a "no namelist" error from the **ps** commands, the kernel may have the wrong name (not vmunix) or the wrong permissions, or the database didn't link correctly. If your **ls** commands fail, then you probably have bad partition tables. Never run the **strip** command on any kernel file, since this command removes symbolic information that several commands depend on.

You should also check the operation of the device or devices that were added or changed. If everything seems to be working, notify the users via the motd file that there is a new kernel and to inform you of any problems that they may encounter. The final step is to document the configuration file with the reason for all changes.

2.3   RECONFIGURATION OF THE HP-UX KERNEL

The HP-UX kernel is fairly easy to work on compared to BSD and SVR4 kernel reconfigurations. This is because of its automated database administration tool, called SAM. SAM is a forms/GUI-based system that allows respecification and reconfiguration of the HP-UX kernel as well as general system administration.

The SAM module must be run from a root privileged account. Usually, the kernel supplied with the HP-UX system is sufficient to meet most needs; however, sometimes reconfiguration of kernel setup parameters and addition or deletion of device drivers is required.

The modification of an HP-UX system is generally done through modification of the /etc/conf/dfile for workstations and multiuser systems. The format of the dfile differs between the two. The dfile for a workstation is generally a list of comments and device driver names. It is assumed that the device drivers are located in a central directory. A portion of the dfile for a 700-series HP-UX workstation is shown in Figure 2.5.

Usually, there are several dfiles located in the /etc/conf directory; there will probably be, at a minimum, a dfile.min and a dfile.full. On some systems, usually the multiuser ones, the configuration files may be stored in the /etc/conf/system subdirectory, where *system* is the uppercase name for the system, such as S800. The actual dfile may be called config.sys on multiuser systems. I suggest starting with the dfile.full and commenting out each driver that you don't need for changing a configuration. This ensures that you

```
* installed software drivers and I/O interface cards
* SCSI Interface Driver
c700
* SCSI disk
scsi
* SCSI tape
scsitape
*SCSI floppy
scsifloppy
  .
  .
  .
*
* Tunable parameters
*
*dskless_node    1
*server_node     1
*Swap info
swap auto        /*Swap after fs on root device -
default.*/
```

FIGURE 2.5 Portion of a HP-UX Workstation **dfile**.

always start from a known configuration and move toward your optimal one. If you start with the dfile.min and try to add and patch your way to an optimal configuration, you may overlook some required drivers.

The general procedure for modifying or reconfiguring the kernel is to use the SAM interface; you should never have to manually modify the dfile. SAM allows you to modify drivers, subsystems, configurable parameters, and root and swap devices. Figure 2.6 shows the kernel configuration menu.

2.3.1 Modification of the HP-UX Kernel with SAM

As you can see by a review of Figure 2.6, virtually any section of a kernel configuration can be modified. Selection of the modify or

Options	Purpose
Drivers	• Add driver to kernel.
	• Remove driver from kernel.
	• View driver defaults.
	• Create new kernel.
Subsystems	• Add subsystem to kernel.
	• Remove subsystem from kernel.
	• View subsystems details.
	• Create new kernel.
Configurable parameters	• Modify configurable parameter.
	• Create new kernel.
Root and swap devices*	• Modify root and swap devices.
	• Create new kernel.

*For 800-series HP-UX machines the last option is Root, Swap, and Console Devices.

FIGURE 2.6 SAM Kernel Configuration menu options.

remove options for the devices' or subsystems' menus displays a list of all possible drivers and allows you to choose those you wish to either install or drop from the kernel. The view options allow you to see the details for devices or subsystems that you have chosen. As is logical, each of the modification menus ends with a Create New Kernel option. Naturally, should you choose to add or remove a driver or subsystem, you will need to rebuild the kernel.

In addition to drivers and subsystems, the menus also allow you to configure parameters for the kernel which govern the maximum number or users, files, processes, and memory usage. These parameters have a direct effect on application and system performance, so be sure you know what you are doing before you modify them. Most of the parameters you can reconfigure can be checked with the **getconf parameter_name [pathname]** command. To see a list of the parameters you can check, pull up the man page for getconf.

You can also modify the root, swap, and possible console devices from this menu. When a modify menu option is selected, the defaults are shown for each device and you are allowed to alter them as needed. Again, after modification the kernel must be rebuilt for the changes to take effect.

2.3.2   Manual Reconfiguration of the HP-UX Kernel

I don't suggest attempting a manual rebuild of your kernel unless you are experienced with C programming and compiling. The general procedure will be the same as the procedure we discussed with the other kernels. This is

1. Alter the configuration file.

2. Run the **config** command against the new configuration file. This command has the format

```
/etc/config [-t] [-m master] [-c c_file] [-l m_file]
   d_file
```

or

```
/etc/config -a
```

where

-c c_file is the name of the C source file that will be generated; it defaults to /etc/master/mkdev.sys.

-l m_file is the name of the Makefile to be generated; it defaults to /etc/master/config.sys.

-m master specifies that the file master contains all the data for the supported devices. If not specified, it defaults to /etc/master.

-t specifies that a short table of major device numbers for all of the character and block device files named in d_file be created. This will help with later creation of special files.

d_file is the name for the configuration file itself.

The default make script is placed in the user's current directory as config.mk.

2. Once a configuration file has been run through config, a Makefile and a C language source file are developed. The process to compile these files into a usable kernel is make, which is started with the **make -f makefile** command. The **makefile** argument is the name of the file with the .mk suffix that results from the config process.

3. Once the new kernel has been created with the make process, it should be tested and then implemented. The testing will consist of moving or renaming the current kernel file, then placing a link file in its place that points to the new kernel, and then rebooting. Once the system boots, test whatever was added, deleted, or modified. When you are satisfied with the change, you can either leave the link file in place or remove it and replace it with the actual kernel that was generated. The kernel for the HP-UX system is generally located in the / directory under the name hp-ux. The procedure delineated above is

```
$ mv /hp-ux /hp_ux.works
$ ln -s /etc/conf/S800/s800.new /hp-ux
```

Shut down to maintenance mode and do a **fsck -f**.

Reboot.

Test.

Once the testing is complete:

```
$ rm /hp-ux
$ cp /etc/conf/S800/s800.new /hp-ux
```

If you use SAM, all of this is done for you (except the testing, of course.)

3

System Startup and Shutdown

Startup and shutdown of the UNIX system are two of the critical operations that system administrators perform. Improper shutdown can result in corrupted files and a system that won't start up. Improper startup can result in a corrupted file system not being detected or repaired, thus resulting in further, perhaps irreparable, damage.

Startup consists of an automated series of operations that result in the hardware being checked for failures, the kernel being loaded into memory, disk systems being prepared for access (mounted), and required processes being started. How each type of UNIX system accomplishes this is similar, but all have their own unique twists that require a system administrator to be well versed in his or her own flavor of UNIX.

The kernel program can go by one of several names. On SVR4 it is called UNIX; under BSD it is called vmunix. The UNIX kernel is always stored on the root file system. It contains all of the core programs for operation and pointers to where more complex programs are stored on disk. The kernel first initializes its internal tables. Next it checks its hardware by use of diagnostic programs. Some configurations, such as AIX, may check just memory, while others run full hardware checks, check for new devices, and may even build the required support files for these devices if they don't already exist.

Clearly, these operations need to be covered in detail. We will begin with system startup.

3.1 STARTUP—THE BOOTSTRAP PROGRAM

Startup is generally called *bootstrapping* (Some IBM systems may use the term *IPL*, which stands for initial program load). This term comes from the old adage about pulling oneself up by one's bootstraps, which is appropriate for the process that occurs. On a modern system the initial boot program is stored on a read-only-memory (ROM) chip or under read-only storage (ROS) for IBM under AIX. After some initial hardware diagnostics on some systems (like On Chip Sequencer (OCS) in AIX), this program tells the CPU to read a specific sector of the root file disk—the boot sector—and execute the instructions found there. Usually this is block zero of the root system.

3.1.1 The AIX Boot Process

This process differs a bit for AIX, as you can see from the comments in the previous paragraph. AIX goes through three phases during startup:

- Kernel init phase: known as the ROS phase or IPL.
- Configuration phase 1: configuration of the base devices.
- Configuration phase 2: actual system bootup.

During the kernel init phase in AIX the following steps are performed:

1. AIX runs the OCS to find any motherboard problems.

2. ROS performs the power-on self test (POST).

3. ROS executes the user boot list (UBL). This is a set of available devices that the system administrator is able to modify as required. If no UBL is specified, the default UBL is used. The UBL is stored in nonvolatile random access memory (NVRAM), and the backup or default UBL is kept in the ROS. The system will use the first valid UBL found. If the key is placed in the service position on the system, a different UBL from either of these is used.

4. If the UBL is found to be valid, it is loaded sequentially into memory, followed by the boot image. The boot image consists of a valid kernel and a RAM file system.

5. Once the boot image is loaded, control is passed to the kernel, which begins executing the commands found in the RAM file system.

During configuration phase 1 (base configuration) in AIX the following steps are performed:

1. This phase uses the object data manager (ODM), which is a list of devices present. The cfgmgr program automatically configures all devices found in the ODM.

2. The disks containing the root file system are mounted and the root volume group (RVG) is activated. In IBM-AIX parlance this activation is called "varying" and the RVG is said to be "varied on."

During configuration phase 2 (The system boot) in AIX the following steps are performed:

1. The pager is started to begin what is called "swapping" on other systems.

2. The rest of the file systems are mounted.

3. The init process is started and immediately begins calling the programs listed in the inittab table. The getty process and any required network programs are also started. Once this phase completes the system is booted.

One major difference between AIX and other systems is that AIX startup doesn't clean up /tmp files. Cleanup is accomplished under AIX by the skulker script run nightly by cron. This process is not initially enabled and should be started as a part of the inittab operations.

3.1.2   The System V Release 4 (ATT) Boot Process

Under SVR4 the boot is a bit less complex.

1. A program is loaded from ROM that is just complex enough to check for the boot program disk, perform a minimal hardware status check, and possibly check major peripherals. The program's last step is to call the mboot program.

2. Under system SVR4 there are two boot programs on the boot disk, called mboot and boot. They are stored in partition 7 of the root file system, and UNIX, the kernel, is stored in partition 3. *The presence of these partitions is what defines a bootable disk under SVR 4.* The mboot program starts the boot program.

3. Boot loads the kernel and starts several processes.

4. In most cases swapper will be started as process 0. This process acts as a traffic cop for the system. Without swapper, processes would swap in and out of memory in a random manner. This could result in a condition known as *thrashing*, where you have

too many processes and too little memory and the CPU uses all of its cycle time swapping memory contents to and from disk instead of processing. The swapper process determines the optimal method for swapping out processes to maximize resource utilization and prevent trashing. Not all systems utilize **swapper**.

5. The next process, process 1, will always be init. The init process initiates all system and user processes, using the inittab table to determine which processes to start. The system is started up in multiuser mode unless told otherwise in the inittab table. Once the processes delineated in the inittab table are taken care of, the programs stored in the /etc/rc area are executed. The init process usually performs the following series of operations:

   ■ Setting computer name and environment variables usually found in /etc/rc.local.

   ■ Checking file systems using the fsck utility.

   ■ Mounting local disks.

   ■ Designating paging areas.

   ■ Performing file system cleanup, which consists of checking disk quotas, preserving editor files, and deleting /tmp files and other temporary files.

   ■ Starting system servers (daemons) such as printing, mail, accounting, and cron.

   ■ Starting network daemons and mounting remote disks (if required).

   ■ Enabling user logins by starting the getty process.

6. Once the init process completes, users can log in to the system. If problems occur, the system may fail to start up or may come up in single-user mode. Single-user mode is also know as maintenance mode on some systems.

3.1.3   **The BSD Boot Process**

Under BSD the boot process consists of the following steps:

1. The program located in the ROM chip loads the UNIX kernel, usually called vmunix under BSD. The kernel knows how much memory it will require and will not load if resources are insufficient.

2. The kernel is executed and control passes to it. The kernel initializes itself. This process involves setting up internal data storage areas and I/O buffer areas.

3. The kernel will look at the system in this step and see what devices it holds. When the kernel is built the system administrator tells it what devices should be present. The kernel seeks out the device drivers for these devices and gets most of its configuration data from them.

4. The kernel starts several processes. Generally, at least three will be invoked: swapper as process 0, init as process 1, and page-daemon as process 2.

5. Once step 4 finishes the kernel is done as far as startup is concerned. This leaves the system in the single-user mode if no further action is taken. Generally, the goal is to get to multiuser mode, which requires execution of the initialization scripts.

6. The initialization scripts are stored in the /etc/rc directory. They are normally executed by the init process. Once init is started it uses the rc files to start other required processes. The rc scripts can perform the following actions:

   ■ Setting the name of the node (computer).

   ■ Checking the disks for corruption using **fsck**.

   ■ Mounting all required disk partitions.

   ■ Removing /tmp files.

- Invoking daemons and network services.

- Starting other services such as accounting.

- Performing other configuration tasks such as network configuration.

7. Finally, the getty process(s) begins. Remember, unless getty is started, no users will be able to log in to the system. The /etc/nolgin file is also removed. *Until this file is deleted no logins are allowed.*

3.1.4 The Diskless Workstation Boot

In some configurations the CPU that is booting may have no disk drives of its own. This is known as a diskless workstation (many graphics workstations are of this type.) Diskless workstations have a slightly different ROM program that tells them to seek out the network or file server drive and boot from it instead.

Booting can be either automatic or manual. Most up-to-date systems boot automatically (autoboot) on powering up unless the operator has set a switch or issues an interrupt from the main terminal, known as the *console*. On large UNIX installations the console should be in a restricted area, since access to it can give users many more abilities than they would normally have. The extra privileges operating from the console are dependent on the version of UNIX being used.

3.1.5 Nonautomatic Boots

If your system doesn't boot automatically, there usually are simple commands to perform from the console to carry out the boot operation—for example:

> <cr>   A simple carriage return at this prompt works on some consoles.

> b   Typing a simple b followed by a carriage return will do the trick on others.

> boot   Some consoles may require a more verbose command.

Most systems will allow the -s modifier to boot standalone:

> -s <cr>   If all that was required to boot was a carriage return.

> b -s   If you needed a b to boot.

> boot -s   If your system is verbose.

On other systems a multistage boot may be required:

> b   This comes up in single-user mode.

> unix   This boots the full multiuser kernel.

3.1.6   Run Levels

UNIX systems use the concept of *run levels* to describe the computer's state. The general run levels are single-user (or maintenance) and multiuser. Somewhat facetiously, you could also call the shutdown state a run level, giving a total of three. However, we will use only the two listed above in our discussion.

System V Release 4 Levels   On non-System-SVR4 installations there are generally only single-user or multiuser levels. This is not the case on SVR4. On SVR4 there are several additional levels:

0—Power-down mode, which indicates that the system may be shut down safely.

1—Administrative mode, which is equivalent to single-user mode.

s or S—Single-user mode.

2—Multiuser mode, the normal mode for nonnetworked systems.

3—Remote file-sharing mode (RFS), the normal mode for networked systems.

4—User-definable system mode, which is not normally used.

5—Firmware mode, used for maintenance and diagnosis.

6—Shutdown and reboot mode.

These run levels will appear on some systems after the colon in table entries. In most versions states 1 and s are indistinguishable. Not all states are implemented in all SVR4 implementations. Sometimes run levels 2 and 3 are collapsed and the system will run networked out of state 2. The command **who -r** may be used to show the state.

Here are some examples of movement between states on SVR4. Assuming we start at a normal state 3:

Shutdown—Moves from 3 to 0.

Startup—Moves from 0 to 3.

Reboot—Moves from 3 to 6 to 0 to 2 to 3.

Shutdown to single-user—Moves from 3 to 0 to s.

The init process handles the movement from one state to another.

AIX Run Levels   AIX also uses the run level concept. AIX run levels are defined for version 3.2 as follows:

0-9   Changing from run level to run level within 0–9 will kill all processes at the current run level and start processes for the new level. This is done by the init process.

0-1   These levels are reserved for the future use of the operating system.

2   This is the default run level for AIX, comparable to the SVR4 combined 2–3 mode (multiuser).

3-9   These run levels are defined according to the user's needs and preferences.

a, b, c   If init changes to levels a, b, or c, current processes are not killed; this only starts the new processes.

Q,q   These run levels force init to examine the /etc/inittab file and make adjustments as required.

To change levels on the AIX system, the **smit telinit** command is used. This command will invoke the smit "Set System Run Level" menu displays. Run levels control what processes are running under AIX. The run levels for system processes are listed in the inititab table. Under AIX the records in the inittab table can be altered, viewed, or added to by use of the following commands:

chitab changes records in the table.

lsitab lists records in the table.

mkitab adds records to the table.

rmitab removes records from the table.

The general format for using the commands is

```
command identifier:run Level:Action:Shell Command
```

This is excluding the **lsitab** command, which uses the format **lsitab identifier** for a single record or **lsitab -a** for all records.

We've touched on single- versus multiuser operation. Let's look at these in more detail.

Single-User   On most systems if a problem is detected during startup, the system will be placed in single-user, or maintenance, mode. This mode is designed for administration and maintenance tasks. The init process will fork to create a new process that executes the Bourne shell as user root to accomplish a single-user startup. The prompt for the single-user mode is a pound sign (#). More experienced users will remember that this is also the prompt for the super user account. These accounts share a prompt because they are the two most powerful account states to deal from. Whenever you see the pound sign (#) prompt you must exercise great care in whatever you do, since you could inadvertently destroy the file system with a poorly executed command.

Problems with the fsck program can also result in it exiting to single-user or maintenance mode. If fsck finds an error that is other than a simple non-data-corrupting one, it will exit to single-user mode. The fsck program must be run by the system manager if more serious fixes are required. Usually, once the problem is fixed, the system administrator can resume the boot process by pressing the **Control (Ctrl)** and **d** keys in sequence to exit the Bourne shell. If the fixes are substantial, or the version of UNIX you are on doesn't support this feature, a complete reboot may be required.

Single-user startup is in some ways a more limited condition than full multiuser startup. There are usually several things that haven't been done if the startup exits into single-user mode before completing. Tasks left uncompleted by the startup can include the following:

The search path and terminal type may not be defined.

Most likely, only the root file system will be mounted.

UNIX commands that may reside in the /usr file system will probably be unavailable.

In some versions commands that depend on libraries in the /usr directories will not work.

Some or most daemons won't have been started: printing, cron, and networks.

There are also security issues with single-user startup. On older systems single-user startup didn't require a password. This meant that an intruder could gain access to your system simply by pushing the Reset button or unplugging and replugging in the system and then using the console to halt the boot process and enter single-user mode. On modern systems the single-user mode is password-protected or can be locked out by use of a key switch (since most sites leave the key in place this is of limited use). This lock feature forces the system into multiuser mode following the fsck process. To see what security features are available on your system consult the administration manual or the man pages, or look in the init files.

Multiuser As its name implies, this mode allows multiple users to access the system simultaneously (actually sequentially but so fast it looks simultaneous). In this mode the getty process actually controls user login.

When a user attempts to log in to a UNIX system in multiuser mode the getty process executes the login program, employing the user's login name. The login process prompts for the user's password and then validates the login name and password against the entry in the /etc/passwd file and/or the /etc/shadow file. Once the user is verified the message of the day is printed to his or her screen or device if the /etc/motd file is defined. After the motd is displayed or printed the user shell, as specified in the passwd file, is executed. BSD UNIX will set the TERM environment variable to the value set in the termdef file for the user's login port. For users using the Korn or Bourne shell, the .profile startup file in the user's directory is executed next. For users using the C shell, the .cshrc and .login files are executed. Once all of this is complete, the user prompt ($) is issued and the user is ready to go.

3.2   UNIX INIT SCRIPTS

All UNIX implementations will have one thing in common. At some time during the startup process they will depend on either a single startup script or, more likely, a series of startup scripts to actually get the system to a usable condition. These scripts will usually be written in the Bourne shell language and are normally kept in the /etc area of the disk. BSD implementations have the /etc/rc and /etc/rc.local scripts that are used to bring them to multiuser mode (/etc/rc is used by itself to come up single-user.) In SunOS and AIX3.1 this becomes a little more complex.

Under SunOS the /etc/rc.boot script calls the /etc/rc.single script, after which the single-user shell is started. If multiuser mode is desired, the systems then run the /etc/rc and /etc/rc.local scripts. The AIX3.1 system, even though it is based on System V, has its initialization scripts configured like those in a BSD system. Under AIX the init process will run all scripts in the /etc/rc area. Usually this will include

rc.net   General network configuration.

rc.tcpip   Starts tcpip and local daemons.

rc.nfs   Starts the network computing services.

rc.pci   Starts the DOS interface.

3.2.1   Example rc File

Let's look at an example rc file, shown in Figure 3.1.

So, what is this script doing? Let's dissect it and see.

```
HOME=/; export HOME
PATH=/bin:/usr/bin:/usr/ucb:/etc:/usr/etc
```

The first two statements are setting environmental variables and making them available for use. The variable HOME is set equal to the / directory or root, and the PATH variable is set to a search list consisting of the /bin, /usr/bin, /usr/ucb, /etc, and /usr/etc directories. The PATH is searched whenever a nonfull path command is issued that can't be solved by the kernel itself. The "export" commands make the definitions available to the shell environment.

```
            HOME=/; export HOME
            PATH=/bin:/usr/bin:/usr/ucb:/etc:/usr/etc
            if[-r /fastboot]; then
                    rm-f /fastboot
                    echo Fast boot .... had normal
shutdown>dev/console
            elif [$1x=autobootx];
            then
                    echo Automatic reboot initiated >/dev/console
                    fsck -p>/dev/console
                    case $? in
            0)
                    date>/dev/console
                    ;;
            1)
                    exit 1
                    ;;
            4)
                    /etc/reboot -n
                    ;;
            8)
                    echo "Problem with reboot...">dev/console
                    ;;
            12)
                    echo "Operator Intervention in Re-
boot..">/dev/console
                    ;;
            *)
                    echo "An unknown error has
occured">/dev/console
                    ;;
            esac
            else
                    date>/dev/console
fi
if [-s /etc/ptmp ]; then
        if [-s /etc/passwd ]; then
                    ls -l /etc/passwd /etc/ptmp>/dev/console
                    rm -f /etc/ptmp
```

FIGURE 3.1 Example /etc/rc script.

```
            else
                        echo 'recovering passwd file from
    ptmp'>/dev/console
                        mv /etc/ptmp /etc/passwd
            fi
elif [ -r /etc/ptmp ]; then
                        echo 'removing ptmp file'>/dev/console
                        rm -f /etc/ptmp
fi
/etc/umount -a
cat /dev/null > /etc/mtab
mount -at >/dev/console 2>&1
/etc/swapon -a>/dev/console 2>&1
            echo -n 'checking quotas:'>/dev/console
quotacheck -a -p >/dev/console 2>&1
            echo 'done.' >/dev/console
quotaon -a
/bin/ps -U>/dev/console 2>&1
            echo 'Enabling logins.'>/dev/console
rm -f /etc/nologin
            echo "Enabling modem logins.'>/dev/console
rm -f /usr/spool/uucp/LCK.*
if [ -f /dev/ttyp0]; then
            chown root /dev/tty[pqrs]*
            chown 666 /dev/tty[pqrs]*
fi
sh /etc/rc.local
echo 'Saving editor files.'>/dev/login
            (cd /tmp; /usr/lib/ex3.7preserve -a)
echo 'Cleaning tmp directory.'>/dev/console
(cd /tmp; find . ! -name . -exec rm -r {} \; )
echo -n 'Invoking standard Daemons:'>/dev/console
            /etc/update; echo -n ' update'>/dev/console
            /etc/cron; echo -n ' cron'>/dev/console
            echo 'done.' >/dev/console
/etc/accton /usr/adm/acct;
date > /dev/console
exit 0
```

FIGURE 3.1 Continued.

The if, elif, then, and fi statement combinations and the case, esac statement combinations are used to control branch logic. The if and fi denote the start and stop of the if construct. In this situation the first line in the construct:

```
if[-r /fastboot]; then
```

checks for the existence of the fastboot file. This file is created during shutdown if (1) the -f option is used on the shutdown command and (2) the shutdown concludes normally with no problems. The next line:

```
rm -f /fastboot
```

removes the fastboot file. And the next line:

```
echo Fast boot .... had normal shutdown>dev/console
```

sends a message to the system console telling it that a fastboot is in progress and the operator should realize no file check is being performed. The elif tells the system that since the if condition was fulfilled, go to the fi statement. If the if hadn't been evaluated to true (i.e., fastboot didn't exist), control would have jumped to the elif statement immediately. What is the following statement saying?

```
elif [$1x=autobootx];
then
```

It is checking for the existence of the first argument passed to rc "$1". If this argument is **=autoboot**, then the system continues execution at this point. If **=autoboot** isn't passed to rc, then execution will pass either to the next elif, the next else, or fi—whichever it finds first within the same level of the if construct that this elif is in. The rc script next sends a message to the console and then issues the **fsck** command:

```
fsck -p >/dev/console
```

This **fsck** command uses the **-p** (preen) option, which tells **fsck** to perform all non-data-altering fixes it can. The next set of statements forms the case-esac construct that takes actions based on the variable returned by the **fsck** command. The possible results are

0	Normal exit, no problems.
1	Bad root disk, can't fix problem.
4	Fixed root disk problems.
8	Failed on nonroot disk.
12	Operator-interrupted reboot.
other	Unknown errors.

As you can see from the script, in the case of 0, no problem; send the time to the console and exit. In the case of 1, exit before any further damage is done. In the case of 4, automatically reboot the system. In the case of 8, inform the operator and exit. In the case of 12, tell the operator that someone (probably the operator) interrupted the reboot. In the case of any other error, notify the operator and exit.

The final else statement catches the case where any argument other than **autoboot** was passed to rc. In this situation simply pass the time to the console and exit at the fi.

The next section of the rc script checks to see if someone was in the password file /etc/passwd when the shutdown occurred. If this was the case, the /etc/passwd file could be corrupt. The password file editor will make a file, /etc/ptmp, before performing any changes on the password file itself. This temporary file contains the contents of the passwd file. Once editing is complete, the ptmp file is deleted. *Therefore, if ptmp exists, the passwd edit operation was interrupted.*

```
if [ -s /etc/ptmp]; then
        if [ -s /etc/passwd ]; then
                ls-1 /etc/passwd/etc/ptmp>/dev
                /console
                rm -f /etc/ptmp
```

The first line in this section of code checks for /etc/ptmp and if it is greater than 0 length. If this is so, it then checks to see if /etc/passwd exists and if it is greater than 0 length. If both of these conditions are true, the script displays the file data to the console and then removes the /etc/ptmp file.

```
else
        echo 'recovering passwd file from ptmp'>/dev
          /console
        mv /etc/ptmp /etc/passwd
fi
```

This section of the script tells the console that recovery is required and proceeds to move the contents of the ptmp file into the passwd file. You will only get to this section if the passwd file length was 0 or the passwd file doesn't exist and the ptmp file exists and is greater than 0 in length.

```
elif [ -r /etc/ptmp ]; then
                echo 'removing ptmp file'>/dev/console
                rm -f /etc/ptmp
fi
```

This section of the rc script is reached if the first if determines that passwd exists and is not 0 length and that ptmp exists and is 0 length. The system assumes that the passwd file is valid. The ptmp file is removed.

```
/etc/umount -a
cat /dev/null > /etc/mtab
mount -a >/dev/console 2>&1
```

This next section begins with forced unmount (**umount** command) of "all" file systems using the -a option. This option will not unmount the root partition. Once the unmount is accomplished the mtab table, which contains the data on mounted file systems, is truncated to 0 length to ensure that there are no "ghost" entries that could cause problems. Finally, all file systems are mounted by use of the -a option with the **mount** command. You will note the use of the "2>&1" option with the redirection command in this statement and in subsequent statements. This option forces diagnostic as well as regular output from the command to the console. Once the disk file systems are up and operating the swap feature is turned on with the command

```
/etc/swapon -a >/dev/console 2>&1
```

The next set of commands deals with the use of disk quotas. If you don't have quotas set on your system, this code may or may not be present.

```
        echo -n 'checking quotas:'>/dev/console
quotacheck -a -p >/dev/console 2>&1
        echo 'done.' >/dev/console
quotaon -a
```

The first command is an operational information message. The next command, **quotacheck**, checks if quotas are set for any disk volume (the -a option again) and updates entries as required. The **quotaon -a** command enables quotas on all volumes as specified in the /etc/fstab table.

```
/bin/ps -U>/dev/console 2>&1
        echo 'Enabling logins.'>/dev/console
rm -f /etc/nologin
        echo "Enabling modem logins.'>/dev/console
rm -f /usr/spool/uucp/LCK.*
```

These next few commands tell the operator what the system status is: **/bin/ps -U>/dev/console 2>&1**, and that users are about to be allowed on the system: **echo 'Enabling logins.'>/dev/console**;

then it removes the multiple user lock file, **nologin: rm -f/etc/ nologin**. The -f option causes no error message output should there be no nologin file to remove. Finally, modem logins are enabled by removal of the LCK files from the /usr/spool/uucp directory.

```
if [ -f /dev/ttyp0]; then
        chown root /dev/tty[pqrs]*
        chown 666 /dev/tty[pqrs]*
fi
```

These commands check for and correct any access problems for the system's virtual terminals. Access problems could be caused by an abnormal termination of a virtual terminal process during a system crash.

```
sh /etc/rc.local
```

This command starts the rc.local procedure. This procedure is started in its own subshell with the **sh** command, which allows rc to continue processing. The rc.local file, an example of which is shown in Figure 3.2, will set its search path and set the hostname variable, and its tcp/ip address will be loaded into the hostid variable via a lookup from the /etc/hosts file by the **hostid** command.

Next, rc.local configures the loopback ip address used for testing, 1o0, and two addresses for other nodes, de0 (or dixie) and de1 (or jackson). The next few lines load information into the motd file about the current kernel and date. Actually, rc.local **greps** the data out of the kernel file and places it in the temporary file tmotd. This file is then combined with the existing motd file, replacing the first two lines. Lastly, the file replaces the existing motd file. The final lines use the **savecore** command to save off an image of any crash dumps that exist.

Let's get back to the sample rc script shown in Figure 3.1 to look at what it does while rc.local is doing its thing.

```
PATH = /etc:/bin:/usr/ucb:/usr/bin
hostname master
hostid 'hostname'
/etc/ifconfig lo0 localhost up arp >/dev/console
/etc/ifconfig de0 125.134.244.3 up dixie netmask \
        0xffffff00 arp broadcast 125.134.244.255 > /dev/console
/etc/ifconfig de1 125.134.244.4 up jackson netmask \
        0xffffff00 arm broadcast 125.134.244.255 > /dev/console
strings /vmunix | grep UNIX > /tmp/tmotd
tail +1 /etc/motd >> /tmp/tmotd
mv /tmp/tmotd /etc/motd
echo 'Saving COREDUMP' >/dev/console
savecore /users/crash > /dev/console 2>&1
```

FIGURE 3.2   Example rc.local file.

```
echo 'Saving editor files.'>/dev/login
        (cd /tmp; /usr/lib/ex3.7preserve -a)
echo 'Cleaning tmp directory.'>/dev/console
(cd /tmp; find . ! -name . -exec rm -r {} \; )
```

These lines ensure that any files that were being edited when the system went down can be recovered and that any temporary files are cleaned up. This general housekeeping prevents excess file buildup and ensures that users don't lose work because of a crash. On AIX the skulker process will clean up the temporary files, but the saving of the editor files should still be done.

```
echo -n 'Invoking standard Daemons:'>/dev/console
        /etc/update; echo -n '  update'>/dev/console
        /etc/cron; echo -n '  cron'>/dev/console
        echo 'done.' >/dev/console
```

Get out your caldrons. These lines invoke basic system daemons, which are processes that perform specific actions for the system. For example, cron executes periodic tasks as specified in the crontable.

```
/etc/accton /usr/adm/acct;
date > /dev/console
exit 0
```

These final three command lines turn on accounting (if you don't use accounting, this line shouldn't be here), send the date and time to the console, and exit rc. The init process will now run any other scripts located in rc that are specified in the initab file.

Your system's rc file should resemble the one we just examined. However, don't expect it to look exactly like this one, and, for heavens sake, don't modify or delete entries based on this example. Use your system documentation for proper formats and layouts.

3.3   WHEN THE SYSTEM WON'T BOOT

The UNIX system, like any other, will sometimes have startup problems. The first thing to remember is that it is not the end of life as you know it. Think of it as a learning experience. The most important thing is to keep good records of what the symptoms were, what the problem was, and how you fixed it. The one thing you don't want to do is start messing with things you don't understand—don't dismantle systems, don't unplug chips, and don't take apart disk drives. Boot problems generally fall in one of several categories:

Hardware problems

Defective boot media (tapes or floppies)

Errors in the initialization script

Kernel errors

File system errors

The first indication of a problem may be a series of console messages followed by a crash dump and/or a boot to single-user. As I said before, the first thing you do when your system fails to start up or crashes is log what the symptoms are in your log book. If the system comes up to single-user, the /usr/adm/messages file should be checked for information on the cause. You should also make a copy of the crash dump if it is present. If you need to call in the experts, the crash dump will be a valuable source of information for them.

A crash dump contains an image of the kernel at the time of the crash, and while it may look like Sanskrit to you (unless you are a kernel guru), it is an invaluable look into the kernel to an expert. Any error messages and codes displayed to the console should also be logged. Only after preserving as much information as you can about the causes of the crash or failure to start up should you attempt a reboot. *Remember, the very act of rebooting the system may erase valuable troubleshooting information.*

In one case we had a problem that prevented a key operation from performing as expected. A quick review of the log found an entry from almost a year before with the same exact error, what we had to do to fix it, and how to prevent its reoccurrence (it turned out to be a disk maintenance problem easily fixed by running a disk cleanup and defragmentation utility). Your system log should be a living document that is updated for every problem, not just major ones.

If a system fails to start up, or comes up to single-user when it should be multiuser, do the following:

1. Check all connections and power sources. (In one case we had a class of operators who couldn't log in to the system; it turned out that the main connection to the network had come loose for their room. Of course, we didn't discover this until we had wrung the system out for poor performance!)

2. If the system came up single-user, check console messages and log them.

3. If the system came up single-user, check the /usr/adm/messages file for possible errors.

4. Before attempting restart, save off a copy of the crash dump (again, assuming the system reached single-user).

5. Log all of your actions, and try things one at a time, not in multiples; otherwise, how will you know what really fixed the problem?

6. Once the problem is solved, don't forget to write down both the problem and the fix in your log.

Let's examine each of the above types of failure and make a few suggestions on how to go about fixing them.

3.3.1 Hardware Problems

Something we all dread is an error inside the microscopic world of the CPU. These errors are usually shown by error messages that are displayed when the system tries to boot, if it can boot at all. Another error that points to a second dreaded area is one involving memory parity. Generally speaking, unless you are a hardware guru who is familiar with micro-circuits and board-level analysis, these types of errors mean one thing: Call the vendor! However, if the message isn't exactly clear, sometimes shutting off the power for a couple of minutes and then restarting the system will fix them. Even so, if this occurs on every warm start, there is a definite problem that should be corrected.

At the nuclear prototype I qualified on in the Navy there was a certain cabinet that, if you kicked it in just the right spot, would shut down the entire reactor. They could never figure out why, and eventually the entire set of circuits inside the cabinet had to be replaced.

Somewhere there was a loose connection. This is an example of the type of failure that can cause periodic CPU and memory errors, and usually the fix is just as drastic: You have to replace the faulty board lock, stock, and barrel. Anything from a cold-soldered joint to a flakey chip that fails when it reaches 97.56°F can cause failure. These problems are usually also the cause of the failure when you can't get the system to fail for the repairman.

Other hardware errors are numerous, from crashed disks to loose connectors and blown fuses. A general hardware troubleshooting guide would be as follows.

1. System connections, power cords, cables, and so forth. Recently we were trying to connect a compact laser disk to a system. No matter what we did, the system wouldn't recognize the drive as being present. All connections were correct, all initialization scripts were proper, and the drive would test out fine standalone. It turned out that the brand-new, factory-supplied connection cable was bad. I've also answered trouble calls from users whose system wouldn't start up no matter what they tried, until I had them flip on the power strip power switch. You may laugh—until it is you caught red-faced because the same silly thing happened to you.

2. Defective boot media. If you are a good system administrator, this is easy to detect. A good system administrator will have up-to-date backup copies of the boot media. If defective boot media are suspected, boot from your backup. If the boot succeeds from the backup media, then something has happened to corrupt the regular boot media or something you recently changed needs to be changed back. If you don't keep your backup disk current, it will be useless. Once changes are made to the boot media and tested they must be placed on your backup media as well.

3. Initialization script errors. Again, if you are a good system administrator, you will make copies of existing scripts to either a backup disk or a backup directory area. Of course, all initialization script changes are also logged in the system log and you only change one script at a time before testing, right? Then, if the initialization fails, you only have to bring one script back, not several. You will also have a precise idea of what not to do next time.

4. Kernel errors. Kernel errors can only occur after a change to either the kernel or the physical memory system. For example, if you configure your shared memory area too large, the system won't start up. If, on the other hand, you remove memory and then try to boot up without lowering kernel requirements, the same thing can happen. There are numerous configuration parameters that were covered in Chapter 2 on kernel configuration that can have as devastating an effect on system startup if set improperly. These can be mitigated by ensuring that you have a good backup of the kernel to restore from.

3.3.2 ■ Common Error Codes during Startup

There are numerous errors that can occur during system boot. The following list is for SCO UNIX and is representative of what you can expect on most other UNIX flavors.

BAD TBL   One of the bootable partition indicators for one of the operating systems in the fsck table has a bad or unrecognized code.

IO ERRM   When masterboot tried to read the partition boot of the operating system an error occurred.

NO OS   An unrecoverable error prevented the system's partition boot from executing.

The above errors are displayed by the SCO UNIX masterboot program. In addition, there may be errors from the boot process itself. The most common of these are

bad magic number	The file that boot tried to run wasn't an executable file.
boot failure stage 1	The boot file couldn't be found by the bootstrap loader, usually because the boot program was not in the root file system.
can't open "path"	The indicated path doesn't exist—perhaps the file system hasn't been mounted.
float:read(x)=y	A premature end of file or a corrupted file. It indicates that x bytes were asked for, but only y bytes where returned.
not a directory	The program attempted to read an area on a device that didn't contain a valid file system.
zero length directory	An attempt was made to read a file in a directory that had no contents. It can indicate an improper file specification or a corrupt file system, usually due to an old-version UNIX file system being read by a new version.

3.4   UNIX SYSTEM SHUTDOWN

Shutdown is another important aspect of system administration. An improper shutdown can result in a corrupted file system that won't boot. There are several methods for shutting down UNIX.

Turning off the power (not recommended except in dire emergencies). Don't use this one unless there is no other way. An example would be a flood, fire, or other disaster where there isn't time to do a proper shutdown.

*Using the **shutdown** command.* This is the best method to shut down UNIX. The general format is **shutdown time (message)**.

Shutdown has -h (halt), -r (reboot), and -k (kidding) options. The -k just sends out a warning, but doesn't cause a reboot or shutdown. Use of **shutdown** warns users every so many minutes; at five minutes to shutdown it creates the /etc/nologin file to prevent further logins and then brings the system to single-user mode in the proper manner and removes the /etc/nologin file.

*Under BSD using the **halt** command or under SVR4 the **haltsys** command.* The **shutdown -h** and **halt** or **haltsys** commands are usually synonymous. The **halt** command usually logs the shutdown, kills the system processes, and issues the **sync** command via a system call. If -n is used, no **sync** command is issued. If -q is used, the system performs an immediate halt without synchronization, killing of processes, or writing of logs—rather like pulling the plug. The flags shouldn't be used unless fsck has just been run or you are absolutely positive the file system is completely in order.

*Under BSD or AIX, using the **reboot** command.* The **reboot** command is identical to **halt** or **haltsys** except that it executes an immediate reboot. This is synonymous with **shutdown -r**. The **reboot** command supports the -n and -q flags.

*Sending **init** a **TERM** command.* Sending a **TERM** command to init is rather like shooting yourself in the foot. You know there will probably be damage, but you don't know how much. The init process is always pid 1, so the command will be

```
sync
kill -15 1
```

This kills all processes, getty, and daemons, and goes to single-user mode. The exact value to send init can be found in the /include/signal.h file. This is how shutdown does this operation.

Using the BSD ***fasthalt*** *or* ***fastboot*** *command.* Using the BSD **fasthalt** and **fastboot** commands causes the /etc/fastboot to be created. This results in no fsck being run upon restart. Use these commands only when you need the system to come back up quickly and you are sure that the file system is in excellent condition. Never attempt to create the /etc/fastboot file yourself, as this could result in serious file system damage if done improperly.

Killing init. Killing init will result in automatic reboot of UNIX, which is not a suggested method. Use **reboot** instead. This works because init is the single most important system process and the system will be forced to boot if it is removed.

3.4.1   Shutdown Techniques

As with all things in life, there are proper techniques for shutting down UNIX. These techniques vary little between systems and there are several general steps that apply to all UNIX system shutdowns. These are

1. Warn users—This should be done well in advance of shutdown to allow users time to close files, exit editors, and log off on their own. Doing so ensures that files are in a safe state when the shutdown occurs and thus preserves file system integrity. The **shutdown** command allows a message to be sent to all users and then warns users up to the point of shutdown at periodic intervals. On some systems the /etc/nologin file is created at five minutes prior to shutdown to prevent new user logins.

2. Kill active processes—This closes open files and ensures that all buffers are flushed back to disk. Again, this helps preserve the integrity of the disk system so that a proper startup can

occur at a later date. The kill function is taken care of via the **/usr/lib/lpshut** and **/etc/killall** commands.

3. Unmount the file systems—The file systems (excluding root, of course) are unmounted to ensure that all pointers and files are closed in order to prevent file system corruption. This function is performed by the **unmount** command, which utilizes the /etc/mnttab file to know which file systems to unmount.

4. Go to single-user mode—Once the shutdown script has warned the users, killed active processes, and unmounted all file systems except root, it sends a command to the init process, forcing it into single-user mode.

5. Copy memory-resident files to disk—This is the final step of a shutdown, performed via the **sync** command. The **sync** command is usually done several times. It closes all accounts and writes the memory-resident files to disk. Once **sync** completes it sends an appropriate message to the terminal indicating that it is safe to turn off the power.

3.4.2   Rapid Shutdown

There are times when it is desirous to rapidly shut down UNIX. As shown above, there are several techniques for doing this with varying degrees of risk. Let's look at some of these and see when they may be applicable.

Turning off the power (not recommended except in dire emergencies). About the only time it is a good idea to use this method is when actual physical damage will happen to either a person or your system should the equipment remain energized. For example, you or your assistant may grab a live area of the power supply or something may turn on the room's sprinkler system. Another example is a fire or other physical threat that prevents you from reaching the console terminal.

*Sending **init** a **TERM** command.* Sending a **TERM** command to init is rather like shooting yourself in the foot. You know there will probably be damage but not how much. The init process is always pid 1, so the command will be

```
$ sync
$ kill -15 1
```

This kills all processes, getty, and daemons, and goes to single-user mode. The exact value to send init can be found in the /include/signal.h file. This is how shutdown does this operation. It begs the question, if you can afford the time to issue the above two commands, why not just issue a proper **shutdown** command in the first place? Probably the only time **TERM** should be used is when for some reason the **shutdown** command is not available.

Killing init. This is rather like item 2, except that it is a more radical method. Killing init outright will force all UNIX systems to reboot or shut down. The init process is the most important of the UNIX processes; thus its loss will force a shutdown. Again, why not just issue the normal shutdown command? The only time either item 1 or item 2 may be applicable is in the case of another operator having control of the system who you know is intent on damaging the system or perhaps stealing information.

UNIX File Systems

With the many versions of UNIX there are several ways that disk resources can be divided. There are physical volumes, logical volumes, logical volume groups, and file systems. Depending upon which version of UNIX you are using, you may have all or only a subset of these. Figure 4.1 is a schematic of a UNIX file system.

Physical devices correspond to the actual disk assets and are at the lowest, or least granular, of the divisors for disk assets. Logical volumes, or logical disks, can correspond to more than one physical disk. A volume group is a collection of logical volumes. To summarize, physical volumes, which correspond to disks, are mapped into one or more logical volumes that are then mapped into logical volume groups. File systems are built within logical volume groups. Depending on how the physical storage maps into the other areas, a file system can be spread over several physical volumes even though it appears as a contiguous system to users.

Under UNIX the main divisor for disk areas is the file system. UNIX has an inverted-tree directory structure with the root at the top

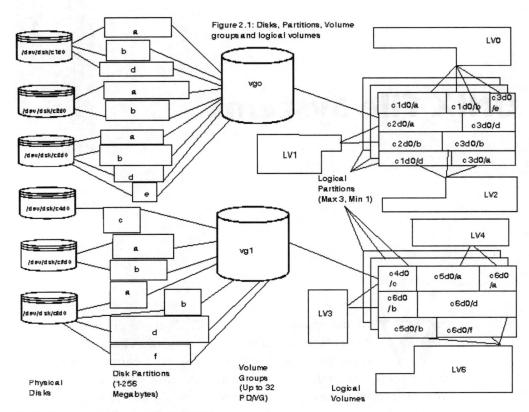

FIGURE 4.1 Schematic of a UNIX file system.

and the branches at the bottom. This inverted tree, also known as a hierarchical structure, is used by most of the other operating systems as well. What makes UNIX unique in its use of the inverted tree is the concept of file systems.

A file system is a collection of generally related files. The actual physical location of a branch of the file system can be anywhere; in the case of a network file system (NFS) it can even reside on a separate node of the network. This set of related files can be "grafted" onto a local directory via the **mount** command, in much the same way a limb from one tree can be grafted onto another. The graft point is known as the mount point, and the file system is said to be mounted once it is attached to the mount point. Consequently, when you view a UNIX directory structure you usually don't see separated disk volumes; these are hidden from sight by use of mount points.

This can lead to problems if the system manager doesn't have a detailed understanding of the physical and logical volumes and file systems within the UNIX directory structures he or she manages. For instance, ORACLE Corporation's ORACLE™ relational database management system requires physical separation of certain of its files if it is to run safely and properly. Without a good knowledge of the actual physical layout of the disk farm and how it maps into the file systems and directory trees, this required separation cannot be accomplished.

It is vital that system managers take adequate time to design and lay out their file systems. Periodic re-evaluation of file systems, mount points, logical volumes and their relation to physical volumes, usage, and required separations should be done.

This chapter will cover the commands to create, destroy, mount, unmount, and check the consistency and health of UNIX file systems. It will also cover the basic UNIX file systems and what they contain.

4.1 DISK SYSTEMS

4.1.1 Adding a Disk

A disk in the shipping carton is useless. Disks must first be added to the physical computer system before they can be used. How the disk is interfaced (DASD, DSSI, SCSI, ESD, etc.) will determine how this is accomplished, and the system administrator should read all instructions included with the disk by the manufacturer and included with his or her system before performing the actual disk installation.

You don't connect a disk directly to the CPU; there must be a disk controller present that handles the input and output from the disk. Some disk controllers can handle chains of disks; that is, instead of being physically coupled to the drive controller, subsequent disks are attached to the last disk in the chain. Once a disk is physically installed, you must tell the operating system about it for it to be used. Before buying the greatest new disk to come down the line, be sure your system can handle it. This means be certain that the proper interface is available and that you either have the expertise or can get it to install it.

4.1.2   Disk Formatting

Some drives are preformatted; some are not. Before a drive can be used it must be formatted. Generally speaking, a drive's formatted capacity can be as much as 20 percent less than its quoted capacity. Be sure you compare formatted capacities when considering similar drives for purchase. During formatting the imperfections in the disk surface are located and any disk tracks or sectors affected are remapped into other disk areas, or simply marked, so they are not used for data storage. Disks are subdivided into radial tracks, which are subdivided into sectors that correspond to block size for a specific system. Block size is usually 512 bytes, but can be 1,024 or even 2,048 bytes. Each set of tracks at the same radial distance out from the disk center, or in from the disk edge, that is on the platters in a multiplatter disk drive is known as a cylinder. BSD groups cylinders into cylinder groups of 1 to 32 contiguous sets in its fast file system.

Disks are formatted with the **format** command on most UNIX implementations. On HP-UX this command becomes **mediainit**. An example of the use of **mediainit** follows.

```
mediainit -v -i interleave -f format block-dev-file
```

where

> **-v** means tell us everything there is to know about what you are doing. It is short for *verbose*.

-i interleave allows you to specify the interleave factor.

-f format is used with devices such as floppies where formats may vary; it isn't used with hard disks.

block-dev-file is the block device file to be used for **mediainit**. This is required. Block device files should be contained in the /dev/diag/dsk directory.

In a more concrete example, the command

```
$ mediatinit -v /dev/diag/dsk/c1d0
```

initializes the disk c1d0. Before this step can be performed the disk has to have been physically installed and the device file c1d0 created. The file c1d0 is known as a block device file and under the HP-UX system will always be located in the /dev/diag/dsk directory. Usually this process will be handled under the smit utility for AIX or the SAM utility for HP-UX. A block device file handles the movement of blocks of data between processes and devices such as disk drives. Another type of device file, the character device file, moves single characters between processes and devices such as terminals.

Generally, disk formatting is accomplished with the system shut down into single-user, or maintenance, mode. Some systems even require complete shutdown and use of special interfaces. For chained drives or drives on the same controller, detach those drives not being formatted just to be sure that you don't accidentally destroy an active drive. Once a disk is formatted, run the **bad144** and **badsect** commands under BSD or the **badblk** command for ATT to fix bad blocks that appear after the formatting process.

On older UNIX versions such as SRV4 and BSD 4.3, once disks are formatted and the bad blocks mapped, the disk is divided into partitions. Modern systems such as AIX and HP-UX don't use partitions. Usually each disk is limited to eight partitions, specified as a,b,c, . . . h. Figure 4.2 shows how these partitions are used. Change this at your own peril, since many programs depend on this structure.

Partition	Function
a	Root partition
b	Swap and paging area
c	Whole disk
d to h	Partitions that subdivide the rest of the disk into multiple, perhaps overlapping areas

FIGURE 4.2 Disk partitions and their uses.

You should not have overlapping partitions active at the same time; to do so could result in data loss and system corruption. The c partition overlaps all other partitions by convention and, as stated below, is considered to be the "whole disk." This implies that the c partition should never be used unless all other disk partitions are currently not in use.

Once the drive is formatted and partitioned, the system must be told about the partitions via the /etc/disktab table. The system treats each partition as a separate disk.

This discussion of partitions is included so that older systems will be covered. Under most modern systems, such as HP-UX, that use logical volume manager (LVM) technology, partitions are no longer used (or at least no longer accessible by the user).

4.2 FILE SYSTEMS

4.2.1 File System Creation

File systems are created with the **mkfs** or **newfs** command under BSD and SVR4 systems. Under AIX the System Management Interface Tool (smit) process can be used to facilitate file system creation by use of the fast path command **smit mkfs**. Under HP-UX the System Administration Manager system (SAM) is used to perform these functions; however, they can be manually performed using **newfs** for hierarchical file systems and **mkfs** for other types of file systems. The **newfs** and **mkfs** commands have the following general format:

```
newfs -s size -b block-size -f fragment-size -i
   bytes/inode -m %-freespace char-device-file disk-type
```

where

> **-s size** is the size in operating system blocks.
>
> **-b block-size** is the size for the blocks if you want other than default-operating-system-size blocks. 8k blocks are typical.
>
> **-f fragment-size** specifies the size of allowed fragments. Generally, 1k is used. This is application-dependent.
>
> **-i bytes/inode** determines the number of inodes created. Generally, the default values are fine unless your file system is to hold numerous small files.
>
> **-m %free-space** is free space that is reserved for the superuser. This defaults to 10 percent, which is usually sufficient.
>
> **char-device-file** is the character device file for the device upon which you are creating the file system.
>
> **disk-type** specifies the entry in the /etc/disktab to use. Almost every disk has a model in /etc/disktab that you can use.

```
mkfs (-y or -n) (-f ftype) (name) (blocks) (:inodes) (gap
   inblocks) (-b blocksize)
```

(get your man page for actual format on your system)
where

> **-y** forces the system to overwrite any existing data.
>
> **-n** stops the mkfs process if any data is present in the first block of the proposed file system.

-f specifies the type of file system this is to be; the choices are root and jfs (journaled file system).

name is the name of the file system.

block is the size of the file system, in operating system blocks (some systems require this size to be in multiples of four megabytes).

:inodes is the number of inodes that the file system is to have. This usually defaults to somewhere around one for every four blocks.

gap inblocks

-b can specify the block size for the file system. This is generally 512, 1,024, 2,048, or 4,096 bytes. If specified, this has to be the last option on the command.

Generally speaking, it is better to err by making a file system too small than by making it too large. A file system can always be extended, but has to be rebuilt in order to shrink. Once the file system is created it must be mounted to be of use. This mounting is accomplished with the **mount** command.

4.2.2   The mount Command

The **mount** command can only be invoked by the superuser. The root file system, designated by the slash (/) symbol, is the top level of all file systems and is always mounted. All other file systems are mounted downward from the root directory. The format for the **mount** command is shown below.

```
mount (-v) (-r) (-f ftype) filesystem (SVR4, BSD)
```

or

```
mount (-option) (-o option) (filesystem) (directory)
```

For the first version of the command:

-v gives verbose information about the mounted file system.

-r indicates that the file system is to be read-only. If a file system that is being mounted consists of write-protected media (such as a floppy with the write-protect tab in place or a CD-ROM drive), it must be mounted read-only. This requirement is due to the system having to update access times; if it attempts to do so on write-protected media, errors will result.

-f ftype tells the system what type of file system is being mounted. The default type is root.

filesystem is the name of the special file that is the mount point of the file system.

For the second version of the command:

-option has several values:

-a	Mount all file systems listed in /etc/fstab.
- t type	Mount file system by specified type (nfs, 4.2, remote).
-v	Verbose mode, tell what is being mounted.

-o option also has several options:

rw	Mount for both reading and writing.
ro	Mount as read-only.
suid	Set to execution allowed only.
nosuid	Set to no execution allowed.

For example, if you have a file system that contains source code (source), object modules (obj), and resulting linked code (bin), as shown in Figure 4.3 and you wish to mount it to the existing "work" branch of the file system shown in Figure 4.3, the command is

```
#/etc/mount /dev/dsk3 /work
```

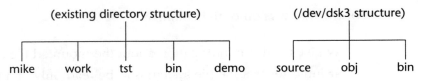

FIGURE 4.3 Existing disk layout.

The resulting structure will look like Figure 4.4 to users, even though it is actually two (or more) file systems.

To see what file systems are mounted in the current directory structure, the user can enter the **mount** command with no arguments, and all of the currently mounted file systems, along with their disk association and when they were mounted, will be displayed. To take a file system out of service, the **umount** command is used. There are also the **df** and **bdf** commands, which will give the system administrator information on mounted file systems, their sizes, and their percent-full statistics.

Under modern UNIX implementations such as AIX and HP-UX there is seldom any call for a system administrator to use the manual **mount** command. Instead, the smit utility under AIX and the SAM utility under HP-UX are used. Other, newer implementations of UNIX may have their own system administration utility.

4.2.3   The umount Command

The **umount** command unmounts a file system from the directory structure. Active file systems cannot be unmounted. In some UNIX versions, if a user has **cd**'ed to the file system, the system is considered in use and thus cannot be unmounted. Since unmounting a file system results in loss of the ability to write or read from the file, all buffers should be flushed with one or more **sync** commands to force synchronization of the file system with the UNIX file buffers. To unmount the file system we mounted in the above example, the following commands are used:

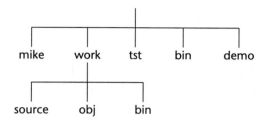

FIGURE 4.4 New layout.

```
# sync
# /etc/umount /dev/dsk3
# /etc/mount
```

The **sync** command forces all pending disk I/O to conclude. Then the file system is unmounted via the **umount** command and the system status is checked with the **/etc/mount** command with no arguments. The **umount** command is passed two arguments, an option code, and the special device file name.

```
umount (-option) (filesystem)
```

The options are

-a   Unmount all mounted file systems that are listed in the /etc/mtab file.

-h host   Unmount remote mounted file systems that are mounted to "host."

-t type   Unmount only the file systems specified by the type argument (nfs, 4.2, remote, etc.).

-v   Verbose—show all file systems as they are unmounted.

The options can be combined to provide for many possible command scenarios.

Under modern UNIX implementations such as AIX and HP-UX there is seldom any call for a system administrator to use the manual **umount** command. Instead, the smit utility under AIX and the SAM utility under HP-UX are used. Other newer implementations of UNIX may have their own system administration utility.

4.2.4   Super-Blocks

Under UNIX a super-block is the 512-byte area that usually starts at byte number 512 of the file system. The super-block contains

- File system name
- File system size
- Address of the first data block
- Count of inodes
- List of inodes
- Count of free data blocks
- List of free data blocks
- Time the super-block was last updated

The super-block for each mounted file system is usually kept in the computer's memory. Memory residency of super-blocks is for speed of access; it can, however, lead to inconsistencies between the disk and memory images of the super-block. These inconsistencies are one of the main reasons the **sync** command is so important. The **sync** command forces the write of all super-block memory images to their respective disk areas. If a system is shut down with the use of **sync**, this will lead to file system inconsistencies and required repairs.

On many systems the cron process automatically issues **sync** commands periodically to ensure that there isn't too great a disparity between the memory and disk images of the super-blocks.

4.2.5   **What Are Inodes?**

In previous chapters and paragraphs I bandied about the term *inode* as if everyone instinctively knew what I was talking about. For those of you who do, jump to the next section; for those who aren't sure or don't have a clue, read on.

The term *inode* refers to the index nodes for a file system. An index node on disk contains

- File owner identifier.

- File type.

- File access permissions.

- File access information (such as when the file was last accessed or modified).

- Time the inode was last modified.

- Number of names the file has in the directory hierarchy (number of links).

- Data addresses for the file (a single file may occupy several areas of a disk).

- File size in bytes.

In addition, the same index node in memory may contain

- Whether the file is locked.

- Processes that may be waiting for the inode.

- If the inode in memory is different from the disk inode.

- Access status of the file (is it a real file or only blocks on the disk?).

- File system id number.

- Relative disk position information for the inode.

■ Pointers to other inodes in memory.

■ Active file instance count.

As you can see, the inode is critical for file access. The memory image of an inode may be different from that of the disk version. Again, the **sync** command forces the memory image and the disk image of an inode to synchronize.

4.2.6 How Are Inodes Used?

When a user or system process requests access to a file, several things occur. First, the file subsystem is passed the **file open**, **read**, or **write** command; next, it accesses the file descriptor table and gets the information needed to access the file table; finally, the file table points to the appropriate inode. Once the file subsystem has the inode information it can handle the user or system process request and access the proper file.

4.3 FILES

4.3.1 File Types

Under UNIX there are at least eight types of file. The BSD special file types are UNIX domain sockets and symbolic links. The ATT special file types are named pipes (FIFOs). And the Common file types are regular files, directories, character device drivers, block device files, and hard links.

4.3.2 Definitions of File Types

Files are the building blocks upon which rests the entire UNIX system. The kernel only sees files; it doesn't see disks, users, or terminals. It used to be said that there were only three types of files under

UNIX: *directory, ordinary,* and *special.* Now there are several more types on this simple list, although purists could argue that the newer types are actually nothing but subtypes under the original three. The decision as to the accuracy of this supposition is left to the reader.

The new types of files are *regular, directory, character device, block device, UNIX domain sockets, named pipes (FIFOs), hard links,* and *symbolic links.* Their definitions follow.

Regular Files   This is the most common file type on any UNIX system. Regular files just hold data, which can be a program, a text listing, source code, or anything that has to be stored. For regular files both sequential access and random access are supported. Files are created by system processes and by editors—text editors, word processors, compilers, and linkers. They are deleted by use of the **rm** command. Other operations involving files include copying (**cp**), moving (**mv**), printing (**lp**) typing to screen (**cat**), or simply listing in a directory (**ls**).

Directories   Directories are like regular files in that they contain a list of data bytes. This list is restricted to other files that are contained within the directory. There are no restrictions on the types of files a directory can contain. Directories are not write-accessible to users, but are kept up by the operating system. BSD directories support variable-length filenames and have a more complex structure than ATT directories have. Both BSD and new ATT releases provide library routines to read directories. On older ATT UNIX-based systems the **read** command is used. The **mkdir** command creates directories, and the **rmdir** command removes empty ones. Nonempty directories are removed with the **rm -rf** command; the contents of a directory can be listed with the **ls** command. The **ls** command has several options to list file statistics at varying levels of detail as shown in Figure 4.5.

File types are also listed by some versions of the **ls** command. Under the ATT and BSD versions of UNIX the **ls** command may show the file type codes listed in Figure 4.6.

Character and Block Device Drivers Character and block device drivers are used by UNIX for communication between devices and UNIX processes. These files are linked into the kernel and provide the required calls and codes to communicate with the devices.

Character drivers are used to communicate with devices that can do their own buffering, such as terminal and pseudo-terminal drivers. Block drivers are associated with device drivers that perform I/O in 512- and 1,024-byte chunks and that want the kernel to perform buffering for them. Some devices, such as disks and tapes, can be represented by both block and character device files.

ls Option	Purpose
-l	Lists the "long" version of a file list, showing mode, size, last modification date, owner, group, link count, and type (this is for ATT versions).
-lg	Lists the "long" version of file list, showing mode, size, last modification date, owner, group, link count, and type (this is for BSD versions).
-a	Lists all entries, including those that begin with period (.).
-b	Forces printing of nongraphic characters in the /ddd format.
-c	Use the time of last inode modification for a sort with -t or -l options.
-d	If file is a directory, lists only its name. Used with -l to get directory status.
-f	Forces each argument to be interpreted as a directory and ignores -i, -t, -s, and -r arguments; enables -a.
-g	Same as -l, except that only the group is printed.
-i	Print the inode number for each file listed.
-l	Prints in long mode (all file inode data).
-m	Puts output as a comma-separated list.
-n	Same as -l, but lists uid and gid as numeric instead of character data.
-o	Same as -l, except only the owner is printed, not owner and group.

FIGURE 4.5 ls command arguments.

ls Option	Purpose
-p	Puts a slash after each directory name.
-q	Forces nongraphic characters to print as (?).
-r	Reverses the sort order.
-s	Gives the size in blocks, including the indirect blocks, for each file.
-t	Sorts by last modification time (inode).
-u	Sorts by time of last access instead of last modification.
-x	Uses the COLUMNS environmental variable to determine number of columns to put the output in; sorts across the page.
-A	Same as -a, except the (..) and (.) files aren't listed.
-C	Uses the COLUMNS environmental variable to determine number of columns to put the output in; sorts down the page.
-F	Puts a symbol that corresponds to the file type with the mode listing: / Directory @ Symbolic link * Executables	FIFO (Named Pipe)
-H	Puts a (+) sign after each hidden directory; also shows cnodes.
-L	Translates all symbolic links into the filenames they point to.
-R	Recursively lists all subdirectories.
-1	(numeral one) Forces 1-column output.

FIGURE 4.5 Continued.

Symbol	File Type
b	Block device file
c	Character mode file
d	Directory
l	Symbolic link (BSD)
p	Named pipe (ATT)
s	UNIX domain socket (BSD)
-	Regular file

FIGURE 4.6 File type codes.

Device drivers may handle more than one device. Device files are always identified by two numbers, a major device number and a minor device number. The major indicates the device driver, while the minor indicates the device. For example, a VAX terminal driver is device 12; physical devices begin numbering at 0, so the fifth device is 4 and thus its device number is 12,4.

The minor number can also be used to specify messages to the device driver. In the case of a tape drive it could be used to specify density, if the tape should be rewound, or other operating parameters. For a modem it could be used to indicate dialers for incoming calls only.

Device files are created with the **mknod** command and eliminated with the **rm** command.

UNIX Domain Sockets (BSD)   UNIX sockets are connections between processes that allow them to communicate quickly and effectively. There are several types, and most require a network. UNIX domain sockets are local to a specific host and are referenced through the file system rather than a network port number. Although they are visible to other processes, only the processes involved in the socket connection can read or write to them. The only standard UNIX processes that deal with domain sockets are printers.

UNIX domain sockets are created with the **socket** system call and can be removed with the rm or unlink system call when no longer in use.

Named Pipes (ATT)   Named pipes are like UNIX domain sockets in that they allow communications between two unrelated processes running on the same host. They are created with the **mknod** command and removed with the **rm** command. Named pipes are also called FIFOs because of the way they handle information sent to them—first-in-first-out.

Hard Links   Links are additional names for a file, not really another file type. Each file has at least one link, the name it was created under. Other links may be made, and the file space can't be freed until all links are dissolved. Hard links cannot exist across file system boundaries. Links and hard links are usually synonymous.

Symbolic Links Symbolic links are files that contain the name of another file. When the kernel looks at a symbolic link it is redirected to the other file. A hard link is a direct link, while a symbolic link is a link by reference. Symbolic links are files with owners and permissions.

Don't use ".." in path names that involve symbolic links, since ".." always references the true parent directory. Symbolic links are created with the **ln -s** command.

4.3.3   Files and Their Relationship to File Systems

Files are stored in file systems. File systems use a certain structure and logic in the placement of files, which should be respected. If the file placement rules that have been established over the years are ignored, it can lead to problems, especially for updates and attempts to use programs that assume that the common structure is in place. The common file systems and their uses are shown in Figure 4.7.

4.4   FILE SYSTEM SECURITY

One of UNIX's major shortcomings is in the area of security. Its design as a portable research and instructional operating system has resulted in the downplaying of its security aspects. Now everyone is trying to use UNIX, beyond the wildest dreams of its creators, for purposes that they probably never even thought or dreamed would come to be. Luckily, several vendors are offering enhanced security features for UNIX, such as login attempt limits, password aging, and other high-level schemes. Unfortunately, we are still stuck with vir-

File System	Purpose
/	Root; contains kernel binary and other important files.
/bin	Commands needed for minimal system operability.
/5bin	SVR4 compatibility commands for BSD-based system.
/dev	Device entries for terminals, disks, modems, etc.
/etc	Critical system configuration files and maintenance commands.
/lib	C compiler and preprocessor.
/sys	Kernel-building work area, kernel configuration files (BSD).
/stand	Standalone utilities (disk formatters, etc.).
/tmp	Temporary files, usually a small amount of space.
/usr/adm	Accounting files, records of resource usage.
/usr/bin	Executable files.
/usr/dict	The spelling dictionary (BSD).
/usr/doc	Larger UNIX-related documents, no manual pages.
/usr/etc	Where SUN-OS puts things that everyone else puts in /etc.
/usr/games	Games and diversions.
/usr/include	All UNIX-defined C header files.
/usr/lbin	Local binaries (ATT).
/usr/lib	Support files for standard UNIX programs.
/usr/local/adm	Accounting log files.
/usr/local/bin	Executables.
/usr/local/etc	System maintenance commands.
/usr/local/lib	Support files.
/usr/local/src	Source for /usr/local/bin, /usr/local/lib, and /usr/local/etc.
/usr/man	Online manual pages.
/usr/new	New software that will soon be supported (BSD).
/usr/old	Obsolete software that will soon be unsupported (BSD).
/usr/preserve	Backup copies of files created by the editors vi and ex.
/usr/spool	Spooling directories for printers, uucp, mail, etc.
/usr/src	Source code for UNIX standard commands.
/usr/src/local	Alternative location for /usr/local/src.
/usr/src/uts	Kernel-building work area, kernel configuration files (ATT).
/usr/tmp	More temporary space.
/usr/ucb	Berkeley utilities and programs (BSD).

FIGURE 4.7 Standard file systems for BSD and ATT UNIX.

tually the same file-level security scheme that has been with UNIX since the beginning.

The file security methodology used by UNIX is based on the concept that there are three types of access; world, group, and owner. World-level security, as its name implies, refers to the entire user community on the UNIX platform. Group-level security refers to users who are given a specific group identifier. A user can belong to as many groups as specified in the /etc/group file. The user's base-level groups are defined in the /etc/passwd file. Owner-level security is what the owner of the file can do to it. Of course, since the owner can change the security of his or her own files, the owner-based protections are more of a protection from brain lapses than from any security hazard. The combination of world, group, and owner security profiles is stored in the file's inode and is referred to as the file's mode.

The root or superuser account maintains the file security for the entire system. Through use of the group and file mode concept, granularity in how security can be defined, as far as use of the file system goes, can be pushed down to the individual file level. The commands for setting a user's passwords and group-related security options will be covered in Chapter 6, on user administration. Let's look at the commands for file security implementation.

4.4.1   Changing File Ownership

Files can only be owned by one owner and one group at a time. Other users and groups may have access to the file, but can't jointly own it. There are two commands that affect file ownership. These are the **chown** and the **chgrp** commands.

Use of the chown Command   The use of the **chown** command is really quite simple:

```
chown newowner filename
```

where

> **newowner** is the login name of the new owner.
>
> **filename** is the name of the file to change the ownership on.

So, if we want to change the ownership of the file /users/bb/chiefs to the user omaha from the owner kc, the command is

```
$ chown omaha /users/bb/chiefs
```

Use of the chgrp Command   Like the **chown** command, the **chgrp** command is simple to use. Essentially, you specify the group identification number and the filename, and the owning group is changed:

```
chgrp groupid filename
```

Using the file from the example in the section on the **chown** command, let's change the owning group from 10 to 2:

```
$ chgrp 2 /users/bb/chiefs
```

Both the **chown** and **chgrp** commands have C language routines named the same that are used to provide the same capabilities from C on UNIX.

4.4.2   Use of the chmod Command on Files and Directories

As was stated at the beginning of Section 4.4, the particular combination of a file's world, group, and owner permissions is referred to as the file's mode. Therefore, it is logical to call the command that changes the file's protections the "change mode" command, or simply **chmod** for simplicity's sake. In the beginning, the mode was set by setting the different bytes of the mode to different numeric values that corresponded to a particular combination of file characteristics (see Figure 4.8).

These codes—4, read; 2, write; and 1, execute, can be specified as a sum or as individual codes. For example, 7 (4 + 2 + 1) (binary 111) grants read, write, and execute; 6 (4 + 2) (binary 110) grants read and write; and 0 accords no permissions.

The total mode of a file can be expressed as a series of three of these composite codes, with the first number corresponding to the owner, the second to the group, and the third to the world class of users. Hence, 777 means that world, group, and owner all have read, write, and execute privileges; 760, that the owner has read, write, and execute, the group has read and write, and the world has none. The command has the format

```
chmod mode filename
```

An example of the use of this command would be setting the protection on a file such that only the owner could access it:

```
$ chmod 700 /users/bb/chiefs
```

The above command would grant read, write, and execute privileges to the owner but revoke all access to the group and world. Remember, you can't restrict the root user (the superuser) from any file access.

On some current implementations of UNIX you may also use symbolic representations for the permissions. These representations

Mode Code	Binary Representation	Meaning
4	100	Read permission
2	10	Write permission
1	1	Execute permission

FIGURE 4.8 File protection mode codes.

are shown in Figure 4.9. Using the codes, the individual levels of protection can be altered. For example, to add the read privilege to world the command is:

```
$ chmod o+r /users/bb/chiefs
```

To change the mode so that group no longer has execute privilege the command is:

```
$ chmod g-x /users/bb/chiefs
```

The **chmod** command is also used to alter the mode of directories. However, the codes' actual meanings change when dealing with a directory rather than a normal file. Directory read permission allows a user to see the contents of a directory, but not to change the directory, using the **cd** command on the directory they can read. The write permission allows a user to modify the directory contents

Symbol	Meaning
u	User (owner).
g	Group.
o	Other (world); doesn't stand for owner!
r	Read.
w	Write.
e	Execute.
s	SETUID or SETGID is set (depending on position) with search permission.
S	SETUID or SETGID is set (depending on position) and search permission refused.
t	Last position only; sticky bit is set.
+	After permissions, means access control list (ACL) is set.

FIGURE 4.9 Symbolic representation of mode codes.

even if the individual files have a different mode than the directory file has. Write permission should be given with care. The final permission, execute, allows the user to **cd** to the directory.

4.4.3   Use of the umask Command

To assign a default permission mask for a user, the **umask** command can be executed in either the .cshrc or .profile file depending on the user's login shell. The **umask** command is fed a 3-digit octal value that defines what protections should not be given to the user. For example, if the **umask** value is set to 222, the user does not have write permission to any file he or she creates. If **umask** is set to 007, the user has all permissions on his or her and his or her group's files, but none on any other file on the system. This value is subtracted from any file-level modes that may be set.

On systems like BSD there is a default value that can be loaded into the kernel and automatically given to each new user. However, users can issue a **umask** command or edit the **.cshrc** or **.profile** file to reset the value to one more to their liking.

4.4.4   Use of the setuid, the setgid, and the Sticky Bit

There are three special bits that can be set in a file's mode: 4,000— the setuid bit; 2,000—the setgid bit; and 1000—the sticky bit. These are activated by adding their respective values to the octal mode in the **chmod** command. For example,

```
$ chmod 1777 /users/bb/chiefs
```

sets the sticky bit for the file /users/bb/chiefs. This has the effect of keeping the file in shared memory. The sticky bit should only be used for frequently accessed programs such as vi. The setuid (4,000) value appends the user's permissions mode to the file for all users, as the setgid (2,000) sets the file's protection mode to that specified in its group mode for all users. Needless to say, all of these special modes should be used with care.

4.5   MONITORING FILE SYSTEMS

System administrators and general users need to monitor file systems and their contents. The system manager needs to be able to monitor modes, sizes, and other statistics, while users need to look at file locations and modes. For these purposes there are several file and file system monitoring commands. The commands can be used to look at individual files or the entire file system, depending on how they are used and what options are specified.

4.5.1   Commands Used for Monitoring File System

Different flavors of UNIX have different commands that may be used to monitor file systems. For example, the AIX system uses the smit interface for many system monitoring functions. To get a file system list showing the node, mounted file system, mount point, type of file system, date the file system was mounted, and any options used when mounting the file system under AIX, use the **smit fs** command. Alternatively, the command-line command **df -v** will produce a listing of the file system, total kb, used kb, free kb, percent used, inode used, inode free, percent of inodes used, and mount point for the entire file system.

Under HP-UX the SAM system can be used to invoke the HP VUE file manager, which will list a graphical representation of the file system showing mount points and file types. The **df** command works in HP-UX as well, and a variant of the **df**, known as **bdf**, is also available. The **bdf** command provides the block device file name for the file system, total kbytes, used kbytes, available kbytes, available capacity as a percent, and the mount point of the file system. If **bdf** is specified with the -i option, the number of inodes used and inodes free will also be displayed for each file system.

The **df** command is also available under BSD and SVR4 UNIX. Under some versions the -t option replaces the -i option for listing the inode information. Other command options for the **df** command are shown in Figure 4.10.

Another useful command for file system monitoring is **du**, short for "disk usage." As its name implies, this command shows the disk usage in 512-byte blocks for a specified file system. Therefore, a 1-block file on a 1,024-byte block file will show up as 2 blocks when this command is used. The **du** command lists the file names and blocks used. It has several options, just like the **df** command, which are shown in Figure 4.11. Some problems with the **du** command include duplicate counting of link files (if there are too many distinct links, they will be counted more than once); files with holes causing incorrect counts, and, in file systems with block sizes larger than 512 bytes, incorrect file block counts being generated.

Option	Purpose
-t	Prints allocated blocks and total free blocks.
-f	Prints the count of free list blocks and used inodes. Can also be used to report on raw devices if desired.
-v	Causes **df** to print used blocks, free blocks, and the percent of blocks free (512k blocks).
-i	Prints inode data; may be used with -v but not with other options. (Generally, -v and -i are used with SCO UNIX only, but have been finding their way into BSD UNIX versions.)

FIGURE 4.10 **df** command options.

Option	Purpose
-a	Gives data on files. If neither the -s nor -a option is specified, the **du** command lists directories only. If -a is not specified, non directories given as arguments will be ignored.
-f	Shows data only for the current file system; ignores any file systems mounted on the current file system.
-r	Shows files that can't be opened or directories that can't be read. If a file has more than one link, will force a single display of that file.
-s	Gives total blocks for each file.
-u	Forces a file with more than one link to be ignored.

FIGURE 4.11   Options for the **du** command.

QUOTA Commands for BSD   In order to use quotas on a BSD system, the kernel must be relinked, with the following line added to the kernel configuration file:

```
options    QUOTA
```

Once quotas are enabled, a useful command, **quot**, shows usage totals for users rather than files. The **quot** command may not be available on all systems; in fact, it is usually only available on BSD-based systems in conjunction with the **quotaon**, **quotaoff**, and **quotacheck** commands. What **quot** provides is a summary (with the -s option) of the users and their total disk usage for a file system. The **quotacheck -v** command provides the same information as **quot** does. The **edquota** command allows you to edit or modify a user's quota. The **quota *user*** command, where ***user*** is the user name for the user you want information on, gives quota information on specific users. The **repquota** command also reports on a user's quota status. Again, these commands are usually found only on BSD and BSD-derived versions of UNIX and are only useful if quotas have been enabled on the system.

Quotas are enabled by use of the **quotaon -a** command in the /etc/rc script. Then the **quotacheck -a** command should be run to regenerate all quota information for all file systems in the /etc/fstab. This data is written to the /users/quotas file. The following commands show the creation of the /users/quotas file by the root user:

```
$ touch /users/quotas
$ chmod 600 /users/quotas
```

To enable quotas on a specific file system, edit the /etc/fstab file. A normal entry for a read/write-enabled file system looks like

```
/dev/ra1g:/tmp:rw:1:2
```

This entry should be modified to replace rw with rq to enable quotas:

```
/dev/ra1g:/tmp:rq:1:2
```

Of course, only read/write–enabled file systems have quotas; quotas can't be enabled for read-only file systems. The **quotacheck -a** command should be run in the /etc/rc script to ensure proper update of the quota file in case of improper shutdowns, just as the **fsck -p** command is used to ensure that file systems are properly conditioned. On some BSD implementations the **quotatcheck** command also has a -p option to check files in a parallel manner. The **quotaon** command can be used with a file system name to turn quotas on for a newly created file system without rebooting.

Quotas under the HP-UX System   Quotas are also available for HP-UX systems. They are set up by editing the /etc/checklist file to include disk quotas, creating a disk quota file, setting up disk usage limits, applying the limits to users, and, finally, turning on the quotas. Let's look at these steps in more detail.

Editing the /etc/checklist file. For quotas to work, the system must be aware of what file systems quotas are applied to. This is accomplished by placing quota-enabling statements in the file entry of the /etc/checklist file for the file systems for which quotas are to be enabled. For example, if we wish to alter the file system /dev/dsk/2s1 mounted on the /tmp directory, the entry in the /etc/checklist file will be altered to

```
/dev/dsk/2s1 /tmp jfs rw,quota 0 1 #quota on /tmp
```

Creating the quotas file. Next, the file that contains the quota information should be created. The **cpset** command is used to do this.

```
$ cpset /dev/null /tmp/quotas 600 root bin
```

This command creates a quota file for the /tmp disk.

Placing quotas in the quotas file. Once the file is created the **edquota** command is used to place user quota information in it. This command is stored in the /etc/edquota location, so to invoke it the format is

```
$ /etc/edquota proto-man
```

This invokes the vi editor on the file system's quota file. Generally, limits are specified for this proto-man user and then they are applied to other users as required. A typical entry for this prototype user, as shown by Marty Poniatowski in *The HP-UX System Administrator's How To Book* (Prentice-Hall, 1994), is listed below.

```
fs /tmp blocks (soft = 500, hard=700) inodes (soft=100,
  hard=200)
```

According to Marty, you can also restrict the amount of time a user has to correct any problems by specifying a command similar to this:

```
fs /tmp blocks time limit=10.00 days, inodes time limit =
   15.00 days
```

Once the limits are assigned to the prototype user, they are assigned to other users by use of the -p option with the **/etc/edquota -p** command. To assign the limits to users nip and tuck, the following command is issued:

```
$ /etc/edquota -p proto-man nip tuck
```

Unlike in the BSD quota system, for quotas to take effect the system must be rebooted. The **quotaon**, **quotaoff**, and **quotacheck** commands are also available under HP-UX. As in BSD, there is a **quot** command, and the **quotacheck -v** or **repquota** command can be used to get disk quota status and disk usage data for users.

4.6   FIXING BROKEN FILE SYSTEMS

File system damage can be grouped into several general categories:

- Unreferenced inodes
- Incorrect super-block information
- Incorrect link counts
- Unrecorded unused data blocks
- Used blocks listed as free blocks

As we discussed in Chapter 3, on startup and shutdown, the **fsck** command is used to repair damaged file systems. All of the above listed errors can be fixed by **fsck**. File systems can be damaged by improper shutdowns, crashes, and other generally file system-destructive activities (such as turning off unresponsive processes that have control of files.) Normally, this command is run at boot time with the -p (preen) option.

The **fsck** command replaces the commands **bcheck**, **dcheck**, **ncheck**, **icheck**, and **clri**, which administrators may have used on early UNIX releases. On most systems a detailed document on **fsck** over and above the man pages is provided. The system administrator should become familiar with this command.

The **fsck** command uses the /etc/fstab table to obtain a list of file systems in use. The fifth field in the /etc/fstab file entry for a specific file system specifies the order in which the file system is checked. File systems that reside on different physical volumes may be checked simultaneously; therefore, they can be given a fifth entry in the /etc/fstab table that is identical and should since it will speed the fsck process.

The ATT SVR4 UNIX uses the /etc/checklist instead of the /etc/fstab table. The /etc/checklist file is a sequential list of file systems that should be checked.

The **fsck** command, when used with the -p option, will warn the user and terminate if one of the following errors is detected:

■ Blocks not accounted for

■ Various format errors

■ Too small a link count value

■ A file claiming blocks that are outside of the file system

■ More than one file claiming the same block

■ Directories referencing unallocated inodes

If you receive one of these errors, **fsck** must be run without the -p option and you must earn your salary by answering all of **fsck**'s questions manually. You should log all of the files altered, dropped, or fixed by **fsck** so that they can be restored from backups if **fsck** makes an error. Occasionally **fsck** may report that a file has zero blocks and ask to delete it. Before you allow this, try copying the file to another location just in case **fsck** is mistaken. You should not allow **fsck** to work on files in the lost+found directory; these should be fixed manually. If you get an DUP TABLE OVERFLOW or LINK COUNT TABLE OVERFLOW error, answer No to the continue prompt and regenerate **fsck** with larger table sizes.

4.6.1 The fsck Command Options

The **fsck** command has the following syntax:

```
fsck [-bCDfnpPqSty] [-sb:c] [filesystem]
```

The command options have the following purposes:

-b—This option is used when checking the root file system. If the damage is minor, the file system is remounted. If it isn't minor, this reboots the system. Under HP-UX this option is specified with a block number to use as an alternate super-block location. This can save you at 2 A.M. when nothing else has worked.

-C—The -s option must be specified as well as the -C option. -C converts an S51K file system into an Acer fast file system (AFS). No performance gains are realized with nearly full file systems, and file systems within a few blocks of being full cannot be converted. Following the -C option, a cluster size that is a power-of-2 integer less than 16 (2, 4, 8, or 16), and generally 8, is specified.

-D—This option checks for directories with bad blocks. This is useful after system crashes.

-f—This stands for "fast" and performs a fast file system check consisting of phase 1, phase 5, and, if required, phase 6.

-n—Use this option if hardware problems are suspected. It stands for "answer No" and answers No to all questions asked by **fsck**, meaning that no repairs are initiated. In a hardware failure situation, attempting to fix problems may cause more damage.

-p—This is the standard "preen" option and allows **fsck** to perform non-data-altering changes only. This is a noninteractive mode and will fix what it can and exit if a serious data-altering error is found.

-P—This is an HP-UX second preening mode. If a file is unmounted and marked as "clean," **fsck** will not check it under HP-UX.

-q—This stands for "quiet." No phase-1 messages are generated. The counts in the super-block will be automatically fixed and the free list salvaged. Generally, you want to know what **fsck** is doing, so don't use this option.

-S—This option rebuilds the free list on a conditional basis—the free list is only rebuilt if no file system problems are found. This is similar to the -n option in that a No response is provided for all questions normally asked by **fsck**. It can be used to reorganize the free list on otherwise normal file systems.

-t—This option, with a specified filename, will use a scratch file for **fsck**-generated tables instead of keeping them in memory. This is useful on systems with limited memory. One precaution: *If no space is left between the -t and the filename, the entire file system will be used, resulting in loss of the entire disk contents!*

-y—This option answers yes to all **fsck** questions. It can save you time, but can cause problems if it removes bad blocks since you won't know which have been removed and won't then know which to restore if required.

-sb:c—This option ignores existing free lists and unconditionally reconstructs the file system's super-block. The file system is unmounted for this operation. One good feature of this option is that it allows creation of an optimally organized free list.

It is obvious from the list above that, as with most UNIX commands, the **fsck** command has numerous options. Under BSD the /etc/fstab file controls how **fsck** behaves. This file has a line for each file system with up to five entries per line. For example:

```
/dev/ra0g:/work:rw:0:3
```

The first entry is the name of the block device file that describes the partition. The next entry, if populated, tells the mount point—if it is empty, this is a swap partition. The third entry is a two-letter code that describes the file system access (see Figure 4.12). The fourth entry is used in the scheduling of the **dump** command, and the fifth is used to force the order in which the partitions are checked at boot time.

This file can be called /etc/filesystems on other versions of UNIX. It is also used by the **mount**, **umount**, and the **swapon** commands. Before editing the entries in your /etc/fstab or its equivalent, be sure you read the documentation for your system concerning the proper format and positioning of options. There is a real chance of botching up your file systems if you make a mistake when editing this file, so be very careful and read your documentation before making changes. You should make a backup of the system before making any changes to /etc/fstab or /etc/filesystems.

4.6.2   fsck Error Codes

During execution of the **fsck** command you may receive various errors depending on which phase of the file checks is being performed. The following is a list of possible error codes for **fsck**; how-

Code	Meaning
ro	Mount for read-only.
rq	Mount for read-write with quotas.
rw	Mount for read-write.
sw	Do not mount, swap partition.

FIGURE 4.12 Options for the file system code in the **/etc/fstab** table for BSD.

ever, it is not intended to be complete and you should consult your system **fsck** documentation for the entire list.

Errors during Phase 1 In phase 1 of **fsck** the file system's blocks and sizes are checked. This means that the inode lists are verified. Generally speaking, there are 13 possible errors during phase 1:

b BAD I=n—Inode n has block number b with a block number outside the range allowed for the file system. This causes additional errors in phases 2 and 4.

b DUP I=n—Inode n has block b that seems to belong to another inode. This will cause additional errors in phases 2 and 4 and will cause the program to enter phase 1b.

CONTINUE?—A Yes response will continue the program; a No response (the suggested one) terminates it. This isn't an error, but will be used in conjunction with an error to determine actions.

CLEAR?—A Yes response zeros the inode contents, essentially deallocating its resources. This can cause unallocated errors in phase 2. This isn't an error, but will be used in conjunction with an error to determine actions.

DIRECTORY MISALIGNED I=n—Since this is actually a warning, the -q flag will suppress it. It indicates that inode n has a directory size that isn't a multiple of 16.

DUP TABLE OVERFLOW (CONTINUE?)—This indicates that one of **fsck**'s internal tables is full, which means that **fsck** needs to be regenerated with larger table sizes. How to do this regeneration should be covered in your system manual.

EXCESSIVE BAD BLOCKS I=n (CONTINUE?)—Generally speaking, if you get more than ten indications that there is a block number outside of the range allowed for the inode (n), you will get this error (these are shown by the b BAD I=n errors.)

EXCESSIVE DUP BLKS I=n (CONTINUE?)—For most systems if you get more than ten blocks that seem to be owned by more than one inode (n), you will get this error (as shown by the b DUP I=n errors).

LINK COUNT TABLE OVERFLOW (CONTINUE?)—This indicates that another of **fsck**'s internal tables has been filled, meaning that **fsck** needs to be regenerated with larger table sizes.

PARTIALLY ALLOCATED INODE I=n (CLEAR?)—This may indicate an inode (n) whose block list was incomplete or otherwise damaged, leaving the inode in a state between allocated and unallocated. If you clear the inode, all data remaining will be lost. You should attempt to manually fix this problem if possible before clearing the inode.

POSSIBLE FILE SIZE ERROR I=n—Since this is actually a warning, the -q flag will suppress it. This indicates a size mismatch between the actual blocks used by inode n and the size stored in the inode.

UNKNOWN FILE TYPE I=n (CLEAR?)—The mode word for this inode (n) doesn't match any of the known file types. If you clear this, it will eliminate the file. You should try copying the file or looking at it with an editor before clearing it to be sure you don't need it.

Errors during Phase 2 Phase 2 involves the checking of pathnames. This means that for all of the bad inodes found in phase 1 and phase 1b, all directory entries that point to those bad inodes will be removed.

BAD BLK IN DIR I=n OWNER = x MODE = y SIZE = z MTIME= t—This error only occurs if the -D option was specified in the **fsck** command. It indicates that for directory inode n, owned by user x for mode y with size z and last modification time t, there are bad or inconsistent entries. Entries with bad "." and ".."

entries, improper characters such as slashes in the name, or non-zero-padded entries will trigger this error. You should attempt to fix or delete the specified entries or delete the entire directory if required.

CONTINUE?—This is an error inclusion statement. It is included at the end of the error to indicate action. A Yes response will ignore any DUPS/BAD errors from phase 1 or 1b in the root inode and will attempt to continue the checks. A No response terminates the program.

DUP/BAD I=n OWNER = x MODE = y SIZE = z MTIME= t DIR=d (REMOVE?)—This indicates that for directory d, inode n, owner x, mode y, size z, and last modification time t, phase 1 and/or 1b have found duplicate blocks or bad blocks.

DUP/BAD I=n OWNER = x MODE = y SIZE = z MTIME= t FILE=f (REMOVE?)—This indicates that for file f, inode n, owner x, mode y, size z, and last modification time t, phase 1 and/or 1b have found duplicate blocks or bad blocks.

DUPS/BAD IN ROOT INODE (CONTINUE?)—Duplicate or bad blocks have been found in the root inode (usually inode 2) by the phase-1 or -1b check.

FIX?—This is an error inclusion statement. It is included at the end of the error to indicate action. A Yes response changes the root inode type to directory. A number of errors will occur if the inode contains blocks that are not directory blocks.

I OUT OF RANGE I=n NAME = d (REMOVE?)—This indicates that directory inode n for directory d has a file inode entry that is out of range of the allowed inode list.

REMOVE?—This is an error inclusion statement. It is included at the end of the error to indicate action. A Yes response removes unallocated or duplicate blocks. A No response ignores the error. Don't answer No unless you intend to fix the problem some other way.

ROOT INODE NOT DIRECTORY (FIX?)—This error indicates that the mode of the root inode (inode 2) is not that of a directory.

ROOT INODE UNALLOCATED. TERMINATING—This error shows that the root inode has no allocated mode bits. The program cannot continue and stops. Usually, recovery from backup is indicated.

UNALLOCATED I = n OWNER = x MODE = y SIZE = z MTIME = t NAME = d (REMOVE?)—This indicates that directory d has inode n that doesn't have any mode bits allocated. If the file system is unmounted and the inode character size is 0, the inode will be automatically removed unless the -n option has been specified in the **fsck** command.

Errors during Phase 3 Phase 3 of **fsck** takes the new and existing inode reference data for directories generated from previous phases and verifies that the inode references are valid. This is referred to as checking connectivity. The general errors that may occur in phase 3 follow.

DIR I = n1 CONNECTED. PARENT WAS I=n2—This indicates that a directory inode n1 was successfully connected to the lost+found directory. The inode of the parent directory is indicated by n2.

RECONNECT?—This is an error inclusion statement. It is included at the end of the error to indicate action. A Yes response reconnects the directory to the lost+found directory. If there are problems such as no lost+found directory or a full lost+found directory, you will get further errors.

SORRY, NO lost+found DIRECTORY—This indicates that there is either no lost+found directory in the root directory or that there is a problem with the access mode of the lost+found directory. This will cause an UNREF error for phase 4.

SORRY, NO SPACE IN lost+found DIRECTORY—This indicates that the lost+found directory is full. Clean out lost+found or make it larger. This will cause an UNREF error during phase 4. The request to link the directory to lost+found will be ignored.

UNREF I=n OWNER = x MODE = y SIZE = z MTIME = t (RECONNECT?)—This error indicates that inode n was not connected to a directory. The fsck program will force a connect if you answer Yes for a nonempty directory.

Errors during Phase 4 Phase 4 checks the link count information from phases 2 and 3. This is referred to as checking reference counts. The general errors for Phase 4 are

ADJUST?—This is an error inclusion statement. It is included at the end of the error to indicate action. A Yes response replaces the indicated link count with the actual link count in the file's inode. A No response continues with no fix performed. You should only give a No response if you intend on fixing the error some other way.

BAD/DUP FILE I = n OWNER = x MODE = y SIZE = z MTIME = t (CLEAR?)—This indicates that bad or duplicate blocks in the file's inode (n) block list were found during phase 1 or 1b.

BAD/DUP DIR I = n OWNER = x MODE = y SIZE = z MTIME = t (CLEAR?)—This indicates that bad or duplicate blocks in the directory's inode (n) block list were found during phase 1 or 1b.

CLEAR?—This is an error inclusion statement. It is included at the end of the error to indicate action. A Yes response deallocates the node by zeroing its contents. A No response ignores the error condition. Don't answer No unless you are going to fix the error some other way.

(CLEAR)—This indicates that the inode mentioned in the UNREF error immediately prior to the statement cannot be reconnected.

FIX?—This is an error inclusion statement. It is included at the end of the error to indicate action. A Yes response replaces the count in the super-block with the actual count. A No response ignores the error. Only answer No if you are going to fix the error some other way.

FREE INODE COUNT WRONG IN SUPERBLK (FIX?)—This indicates that there is a mismatch between the count of free inodes in the super-block versus the actual number of free inodes. If you specify the -q option in the **fsck** command, the count will be fixed automatically.

LINK COUNT DIR I = n OWNER = x MODE = y SIZE = z MTIME = t COUNT = a SHOULD BE b (ADJUST?)—This indicates that the link count (a) for directory inode (n) should be b.

LINK COUNT FILE I = n OWNER = x MODE = y SIZE = z MTIME = t COUNT = a SHOULD BE b (ADJUST?)—This indicates that the link count (a) for file inode (n) should be b.

RECONNECT?—This is an error inclusion statement. It is included at the end of the error to indicate action. A Yes response reconnects the inode to the lost+found directory. If there are problems with the lost+found directory, more errors will be generated. A No response ignores this error condition.

SORRY, NO lost+found DIRECTORY—This indicates that there is either no lost+found directory in the root directory or that there is a problem with the access mode of the lost+found directory. This will cause an CLEAR error later in phase 4.

SORRY, NO SPACE IN lost+found DIRECTORY—This indicates that the lost+found directory is full. Clean out lost+found or make it larger. This will cause a CLEAR error later during phase 4. The request to link the file to lost+found will be ignored.

UNREF DIR I = n OWNER = x MODE = y SIZE = z MTIME = t (CLEAR?)—This error indicates that file inode n was not connected to a directory inode when the file system was checked. If the file system is unmounted, the directory is cleared if it is empty. Nonempty directories aren't cleared.

UNREF FILE I = n OWNER = x MODE = y SIZE = z MTIME = t (CLEAR?)—This error indicates that file inode n was not connected to a directory inode when the file system was checked. If the file system is unmounted, the file is cleared if it is empty. Nonempty files aren't cleared.

UNREF FILE I = n OWNER = x MODE = y SIZE = z MTIME = t (RECONNECT?)—This error indicates that file inode n was not connected to a directory inode when the file system was checked. The file is reconnected to the lost+found directory if it is not empty; if the file system is unmounted and the file is empty, the file is cleared.

Errors during Phase 5   In phase 5 the free list blocks are checked. The general errors for phase 5 are the following:

BAD FREE LIST (SALVAGE?)—This error is always preceded by several informational errors. If **fsck** was run with the -q option, the free list will be salvaged automatically.

BAD FREEBLK COUNT—This error occurs when the free list count is less than 0 or greater than 50. It will always invoke the BAD FREE LIST error as well.

CONTINUE?—This is an error inclusion statement. It is included at the end of the error to indicate action. A Yes response continues the program execution, ignoring the rest of the free list block LIST. A Yes response will always result in the BAD BLKS IN FREE LIST error later in phase 5. A No response terminates the program.

EXCESSIVE BAD BLKS IN FREE LIST (CONTINUE?)—This indicates that the free block list has (usually) more than ten blocks whose addresses lie outside of the file system boundaries.

EXCESSIVE DUP BLKS IN FREE LIST (CONTINUE?)—This indicates that the free block list has (usually) ten or more blocks listed that are claimed by other inodes or previously listed in the free blocks list.

FIX?—This is an error inclusion statement. It is included at the end of the error to indicate action. A Yes response replaces the count in the super-block with the actual count. A No response ignores the error. Don't answer No unless you intend to fix the problem in some other way.

FREE BLOCK COUNT WRONG IN SUPERBLOCK (FIX?)—This indicates an error between the indicated and actual free block count in the super-block.

SALVAGE?—This is an error inclusion statement. It is included at the end of the error to indicate action. A Yes response replaces the old free block list with one newly generated; the new list is ordered according to the -s or -S option. A No response ignores the error and should not be given unless the user intends to fix the error in some other way.

X BAD BLKS IN FREE LIST—This indicates that X blocks with locations outside of the file system boundaries have been specified in the free block list. This will invoke the BAD FREE LIST error condition.

X DUP BLKS IN FREE LIST—This indicates that there are X blocks listed twice in the free space list or that the blocks are claimed by another inode as well. This will invoke the BAD FREE LIST error condition.

X BLK(S) MISSING—This indicates that X blocks that are unused by the file system are also not listed in the free block list. This will invoke the BAD FREE LIST error condition.

Errors during Phase 6 Phase 6 is where the actions specified in phase 5 are executed. This is the phase in which the free block list is salvaged. It only has one error message, which occurs when there are bad blocks-per-cylinder or gap values. For instance, if gap (blocks-to-skip) or blocks-per-cylinder is less than 1, or the blocks-per-cylinder is greater than 500, or the gap (blocks-to-skip) is greater than blocks-per-cylinder, the error will be displayed and the defaults for the system used (usually 7 for gap and 400 for blocks-per-cylinder).

> DEFAULT FREE BLOCK SPACING ASSUMED—This is a warning and shows that defaults for gap and blocks-per-cylinder are being used. Check the specifications for gap and blocks-per-cylinder.

Cleanup Phase Errors   Once you get through the barrage of possible errors in the other phases, there are also errors in the final, or cleanup, phase of the **fsck** process. These errors deal with the file system and its status.

> CLEANUP PHASE MESSAGES X FILES Y BLOCKS Z FREE—This is an advisory message only. It is just giving you the basic facts about the file system (X, Y, and Z are numbers).
>
> **** BOOT Unix (NO SYNC!) ****—You get this message if you have used **fsck** on a mounted file system. It is telling you not to perform a **sync** command or the changes done by **fsck** may be overwritten by the files resident in memory. If you are going to modify mounted file systems, specify the -b option so an automatic reboot is performed without a **sync**.
>
> **** FILE SYSTEM WAS MODIFIED ****—This message simply tells you that the current file system was modified by the **fsck** command.

General fsck Errors   **fsck** also has several general errors that may appear in any phase of operation. These are usually fatal, and you should stop the **fsck** process when they are received.

> CAN NOT SEEK: BLK x (CONTINUE?)—In this error **fsck** has attempted to move something to block x in the file system and failed. This could be due to mode errors or hardware failure.

CAN NOT READ: BLK x (CONTINUE?)—In this error **fsck** has attempted to read block x and failed. This could be due to mode problems or hardware failure.

CAN NOT WRITE BLK x (CONTINUE?)—In this error **fsck** has attempted to write to block x and failed. This could be due to mode problems or hardware failure.

These errors indicate perhaps significant problems in the file system. You should not continue **fsck** if you get one of them. A No response to the continue prompt will terminate the **fsck** process, while a Yes will force it to continue. Even if the process terminates properly after a Yes response, **fsck** should be run a second time to ensure that the file system is fully checked.

4.7   FILE SYSTEM DEFRAGMENTATION

If you read Chapter 1, you know why this section is of particular interest. If it wasn't for my being unable to locate this information in available references, my motivation for writing this book might have never taken root. Like all dynamically allocated disk systems, the UNIX disk management system suffers from problems with fragmentation. Those UNIX flavors based on BSD UNIX seem to have fewer problems than do those based on SVR4.

4.7.1   SVR4 Fragmentation Control

Under SVR4 and its clones fragmentation can be a problem. The system administrator needs to periodically perform disk maintenance to prevent fragmentation from becoming severe. Depending on how severely file systems are fragmented, there are differing levels of response due from the system administrator. To prevent fragmentation caused by aged free block lists, the system administrator should periodically rebuild the free block lists using the -S option of the **fsck** command. The procedure is as follows.

1. Shut down to single-user mode.

2. Unmount the file system that needs to have its free list reorganized. It is critical that the system be unmounted; there must be no activity within the file system other than that generated by the **fsck** command. Remember that root can't be unmounted, but you can perform this operation against it in single-user mode.

3. Execute the **fsck -S** command against the file system—this rebuilds the free block list.

4. Reboot the system immediately after **fsck** completes.

This procedure only affects future files and doesn't help if files are already fragmented. If you have SVR4, you can use the **dcopy** command to defragment existing file systems. In pre-release-4 releases the only way to defragment the file systems is to perform the following procedure:

1. Back up the file system.

2. Use the **mkfs** command to rebuild the file system.

3. Restore the file system backup.

This procedure will defragment the file system and the free block list. It will have to be repeated as often as the file system becomes fragmented. It is suggested that you upgrade to a version that supports **dcopy**, as this can be a major inconvenience for large systems.

On SVR4 systems and later releases there is a new command called **dcopy**. This command is used to defragment file systems. One version of the **dcopy** command has the following format:

```
dcopy [-Vod] [-sb:g] [-an] filesystem1 filesystem2
```

where

-**V** prints the commands that **dcopy** will generate, but doesn't perform them.

-**o** indicates that the options that follow are system-specific.

-**sb:g** forces a reorganization of the file system using a cylinder size of b and a rotational gap of g blocks between the successive blocks in the same file.

-**an** moves inactive files (files that have been unused for n days) to the end of the reorganized file system. This clusters the frequently used files at the start of the file system for rapid access.

-**d** tells **fsck** not to change the order of the files within a directory.

You will need to check your manual or the man pages for your system to see what options your command has available.

If a file system has adequate file space, a second file system doesn't have to be specified. To use the command, the file system is first unmounted and then the **dcopy** command is issued against the file system with its name as both the first and second file system names. If a file system doesn't have enough space, then it must be copied into a separate file system. In this situation both file systems are unmounted and then the **dcopy** command is issued against them, with the file system to be defragmented as the first file system argument and the empty file system of equal or greater size as the second file system argument.

Logic dictates that you do a full backup before executing something as intrinsically destructive as a **dcopy** command. Always run **fsck** after using **dcopy**.

4.7.2   Fragmentation Control under BSD

Under BSD the fast file system minimizes the fragmentation problems associated with other UNIX implementations. However, as BSD file systems fill their access times can increase dramatically. For this reason the file systems are created with two parameters: *minimum free space* and *optimization style*. These two parameters ensure that BSD file systems perform optimally even when close to being completely full (full is defined as maximum file system size minus the *minimum free space*). Once a file system nears the point at which the *minimum free space* is the only free space available, the users attempting to create files or use more disk space will be given the "Filesystem Full" message.

If users start receiving the "Filesystem Full" message, first, you haven't done your job by being proactive; second, there are two options for you to use. You can increase the amount of space available by reducing the *minimum free space* parameter; however, this is just a temporary measure. Or you can increase the size of the file system or eliminate unneeded files to make more room. You aren't doing your job if you have to resort to any of these measures. You should be watching file system parameters and adjusting as needed to be sure users don't get nasty messages.

The *minimum free space* parameter is usually set at 10 percent of the file system's available space. This parameter can be adjusted with the **tunefs** and **newfs** commands. Use **tunefs** on existing file systems.

The *optimization style* is a choice between time or space optimization. Time is the less picky of the two and places files as fast as it can. Space is more careful about file placement to reduce fragmentation. If a minimum free space of less than 10 percent is specified, space optimization is used by default.

The minimum free space is set by using the **-m** parameter with either the **tunefs** or **newfs** commands. The optimization method is specified by use of the -o option and either the **time** or **space** argument. The file system must be unmounted before the **tunefs** command is used. Before the **newfs** command is used the file system to be modified should be backed up since this command destroys any information stored in the file system.

Here is an example of the use of **tunefs**:

```
# unmount /dev/disk2a
# tunefs -m 15 -o time /dev/disk2a
# mount /dev/disk2a
```

The above commands reset the minimum free space to 15 percent and set the optimization to time-based.

Here is an example of the use of the **newfs** command:

First: back up the filesystem

```
# /etc/umount /dev/disk2a
# newfs -m 15 -o space /dev/disk2a cdc-9715
# /etc/mount /dev/disk2a
```

last: Restore the filesystem from the backup taken above

As I said before, BSD reduces fragmentation but doesn't eliminate it. You will periodically have to back up, re-create, and restore the file systems to eliminate excessive fragmentation under BSD.

System Backup and Restore

5

ou job tenure is only for as long as you can ensure that your UNIX system is recoverable. You might get by once without being able to restore critical files, but I'll be willing to bet that the second time it happens you will need a current resumé.

Backup and its companion, restoration, are two very important parts of a system administrator's job. Backup is more than just copying the system to tape; restoration is more than just retrieving those files and structures from tape. Backup and restoration require planning and careful thought. You need to understand the applications and how they use files. For example, some database systems such as ORACLE can't be backed up, unless they are shut down, with the standard backup programs. Do you want full backups? Incremental backups? A combination? How often? All of these questions need to be answered before you institute a backup policy.

The two major backup utilities are tar and cpio. Both have advantages and drawbacks, which we will explore in the following sections. This chapter will also provide example scripts for using tar and cpio for backup and recovery. We will also cover the different commands such as **dd**, **volcopy**, and **dump** that reside under different forms of UNIX, and we will discuss use of the automated tools smit and SAM for doing backups.

5.1 BACKUP MEDIA

It used to be that you had two choices of backup media: tape or floppy disk. Now you have tape, floppy, CD-WORM, removable hard disk, 8mm DAT, streaming tape, and videotape, and more seem to appear every day.

Each type has its strengths and weaknesses depending upon what kind of backup you are performing. For instance, for a full-system backup CD-WORM is a good choice, but for a single-file backup to take with you to another site, it probably isn't. You see, CD-WORM has huge capacity but the media cost is high, so for a single file a floppy is probably a better choice. You wouldn't choose floppy for a full-system backup because it could take literally hundreds of floppies to perform it. Full backups are better sent to tape, CD-WORM, streaming tape or 8mm DAT tape, since these types are designed to hold large volumes of material.

An advantage that CD-WORM has over almost all other types of backup is permanence. Since the backup image is actually "etched" on the surface of the disk by laser, it isn't susceptible to magnetic fields, fading, or other problems associated with magnetic storage media. CD-WORM backup media don't have to be retensioned or rewritten. The shelf life is conservatively estimated at 30 years for a CD-WORM disk. Unfortunately, the cost of CD-WORM drives is still high in comparison to tape drives and not everyone has them (yet). Tape, in one form or another, is still the major backup medium.

5.2   TYPES OF BACKUPS

Backups are of three general types: partial, as in one file; full, as in all files; and incremental, as in all files since the last full or incremental backup.

Partial backups, usually of a file, a user's set of files, or an application system's files, are a regular part of a system administrator's job. When users are removed from the system, their files should be archived and removed from the system as well. When applications are placed into production it may mean moving them from one machine to another. The **ftp** command can be used for this, but it much easier to **ftp** 1 tar archive file than 50 single files spread across several users' directories. These partial backups can use either partial-path or full-path specifications. Partial-path specification allows all files to be placed in one directory, while full-path allows the tar program to rebuild an existing directory structure. A full-path specification would be of the form /usr/development/TAM/TAM.exe, while a partial-path would be TAM.exe.

Full backups may require you to be in maintenance or single-user mode. If you back up file systems that are in use, your backup may be inconsistent. Full backups start at the root directory (/) and work outward to encompass all mounted file systems. A full backup may require several tapes, hundreds of floppies, or a good chunk of a CD-WORM for a large system.

Incremental backups with tar or cpio require the use of a filter command using the **find** command. The incremental backup's main strength is that it only takes the files that have been modified since a specific date or since the last backup, depending upon how the script is configured.

Normally, a shop will set up its backups so that a full backup is taken at some predetermined periodicity and then incremental backups taken daily between the full backup dates. This permits the system administrator to recover from a minimal set of tapes.

5.3   USE OF TAR FOR BACKUP AND RESTORE

Tape archive and restore (**tar**) is the original tape archiver and restoration program for UNIX. Since its inception it has been expanded in functionality to allow output to other media such as hard drive or floppy disk. The general format of the **tar** command follows:

```
tar [option] [files]
```

where **option** (sometimes called **key**) is **rxtucvfbe**:

r appends files to the end of an existing archive.

x restores files from an archive.

t lists names of specified files if they are present on the archive volume.

u adds files if they do not already exist or if the ones on disk are newer than the ones on the archive volume. This is quite slow.

c forces creation of a new archive volume and forces writing from the beginning of the archive or tape.

v forces more verbose output of tar messages and file specifications.

w allows you to choose if a file is archived or restored from archive; this forces tar to display the filename, and you specify either y to take the action or n to go on to the next file.

f the argument following f is the archive medium name.

b the argument following b is the blocking factor for the records in the archive.

e does not allow files to be split between volumes (not available on all implementations).

files are the files to be backed up. These can either be full-path or partial-path specifications. A full path has the advantage that all directories are recreated when it is restored. A partial path will only restore to the limits of the specified path. An example full-path specification would be /etc/passwd; an example partial-path specification would be passwd.

5.3.1   Single-File Backup with tar

To archive a single file backup, the command is:

```
# tar -cv myfile -f /dev/rct0
a myfile 2 Blocks
```

In this example we back up using a relative pathname, the file "myfile," to a floppy disk on device /dev/rct0. The option cv tells **tar** to write from the beginning of the disk volume or current archive set, and to tell us in verbose mode what it is doing. The v option generates the "a myfile 2 blocks" report telling us that myfile was archived and is two blocks in length.

5.3.2   Archiving an Entire Directory with tar

To archive a user's entire directory an example command is:

```
# tar -cvf /dev/rct0 /usr/mault/.[a-z]* /usr/mault/*
a /usr/mault/.login 1 blocks
a /usr/mault/.profile 1 blocks
a /usr/mault/work.log 420 blocks
a /usr/mault/passwd.c 2 blocks
```

This command takes all of the files from user mault's directory, including the "." files. The **.[a-z]*** syntax allows taking the "." files without including the ".." or parent directory contents, which would be included if we simply specified ".*".

5.3.3 Performing a Full-System Backup with tar

To perform a full-system backup to /dev/rmt0 the commands are

```
# cd /
# tar -cevf /dev/rmt0 > /usr/backup/log/full_bu.log
```

The "e" flag prevents archived files from being split across tape volumes, but may not be available on all versions. Remember that you may be required to shut down to single-user, or maintenance, mode on some versions of UNIX; check your documentation. Even though the output from the -v option is being redirected into the /usr/backup/log/full_bu.log file, all warnings concerning full tapes will still come to stdin (the terminal screen).

5.3.4 Backup of Selected Files with tar

In some cases you may only want to back up selected files—say, all those dealing with the TAM project. Being a clever person, you place the letters "TAM" as a suffix to all files associated with this project so that wherever you are in the file structure you will recognize them. How do you go about locating and backing up all of the files with the ending "TAM"? The next few commands show how this is accomplished.

```
# find . -depth \( -name [a-z]*.TAM -o -name [A-Z]*.TAM \)
  -print > files.TAM
# tar -cvf /dev/rmt0 `cat files.TAM`
```

What we have done here is use the **find** command to search both up the directory tree from our current directory "." and down the directory tree "-depth" for files that start with a–z and end with ".TAM", or files that start with A–Z and end with ".TAM". The names of the files found by the **find** command are placed in the files.TAM file by the redirector ">". The second command tells the **tar** command to take the results of the "**cat files.TAM**" command and use it to feed the file list required by **tar**. Note that the **cat** command is surrounded by backward single quotes (`) (usually found on the same key with the tilde (~), not the normal single quotes (') that are on the key with the double quotes. If you specify the normal single quotes around the **cat** command, you will get some unusual errors but not what you want.

5.3.5   Performing an Incremental Backup with tar

An incremental backup is the backup of files that have been modified since a certain date and time, usually the date and time of the last backup. The **tar** command sets the file access date when it copies the file to tape. Any other access will also reset the date to a newer one.

One disadvantage of a date-based incremental backup is that your tar set will grow each night until a full backup is taken. There are other options that allow you to specify a time period, such as all files accessed or modified in x number of days. If your incrementals are run each night, you can use this option and only back up the files that changed that day. I don't suggest using the -atime (last access time) option since it will alter the access date of the files it touches; and thus they will always be backed up. Instead, use the -mtime qualifier that stands for modified-time and is the number of days since the file was last modified, not accessed, which is what we want, anyway. The -type f option tells **find** that we are only interested in regular files. The commands for this type of backup are

```
# find / -type f -mtime 1 -print > backup.list
# tar -cvf /dev/rmt0 `cat backup.list` >
  /usr/backup/incr.log
```

The commands shown will find all regular files that have been modified in the last 24 hours from the current time and place their names in the file backup.list. The **tar** command backs up the files whose names are in backup.list to /dev/rmt0, with the output from the verbose option - v going to a log file. Another method, once the log file is generated, is to use the date of the log file to drive the files that are backed up by use of the -newer option. An example of this is

```
# find / -type f -newer /usr/backup/log/incr.old -print >
  backup.list
# ren /usr/backup/log/incr.log /usr/backup/log/incr.old
# tar -cvf /dev/rmt0 `cat backup.list` >
  /usr/backup/incr.log
```

This series of commands finds all of the files that have been modified since the date of the last incremental backup and places their names in backup.list. The old log is then renamed to incr.old and the **tar** command backs up all of the files listed in the backup.list file, logging its actions in a new incr.log log file. Even though the output of the command has been redirected to a file, the system will still warn you when it needs another tape or disk mounted.

The method you use depends entirely on how you want to do the backup. I believe the second is more likely to achieve the desired results with less likelihood of missing a file because of a time error.

5.3.6   Checking the Contents of a tar Backup Set

To check the contents of a tar set, you use the command

```
# tar -tf /dev/rmt0 'tar - file name'
```

You should replace the **/dev/rmt0** with your archive media device specification or filename and **'tar - file name'** with the filename you want to check on in the tar set. If you want all the files, then just specify the device name or filename.

5.3.7   An Example tar Backup Script

If you always back up to a single destination, then you can amend the script in Figure 5.1 to remove the options pointing to several media. The script calls a media menu display script that looks like this when printed:

```
Available Backup Media
1.4mm DAT Tape
2.QIC Cartridge Tape
3.1.44 Megabyte 3.5" Floppy
Enter Choice:
```

Figure 5.1 shows a quick and easy script for doing **tar** type backups that uses the above menu. This script allows you to specify whether you want a full or incremental backup, the directory to back up, the device to back up the files to, and whether or not to print a list of the files that were backed up before the list is deleted.

5.3.8   Restoring From a tar Backup Set

In general, restoring from a tar set is fairly easy. The -x option tells tar to restore the files listed at the end of the command. For example, to restore a file named sample.TAM the command is

```
# tar xvf /dev/rmt0 sample.TAM
```

Wildcards can also be used with the file specifier:

```
# tar xvf /dev/rmt0 *.TAM
```

```
#! Purpose:      tar backup script
#! Created By:   Mike Ault 4/8/95 Rev 0.
#! Shell:        /bin/sh
# @(#) tar backup utility script
#! Establish the location for the file list to be generated
budata=/tmp/tbfile
#! Set up for use of the screen file shown above
screen=media_menu
#! Load a local variable with the menu file location
m=/usr/menus
#! Verify users privilege level, if not super user, they're out of here
#! First get user name using the whoami utility
user_name='whoami'
if [ $user_name = 'root' ]     #! If they pass muster, get additional information
then
        echo "\nFile Directory to Backup: \c"
        read file_loc
        if [ -n "$file_loc"]
        then
                echo "\nSpecified Directory: $file_loc\n"
        if [! -d $file_loc]
        then
                echo "Invalid entry, try again\n"
                exit 1
        fi
        else
                echo "No directory specified, try again\n"
                exit 1
        fi
#! Determine if a full or incremental backup
echo "\nFull or Incremental backup? (f or i ): \c"
read bu_ind
if [ $bu_ind = 'f']
        then
                echo "\n Doing a Full Backup of : $file_loc\n"
```

FIGURE 5.1 A sample tar backup script.

```
cd $file_loc
find . -type f -print > $budata
cat $m/$screen | more
read budev
case "$budev" in
        1)
                buname=/dev/rctmini
                break
        ;;
        2)
                buname=/dev/rct0
                break
        ;;
        3)
                buname=/dev/rfd0135ds18
                break
        ;;
        *)
                echo "\nImproper response, try again\n"
                exit 1
        ;;
easc
if [ -n "$buname"]
then
        echo "Entered device: $buname\n"
else
        echo "Improper Device,can't backup...exiting\n"
        exit 1
fi
full_dev = $buname
#! Going to use tar cvf to create a new archive, display names of files archived
#! and f to specify device name.
        tar cvf $full_dev `cat $budata`
elseif [ $bu_ind = "I"]
    then
```

FIGURE 5.1 Continued.

```
                   echo "\n Doing an Incremental backup of : $file_loc\n"
                   cd $file_loc
#! Now get increment period
                   echo "\n Enter number of days since last backup: \c"
                   read inc_per
                   if [ -n "$inc_per"]
                   then
                           echo "Entered Incremental period of $inc_per days\n"
                   else
                           inc_per=1
                           echo "No period entered defaulting to one day\n"
                   fi
                   echo "\n Doing Incremental Backup\n"
                   find . -type f -mtime -$inc_per -print > $budata
                   cat $m/$screen | more
                   read budev
                   case "$budev" in
                           1)
                                   buname=/dev/rctmini
                                   break
                           ;;
                           2)
                                   buname=/dev/rct0
                                   break
                           ;;
                           3)
                                   buname=/dev/rfd0135ds18
                                   break
                           ;;
                           *)
                                   echo "\nImproper response, try again\n"
                                   exit 1
                           ;;
                   easc
                   if [ -n "$buname"]
```

FIGURE 5.1 Continued.

```
                   then
                           echo "Entered device: $buname\n"
                   else
                           echo "Improper Device,can't backup...exiting\n"
                           exit 1
                   fi
                   full_dev = $buname
#! Going to use tar cvf to create a new archive, display names of files archived
#! and f to specify device name.
                   tar cvf $full_dev `cat $budata`
fi
echo "Print the list of archived files before removing it [y/n] \c"
read y_n
do
       case "$y_n" in
              [yY]*)
              echo "\n Printing and removing ...\n"
                     lp $budata
                     rm $budata
              break
              ;;
              [nN]*)
              echo "\n Removing ...\n"
                     rm $budata
              break
              ;;
              *)
                     Echo "Please enter y or n \n"
              ;;
              easc
       done
else
       echo "Cannot execute - not root!\n"
       echo "Check user permissions and try again!\n"
fi
```

FIGURE 5.1   Continued.

This command gets all of the files that end with .TAM from the tape.

Remember, if the full pathname of a file is specified when the file is placed in an archive set, the restore will re-create the full path. If the relative path is specified during an archive operation, the file will be restored to the current directory. Restore operations will write over any existing files with the same pathname and filename.

Restoration of an incremental or full backup requires similar commands:

```
# tar cvf /dev/rmt0 /
```

Of course, you may have to be in single-user, or maintenance, mode to do a full restore. To bring a complete system back from a set of a single full backup and several incremental backups, you begin by applying the full backup and then applying the incremental backups in the order they were taken. If you opt for the style of incremental backup that takes all files from a given date (such as the date of the last full backup) instead of the one that takes only the files modified since the last incremental backup, then only two backup sets will have to be applied: the full and the last incremental.

Figure 5.2 shows a sample **tar** restore script. You can make the scripts as elaborate as you wish; some even use C routines to give you a list of the files on the backup media and allow you to choose which files you want to extract.

5.4   USE OF CPIO FOR BACKUPS

The tar program has been around a long time. While it is a very useful tool, it still suffers from some limitations. The cpio program was designed to overcome the limitations inherent in **tar**. One good point for cpio is that it is faster than the tar program, which translates to less system downtime. Also, it can handle a longer supplied

```
#! Purpose:       tar restore script
#! Created By:    Mike Ault 4/8/95 Rev 0.
#! Shell:         /bin/sh
# @(#) tar backup utility script
#! Establish the location for the file list to be generated
budata=/tmp/tbfile
#! Set up for use of the screen file shown above
screen=media_menu
#! Load a local variable with the menu file location
m=/usr/menus
#! Verify users privilege level, if not super user, they're out of here
#! First get user name using the whoami utility
user_name=`whoami`
if [ $user_name = 'root' ]     #! If they pass muster, get additional information
then
        echo "\nFile Directory to Restore: \c"
        read file_loc
        if [ -n "$file_loc"]
        then
                echo "\nSpecified Directory: $file_loc\n"
        if [! -d $file_loc]
        then
                echo "Invalid entry, try again\n"
                exit 1
        fi
        else
                echo "No directory specified, try again\n"
                exit 1
        fi
        echo "\n Doing a restore of : $file_loc\n"
        cd $file_loc
        cat $m/$screen | more
```

FIGURE 5.2 A sample tar restorescript.

```
read budev
case "$budev" in
        1)
                buname=/dev/rctmini
                break
        ;;
        2)
                buname=/dev/rct0
                break
        ;;
        3)
                buname=/dev/rfd0135ds18
                break
        ;;
        *)
                echo "\nImproper response, try again\n"
                exit 1
        ;;
easc
if [ -n "$buname"]
then
        echo "Entered device: $buname\n"
else
        echo "Improper Device,can't restore...exiting\n"
        exit 1
fi
        full_dev = $buname
#! Going to use tar xvf to extract files, display the file names as they are
   extracted and
#! specify the location of the media via the f option.
$!
        tar xvf $full_dev
```

FIGURE 5.2 Continued.

list of filenames. The cpio program has the following syntax when it is called.

```
cpio -o[acBvV][-C bufsize][[-O file][-K volsize][-M
  message]]
cpio -i[BcdmvtTuvVfsSb6k][-C bufsize][[-I file][-K
  volumsize][-M message]][pattern...]
cpio -p[adlmuvV] directory
```

The main **cpio** arguments are o, i, and p. **-o copy out** reads standard input to get a list of pathnames and copies the files to standard output. **-i copy in** extracts files from standard input and copies the files to the current directory; the standard input must be a cpio-format file. **-p pass** reads standard input to get conditionally created pathnames of files that are copied to the destination file tree based on the selected options.

The secondary options for cpio are listed in Figure 5.3. Let's look at how these options are used to perform backup and recovery operations.

5.4.1 Backup of an Individual File with cpio

Like tar, cpio can be used to back up single files as well as entire systems. A single file is simply specified on the command line:

```
# cpio -(options) file < backup devices
```

So, if you want to back up a file called /usr/book/chapter5.doc to /dev/rct0, the command is

```
# cpio - ocmB /usr/book/chapter5.doc > /dev/rct0
```

In this case the options are -o, c, m, B, copy out, use ASCII header, maintain file dates, and block data to 5,120 bytes.

Option	Purpose
-B	Blocks input and output to 5,120 bytes. The default is 512 if the -B and -C aren't used. The -B option can only be used with character special devices.
-c	Writes the file header information in ASCII; should always be used if the destination machine is different from the source machine.
-C bufsize	Blocks input or output with the value specified by the **bufsize** parameter in a whole integer. This is specified as bytes per record; if K is specified, **bufsize** is in kilobytes. Not used when the -**p** main argument is specified.
-d	Tells cpio to create directories as required; only used with the -**i** and -**p** main arguments.
-f	Copies all files except those restricted by the specified patterns.
-I file	Reads the contents of the **file** argument as input; only used by the -**i** main argument.
-k	Tells cpio to skip files with corrupted headers but to read all possible files.
-l	Links files whenever possible rather than copying them; used only with the -**p** main argument.
-m	Causes cpio to force retention of existing modification dates and times. This is ineffective on directories.
-K volumesize	Specifies the media size in kilobytes. You must use the -C option and the K qualifier on the buffersize. Buffersize must be a multiple of 1k.
-O file	Specifies that output be directed to the file named; only used with the -**o** main argument.
-v (verbose)	Causes the file name to be listed as it is processed.
-V (special verbose)	Causes cpio to print a dot (.) to the screen for each file processed.

FIGURE 5.3 cpio Secondary Options.

5.4.2 Backup of Selected Files with cpio

Since cpio can accept input from a file for its file pathname arguments, it is relatively easy to specify a set of filenames using the **find** command. For example, if you wanted to back up all files that matched the pattern /usr/book/chapter*.doc, the command sequence would be:

```
# find /usr/book/chapter*.doc -print | cpio -ocv >
   /dev/rct0
```

In this case, **find** creates a list of files that match the pattern and prints them through a pipe to the **cpio** command, which then processes the files, placing an ASCII header on the total file and reporting its actions as it processes each file. It then copies the processed file to the /dev/rct0 device.

5.4.3 Backing up a Single Directory

In the case of a single directory or single directory tree, you probably won't want to back up nonfile entities such as device files or pipes (FIFOs). In this situation the **find** command can be used with the type option and with the f option to specify backup only of files. In this example let's back up the /usr/book directory.

```
# cd /usr/book
# find . -type f -print | cpio -Ocv > Mar0895.arc
```

Here we are sending the cpio output to the Mar0895.arc file in the current directory. If a full path was specified, the file would have been created there, assuming that we had the appropriate privileges. Note the use of the -O option.

5.4.4 Full Backup Using cpio

Full backup with cpio is as easy as moving to the root (/) directory and then issuing the **find** and **cpio** commands with the appropriate options:

```
# cd /
# find . -depth -print | cpio -ovc > /dev/rct0
```

In this example **depth** backtracks any lower directories and the dot (.) captures all files (even hidden ones) and then prints the list to cpio, which copies the files in verbose mode with a compatible ASCII header to the /dev/rct0 device.

5.4.5 Incremental Backups with cpio

Incremental backups can only be taken via cpio once a full backup has been accomplished. The full backup marks the files with a backup date that is then used to determine their status for incremental backup. Each subsequent incremental backup increments the dates for the affected files. The commands to perform an incremental backup are

```
# cd /
# find . -type f -depth -mtime 1 -print | cpio -ocv >
  /dev/rct0
```

5.4.6 Example Backup Script with cpio

If you always back up to a single destination, you can amend the script in Figure 5.4 to remove the options pointing to several media. The script calls a media menu display script that looks like this when printed:

```
#! Purpose:      cpio backup script
#! Created By:   Mike Ault 4/8/95 Rev 0.
#! Shell:        /bin/sh
# @(#) tar backup utility script
#! Establish the location for the file list to be generated
budata=/tmp/tbfile
#! Set up for use of the screen file shown above
screen=media_menu
#! Load a local variable with the menu file location
m=/usr/menus
#! Verify users privilege level, if not super user, they're out of here
#! First get user name using the whoami utility
user_name='whoami'
if [ $user_name = 'root' ]      #! If they pass muster, get additional information
then
        echo "\nFile Directory to Backup: \c"
        read file_loc
        if [ -n "$file_loc"]
        then
                echo "\nSpecified Directory: $file_loc\n"
        if [! -d $file_loc]
        then
                echo "Invalid entry, try again\n"
                exit 1
        fi
        else
                echo "No directory specified, try again\n"
                exit 1
        fi
#! Determine if a full or incremental backup
echo "\nFull or Incremental backup? (f or i ): \c"
read bu_ind
if [ $bu_ind = 'f']
        then
```

FIGURE 5.4 Sample cpio backup script.

```
                    echo "\n Doing a Full Backup of : $file_loc\n"
                    cd $file_loc
                    find . -type f -print > $budata
                    cat $m/$screen | more
                    read budev
                    case "$budev" in
                            1)
                                    buname=/dev/rctmini
                                    break
                            ;;
                            2)
                                    buname=/dev/rct0
                                    break
                            ;;
                            3)
                                    buname=/dev/rfd0135ds18
                                    break
                            ;;
                            *)
                                    echo "\nImproper response, try again\n"
                                    exit 1
                            ;;
                    easc
                    if [ -n "$buname"]
                    then
                            echo "Entered device: $buname\n"
                    else
                            echo "Improper Device,can't backup...exiting\n"
                            exit 1
                    fi
                    full_dev = $buname
#! Going to use cpio to create a new archive, display names of files archived
                    find . -type f -print |cpio -ocv> $full_dev
elseif [ $bu_ind = "I"]
        then
```

FIGURE 5.4   Continued.

```
                echo "\n Doing an Incremental backup of : $file_loc\n"
                cd $file_loc
#! Now get increment period
                echo "\n Enter number of days since last backup: \c"
                read inc_per
                if [ -n "$inc_per"]
                then
                        echo "Entered Incremental period of $inc_per days\n"
                else
                        inc_per=1
                        echo "No period entered defaulting to one day\n"
                fi
                echo "\n Doing Incremental Backup\n"
                cat $m/$screen | more
                read budev
                case "$budev" in
                        1)
                                buname=/dev/rctmini
                                break
                        ;;
                        2)
                                buname=/dev/rct0
                                break
                        ;;
                        3)
                                buname=/dev/rfd0135ds18
                                break
                        ;;
                        *)
                                echo "\nImproper response, try again\n"
                                exit 1
                        ;;
                easc
                if [ -n "$buname"]
                then
```

FIGURE 5.4   Continued.

```
                                echo "Entered device: $buname\n"
                else
                                echo "Improper Device,can't backup...exiting\n"
                                exit 1
                fi
        full_dev = $buname
#! Going to use cpio to create a new archive, display names of files archived
        find . -type f -mtime -$inc_per -print > $budata
        find . -type f -mtime -$inc_per -print | cpio -ocv > $full_dev
fi
echo "Print the list of archived files before removing it [y/n] \c"
read y_n
do
        case "$y_n" in
                [yY]*)
                echo "\n Printing and removing ...\n"
                        lp $budata
                        rm $budata
                break
                ;;
                [nN]*)
                echo "\n Removing ...\n"
                        rm $budata
                break
                ;;
                *)
                        Echo "Please enter y or n \n"
                ;;
                easc
        done
else
        echo "Cannot execute - not root!\n"
        echo "Check user permissions and try again!\n"
fi
```

FIGURE 5.4 Continued.

```
Available Backup Media
1.4mm DAT Tape
2.QIC Cartridge Tape
3.1.44 Megabyte 3.5" Floppy
Enter Choice:
```

Figure 5.4 shows a quick and easy script for doing cpio-type back-ups that uses the above menu. This script allows you to specify whether you want a full or incremental backup, the directory to back up, the device to back up the files to, and whether or not to print a list of the files that were backed up before the list is deleted.

5.4.7   Restoration with cpio

Restoration using cpio can be either of the full backup file and all of the files it contains or restoration of a single file or a group of files. If your site uses full and incremental backups, a full restoration will involve several operations using multiple cpio-generated files.

Restoration of a Single File Using cpio   In my experience, most restoration chores involve either a single user's file or a directory structure—for example, a user who does an **rm** * in his or her top-level directory and accidentally deletes all of his or her files or erases the only working copy of a program. To restore a single file, the following commands is used:

```
# cd /(users directory)
# cpio -ivdcmn (filename) <(backup device)
```

So, for a user whose directory is /usr/smith and who has deleted the only copy of a file called bid_response.doc, restoring from /dev/rct0 the commands are

```
# cd /usr/smith
```

```
# cpio -ivcmn /usr/smith/bid_response.doc < /dev/rct0
```

To restore if the user has deleted all of his or her files (probably on a bad day) the commands are

```
# cd /usr/smith
# cpio -ivdcmu /usr/smith/.[a-Z]*,/usr/smith/* </dev/rct0
```

Figure 5.5 shows a sample restoration script for cpio. You can make the scripts as elaborate as you wish. Some even use C routines to give you a list of the files on the backup media and allow you to choose which files you want to extract.

```
# @(#) cpio restoration utility script
#! Establish the location for the file list to be generated
budata=/tmp/tbfile
#! Set up for use of the screen file shown above
screen=media_menu
#! Load a local variable with the menu file location
m=/usr/menus
#! Verify users privilege level, if not super user, they're out of here
#! First get user name using the whoami utility
user_name='whoami'
if [ $user_name = 'root' ]      #! If they pass muster, get additional information
then
        echo "\nFile Directory to Restore: \c"
        read file_loc
        if [ -n "$file_loc"]
        then
                echo "\nSpecified Directory: $file_loc\n"
        if [! -d $file_loc]
        then
                echo "Invalid entry, try again\n"
                exit 1
        fi
```

FIGURE 5.5 Sample restoration script with cpio.

```
        else
                echo "No directory specified, try again\n"
                exit 1
        fi
        echo "\n Doing a restore of : $file_loc\n"
        cd $file_loc
        cat $m/$screen | more
        read budev
        case "$budev" in
                1)
                        buname=/dev/rctmini
                        break
                ;;
                2)
                        buname=/dev/rct0
                        break
                ;;
                3)
                        buname=/dev/rfd0135ds18
                        break
                ;;
                *)
                        echo "\nImproper response, try again\n"
                        exit 1
                ;;
        easc
        if [ -n "$buname"]
        then
                echo "Entered device: $buname\n"
        else
                echo "Improper Device,can't restore...exiting\n"
                exit 1
        fi
                full_dev = $buname
#! Going to use cpio to extract files, display the file names as they are extracted
$!
                cpio -ivdcmu < $full_dev
```

FIGURE 5.5 Continued.

5.5 **USE OF THE DD COMMAND**

The **dd** command, supplied on SVR4-based systems, is a bit-for-bit copy process from one source to another. The command is used to copy and optionally convert a file's format in the process. The allowed conversions are from IBM EBCDIC to ASCII or from ASCII to IBM EBCDIC. The **dd** command is often used to read non-UNIX format tapes. Another use is to allow an easy copy of an entire file system. On some systems the only way to copy raw partitions, if they are used, is via the **dd** command. The syntax for **dd** follows:

```
# dd (options)
```

where the options are from the following list:

if = file specifies the input file name; standard input is the default.

of = file specifies the output file; standard output is the default.

ibs = n specifies the input block size.

obs = n specifies the output block size.

bs = n sets both the **ibs** and **obs** parameters to the same value.

cbs = n sets the size of the conversion buffer.

skip = n tells dd how many records to skip before processing (for example, if there are header records that shouldn't be processed).

seek = n tells **dd** how many records to seek before processing (for example, if there are differences in block size, you may want to process an entire new block's worth of records at a time).

count=n tells dd to process only n records.

conv=ASCII tells **dd** to convert from EBCDIC to ASCII.

conv=EBCDIC tells **dd** to convert from ASCII to EBCDIC.

5.5.1   Example Use of dd

An example of the use of **dd** would be to completely copy one tape to another. In this case we assume that we have two tape drives; if only one is available, **dd** first to a holding file and then to a new tape.

```
#dd if=/dev/rmt0 of=/dev/rmt1 cbs=16b
```

Another example is in the backup of raw devices, assuming that /dev/dsk/6s0 is a raw disk and /dev/rmt/0m is a tape unit:

```
#dd if=/dev/dsk/6s0 of=/dev/rmt/0m
```

While primitive, **dd** is very useful and is, quite frankly, the only way to do some operations easily.

5.6   USE OF THE VOLCOPY COMMAND

The **volcopy** command is used to make an exact copy of a file system. It is available on most ATT-based UNIX systems. The command will automatically adjust block sizes as the file system is copied from one location to another. It has the following syntax:

```
volcopy [options] filesystem source volume1 destination
     volume2
```

where the options are from the following list:

> **-a** requires an operator to respond to the verification request instead of just waiting ten seconds and copying. This gives you a grace period should you give the command a bad volume name.
>
> **-s (default)** fails safe if an improper verification sequence is encountered. The program will ask for information such as length and density for a tape if not on the tape header.

filesystem is the name of the file system to be copied. This is the mounted name.

source and **destination** should be the physical disk section or tape identification.

volume represents the physical volume name, which must be less than six characters.

source and **volume1** are the identifiers for what is being copied.

destination and **volume2** are the identifiers for the destination of the copy operation.

5.7   USE OF THE BACKUP AND RESTORE COMMANDS

The **backup** and **restore** commands are front-end processes for the **cpio** command. However, even though these programs front-end the cpio process, you should only use files generated with **backup** for the **restore** command; do not use general cpio files with **restore** or the results could be unpredictable.

5.7.1   The backup Command

The backup command has the following format:

```
backup [-t] [-p] [-c | -f files | -u "user1, user2..."] -d
   device
backup -h
```

where

-t specifies the backup destination as a tape device. This option must be used with the -d option when a tape device is the destination.

-p tells **backup** to do a partial or incremental backup of files changed since the last run of **backup**.

-c tells **backup** to generate a complete backup of all files changed since system install.

-f files tells **backup** to back up only the specified files. The file-names may contain wildcards such as "." and "*". The arguments must be in quotes, for example:

```
-f "/usr/book/toc.doc,/usr/book/chap*".
```

-u "user1,user2..." tells **backup** to back up the specified user's home directory. If more than one user name is specified, the argument list must be in quotes. If the argument **all** is specified rather than a user name or names, then all of the user's home directory contents are backed up.

-d device tells backup to perform the backup operation to the specified device. This argument must be used. If the device is a tape, the -t option also must be specified.

-h tells **backup** to provide you with a history of backup activity (last backup dates).

A complete backup (-c) must be completed before you can use the partial or incremental option (-p). If floppy disks are used, they must be formatted. If tape is used, the process will format the tape if required, but the tape must be rewound for each operation.

5.7.2 The restore Command

The **restore** command is the companion to the backup command. If a file is generated with **backup**, you must use restore to recover it. Of course, the obverse of this is that **restore** can only be used with files created with **backup**. The **restore** command provides incremental recovery from a backup file. It is generally provided with SVR4-based systems.

The syntax for the **restore** command follows:

```
restore [-c][-i][-o][-f][-d device][pattern, pattern...]
```

where

-**c** tells **restore** to do a complete restore.

-**i** tells **restore** to get the index file off of the backup medium.

-**o** tells **restore** to overwrite existing files.

-**t** tells **restore** that the recovery medium is a tape; if -d specifies a tape device, -t also must be specified.

-**d** tells **restore** the name of the recovery medium. If the recovery medium is a tape, the -t option also must be specified. This is a raw format device.

5.8   USE OF THE DUMP AND RESTOR COMMANDS

The **dump** and **restor** commands are supplied on BSD-based systems. They are used to create and restore an incremental file system backup. Normally, these commands are used in maintenance, or single-user, mode. They may require operator interaction to handle end-of-tape, disk, and other errors. The programs expect all answers to prompts to be Y or N.

5.8.1   The dump Command

The **dump** command checkpoints itself at the beginning of each backup volume. This allows it to restart at the beginning of each volume instead of at the beginning of the full sequence of volumes should there be a problem with the tape. The error threshold for disk errors is 32; any more than that and **dump** will exit. On HP-UX systems, this command is replaced by the **fbackup** command.

The format of the **dump** command follows. (*Note:* Where options have arguments, the arguments are listed in order after the option list.)

```
dump [0-9] [-a[d density] FfkbCc[s size]uWwn] filesystem
```

where

> **[0-9]** tells **dump** the level of dump to perform. The level scheme allows the minimum amount of files to be backed up at one time. The dump levels correspond to
>
> > 0—Essentially a full backup of the system, which should be done when the file system is inactive or errors can result.
> >
> > 1-9—Back up any files that were changed since the last n- (1 to n-1) dumps, where n is the currently specified dump level. Usually, doing an initial level-0 dump and then daily level-9 dumps is sufficient, but more grandiose schemes can be devised, with some involving as many as 14 different tapes (or sets of tapes) used in a rotating sequence. If you like this level of complexity, look into Chapter 18 of *UNIX System Administration Handbook* by Nemeth, Snyder, and Seebass (Prentice-Hall, 1989) for a detailed look at the Towers of Hanoi dump sequence.
>
> **-a** tells **dump** that the device specified in the -d argument doesn't support asynchronous reads and writes.
>
> **-d** interprets the corresponding argument as tape density; the default value is 1,600.
>
> **-F** allows the dump to go on in the background. If an error occurs, the dump is halted.
>
> **-f** specifies the output file, usually a tape. You can specify many with -f. Consult the man pages for details on your system.

-b is the blocking factor that tells **dump** the number of 1-kilobyte blocks to write out at one time.

-C is the total tape capacity in 1-kilobyte blocks (see Figure 5.6).

-o indicates a cartridge tape instead of a 9-track reel-to-reel.

-s is used to pass the size of the tape in feet (see Figure 5.6).

-u tells **dump** to increment the /etc/dumpdates file.

-W prints out the dump status for all file systems as recorded in /etc/dumpdates and /etc/fstab.

-w does the same as W does but only for file systems that require a new dump. If a file has never been dumped, neither W nor w will report on it.

file system is the file system to be backed up.

Tape Type	Length (Actual)	Length (Effective)	Capacity*	Tracks
P5-8mm European	112 meters		2,200 megabytes	
P6-8mm American	112 meters		2,000 megabytes	
QIC-24	600 feet	5,400 feet		9
QIC-120	600 feet	9,000 feet		15
QIC-150	600 feet	10,800 feet		18
6″ reel	200 feet			9
7″ reel	600 feet			9
8.5″ reel	1200 feet			9
10.5″ reel (1.3mm)	2400 feet			9
10.5″ reel (1.9mm)	3600 feet			9

*Capacity in bytes is approximately equal to seven times the specified density times the length in feet times 0.9.

FIGURE 5.6   Relative data on different tape types.

-**n** tells **dump** to post a notification to all users in the operator group when it needs help (tape switch, end of tape, end of dump, errors).

You should keep detailed records of dumps, their levels, and the inodes for the files on each tape (start and stop inode values, which are reported by **dump**) so that it takes a minimum of time to find a lost file. The restor program allows you to generate a list of all files, and their inode values, contained on a dump volume. It is suggested that you run the restor program to generate this list immediately after **dump** completes. This **restor** generates a file list that is stored on-line; it also verifies that the dump volume is readable.

The file produced by the run of **restor** on the dump volume, and your dump log showing level, date, and inode ranges for each tape in the dump sets, will be an invaluable toolset for recovering files.

An example of the use of the **backup** command for a level-2 dump on the /usr file system follows:

```
# dump 2usdf 1200 1500 /dev/rmt0 /usr
```

Note that this command sets the s and d options, with s being the size of the tape in feet and d being the density of the tape in BPI. Notice that s comes first in the option list followed by d, and that 1200 (the argument for s) comes before 1500 (the argument for d) in the argument list.

5.8.2   The restor Command

The **restor** command is the complement to the **dump** command; it can only be used against volumes generated by the dump process. Usually **restor** will require the file system name or a filename to restore a single file or set of files; however, there are some older versions that will require the inode for an individual file recovery operation. The format of the **restor** command follows:

```
restor -crtTxXfF [ arguments ] [filesystem]
```

where

-**c** tells **restor** to compare the contents of the tape to the file system's contents. This is a means of verifying the tape contents after a dump.

-**r** tells **restor** to read the tape and load it onto the file system specified, destroying the previous contents of the file system.

-**t** prints the date the tape was written, and the dumped-from date, so if the dump tape is from today, today is 6-apr-1995, and the last dump was 5-apr-1995, then the tape date is 6-apr-1995 and the dumped-from date is 5-apr-1995.

-**T** tells the same information as -t does, but also includes the names and inodes of all the files on the tape. This is a good option to run immediately after a dump finishes along with the -c option to generate a "Table of Contents" for the tape. This table of contents can then be maintained in a file given a name that ties it back to the specific tape set, so that tracking down the most current dump of a file and its corresponding inode value becomes simple with the **grep** command.

-**x,X** tell **restor** to recover only a specific file. These options may take the filename as an argument or may require an inode; check your man pages for your system.

-**f** tells **restor** to interpret the corresponding argument as the name of the dump tape device.

-**F** tells **restor** to interpret the corresponding argument as the number of the dump to be read.

For example, if we wanted to completely recreate the /usr

filesystem, this command could be used, assuming the proper dump volume was mounted on device /dev/rct0:

```
# restor -rf /dev/rct0 /usr
```

To recovery an individual file—say, /usr/book/chapter5.doc from a dump volume on device /dev/rct0:

```
# cd /usr/book
# restor xf /usr/book/chapter5.doc /dev/rct0
```

So, **dump** and **restor** can be used to provide a complete backup and restoration capability on BSD systems.

5.9   COMPRESSION AND ARCHIVING

Another aspect of backup and restoration is compression and archiving. Compression is the process by which a file or group of files is compressed to take up less space. When the file is needed, it is decompressed to its original state. Archiving is the process by which a file or group of files is compressed and stored in an archive volume. This archive volume takes up far less space than the original set of files takes up and can be updated as the files it contains change. When a file is required, it is simply pulled from archive and expanded.

5.9.1   The compress Command

The **compress** command actually has several additional utilities that go with it. There are the compress, uncompress, and zcat programs as well. The **compress** command is used to generate compressed files, the **uncompress** command decompresses these files, and the **zcat** command allows for viewing of the compressed files without decompression. The syntaxes for these commands are as follows:

```
compress [-dfFqc] [-b bits] file
uncompress [-fqc] file
zcat file
```

where

> **-d** decompresses a compressed file.
>
> **-c** writes the output to the standard output and doesn't remove the original file.
>
> **-b bits** specifies the maximum number of bits to use when encoding.
>
> **-f** overwrites the previous output file.
>
> **-F** writes an output file even if compression doesn't save space.
>
> **-q** generates no output except for error messages. It can be used to check a file for corruption.

The **compress** command can compress files by up to 40 percent, which can show a significant file space savings. Files that are large and infrequently used give the most benefit from compression. Another use is prior to backup. The **compress** command can be used with wildcards.

Other Compression Routines There are other compression programs available, such as pact and compact, that may be quicker than compress but usually do a poorer job of compression—what you save in time you lose in space. In most cases compress will do a 10- to 15-percent better compression than these other two programs.

There may also be one of the zip compression routines on your system. This is usually zip, pkzip, or gzip. Generally, the zip family uses the same program with the -d option to decompress. The files that have been compressed with compress have .Z (uppercase) extensions; the files that use zip generally have a .gz extension, and files that use the pack family generally have a .z (lowercase) extension. To find out what programs are available on your system that deal with compression use the **man -k compress** command.

5.9.2   **The archive Command**

The **archive** command is used to put files in an archive state (usually compressed and stored on tape or other media). An archive can contain numerous files and can be used for versioning in a development environment. For example, the sources for Release 1 of the accounts payable package called accpay could be archived into the file accpayrev1:

```
# cd /usr/accproj/revision1
# pwd >> /usr/accproj/revision/.archived
# date >> /usr/accproj/revision1/.archived
# ls -al >> /usr/accproj/revision1/.archived
# find . -print | cpio -ocvdm > accpayrev1
# archive -m accpayrev1
```

The archive process may take a while to run, so be patient. Once the **trail** command shows that the file has been archived, the file can be removed with the **rm** command. If desired, the files in the archive can be removed as well. The reason for doing cpio on the files before archiving them is to save time and store the files as a group. The several commands (**pwd**, *date*, **ls -l**) that are sent into the archived file give a detailed history of the archive files that are stored in the archive. If you make this a standard practice, you can unarchive the archived file and examine it before unarchiving an entire, possibly incorrect, archive file.

The files sent to an archive can be unarchived by specifying the -r option to the **archive** command:

```
# archive -r filename
```

Thus, for our above example, if someone wants all of the files from revision 1 of the acctpay program, the following commands bring them back in all their glory:

```
# archive -r accpayrev1
# cpio -icvdm < accpayrev1
```

The -r option will unarchive a copy of the archived file, but will leave a copy in the archive. Files can be erased from the archive by use of the -e option. Files erased from the archive cannot be recovered.

UNIX User Administration

Next to backup and recovery, user management is probably the most important aspect of UNIX administration. If the system performs wonderfully, e-mail whistles along merrily and backups work like a charm, but users can't use the system, you fail.

6.1 USER TYPES

There are several types of users on any system. These types fall into three general categories: administration, development, and application.

Administration accounts have groups that are considered administration level, are generally able to become superusers, and can read most files on the system. Generally speaking, there will be few users with this much power, and I suggest limiting the number to one—you.

Development users will be granted access based on their projects. I suggest creating a group for each project and having a "master" account that owns all of the group files. Then you can grant access to the groups' files from a single controlling user and just grant the group id to the individual members. This makes backing up group files easier. You should also centralize the development area to its own directory tree. Centralization of files and control at the group level makes dealing with the project as one entity instead of a collection of multiple files much easier.

Usually, application users will be the largest group within a system. These are the folks for whom you really work. If the applications don't work, neither will you, for long. I suggest creating a group for each type of user, then assigning users to that group as they are created. Permissions should be granted on a group basis, not at the individual level, as far as file access goes. For each major application I suggest creating a controlling account that owns all of the application's files.

6.2   THE GROUP CONCEPT

So far I've said a lot about groups—a group for this and a group for that—they are an important concept in UNIX user administration. Groups allow you to place users in convenient categories. With newer versions of UNIX, you can belong to several groups at one time; thus users whose duties cross group boundaries can be handled as well. Groups are set up via the /etc/group file. In this file you assign a group name, group number (0 to 32,767) and group member list. Users can usually belong to eight or more groups at one time. The default group for a user is assigned via the entry in the /etc/passwd file.

User administration breaks down into three general areas: assignment of users to the system, security of users, and removal of users from the system. Each of these areas is important. Obviously, if you can't assign users, the system is useless. Likewise, if users can destroy the system because of inadequate security, you have problems. The converse is also true—if users can't function once they log on because of too much security, they won't be happy. Lastly, and this is where a number of sites fall down on the job, if users aren't properly removed from the system once they no longer require access, serious problems can result.

The next sections deal with the three aspects of user administration.

6.3 ASSIGNING USERS TO A UNIX SYSTEM

Assigning users to your system is a repetitive and boring chore. Unless you have one of the systems that provide an automated management tool, like smit on AIX or SAM on HP-UX, this task will be a manual one. In view of this, you should automate the task using scripts or get scripts to do it from the UNIX community. We will look at an example script for assigning users, and you can feel free to use it if you desire. First, we will look at the manual method of adding users; then we will examine an example script.

6.3.1 The Manual Method for Adding Users

This is the absolute minimum you need to do to add a user:

1. Edit the system password file to add the user name.

2. Create the user's home directory.

However, if this is all you do, the user will be isolated and, unless he or she already knows UNIX, unable to function. The above steps can be done in any order as long as they are both accomplished prior to the user sign-on attempt.

Here are additional tasks you need to perform to make the users' environment more friendly:

1. Copy in the startup files (.profile (C shell), .csh (C Shell), .login (K shell), and so forth, depending on the shell).

2. Set an initial password.

3. Grant them access to an alternate group by editing the group file (/etc/group).

4. If on BSD, authorize their use of the ingres database.

5. If using a dual OS machine, such as a dual ATT/BSD-capable one, set their universe.

Other tasks you should perform to make your life easier are

1. Setting the user's mail home.

2. Entering the user's information into the user database.

3. Entering the user's information into the local phonebook.

4. Setting BSD disk quotas (if on BSD).

5. Recording accounting information.

Let's examine each of these items.

Editing the /etc/passwd File   First, we will look at editing the password file and creating the user's login directory. The password file is usually located in /etc/passwd. In virtually all UNIX versions the information required by the /etc/passwd file is identical:

1. Login name

2. Encrypted password

3. UID number

4. GID number

5. GECOS entry (usually full name, cubicle, extension, and beeper number or home phone)

6. Login directory

7. Login shell

A typical line from a UNIX - /etc/passwd file looks like this:

```
root:Juf4resBg33ss:0:0:system user,,x6096,:/:/:/bin/csh
```

This entry is for user root who has the encrypted password Juf4resBg33ss, a user-id of 0, a group-id of 0, a GECOS field of "system user,,x6096,", and a login directory of "/", and who logs into the C shell "/bin/csh". Notice that the entries are separated by colons (:). To add a user "mault" with a user-id of 100, a group-id of 10, a GECOS field consisting of "Mike Ault,HBC5-5434,x5204,7576909", a login directory of "/user/dba/mault", and a login shell consisting of the Bourne shell, the entry created would be

```
mault:*:100:10: Mike Ault,HBC5-
   5434,x5204,7576909:/user/dba/mault:/bin/sh
```

Notice that the password entry has been set to "*". This is required for all new users. On BSD systems the **vipw** command procedure can be used to edit the /etc/passwd file. You should then use the **passwd** command to set the user's password. The **passwd** command is passed the user's name and then allows the superuser to modify the password (as long as the "*" is in place, the user will not be able to log on). For no required password on an account, set this field to null.

Administration of Passwords Passwords should not be chosen lightly, especially on networked systems. I once worked at a site that had connection to another site that had been operational for several years; the site's systems were connected to the Internet. The first day there I was able to log in to a powerful account, get access to a critical database system through default passwords, if I had desired to, bring down the entire system. I was able to do this because the system administrator didn't set and enforce password security (the powerful system account had its user name and password the same; the database account had its administration account password set to the default value that was published everywhere).

How do you choose a password? I generally choose a random word and add an underscore and a number. This brings the chances of guessing it way down, and a random checking program generally won't handle letter-symbol-number combinations. Some say you need to completely randomize passwords. This use of randomization makes guessing them hard, but makes remembering them hard as well. If passwords are difficult to remember, people will write them down and there goes security.

On SVR4 the **passwd** command has options to set a password's lifetime (minimum and maximum). For example:

```
$ passwd -n3 -x60 mault
```

This requires user mault to reset his password every 60 days and the new password to be used for at least three days before it can be changed (this prevents a hacker from getting the password, changing it, and then changing it back). Some UNIX versions will round this time into weeks, so be sure you know how your system handles this type of password aging before you implement. Some implementations of **passwd** will complain if the password is in all one case or is too short; however, if you are persistent they will allow it to be set. There are also numerous third-party programs available for UNIX that enforce stricter password rules.

User and Group id Numbers   User and group ids are integers between 0 and 32,767. The UID 0 and GID 0 are reserved for use by root and the root or "wheel" accounts, and shouldn't ever be used for general users because they allow access to sensitive files. GID 1 is reserved for use by the "daemon" group, so it shouldn't be used for general users, either. That leaves 32,766 group numbers and 37,767 user id numbers, which should be more than enough.

Duplicate UIDs aren't allowed. You shouldn't reuse a UID unless you are absolutely sure all files that an old user owned have been removed or assigned to another user. Generally, it is safer just to assign new UIDs.

Under early versions of BSD and ATT UNIX a user could only belong to one group at a time. In newer versions of UNIX the entry in the /etc/passwd file sets the user's initial group, but he or she can belong to multiple groups by having entries in the /etc/group file. The **newgroup** command is used to alter the user's current group. Under the latest releases of BSD multiple group membership is simultaneous, so the **newgroup** command isn't needed. In addition, under BSD the ownership of files is controlled by the ownership of the directory they are in, not by the creating user. The ownership of files can now be reset using **chgrp** at the user level, since **chgrp** is no longer a superuser-restricted command.

The GECOS Field The GECOS (General Electric Computer Operating System) field was originally used on the old GE645 for running batch jobs. Now, it is used for general user information. The GECOS field has no predefined format; users can change their information in it by use of the **chfn** command. The GECOS field is used for user lookups using the **finger** command.

The User's Login Directory (Home) The user's login (or "home") directory should be set. This directory is created with the **mkdir** command (chgrp dba/user/dba/mault). If the user entry is created first, then the ownership should be changed using the **chown** command (chown mault/user/dba/mault); if the directory is created first, perform this command after the user is added to the /etc/passwd file.

The User's Default Shell The user's login shell can be set to C (/etc/csh), Bourne (/etc/sh), Korn (/etc/ksh), and Tenex (/etc/tcsh) on most systems. Under BSD users can use the **chsh** command to alter their shell. The /etc/shells file holds the list of valid shells on BSD. On SVR4 the Korn shell is the default shell if none is specified.

Creating the User's Default, or Home, Directory

The login, or home, directory should be created immediately before or immediately after the /etc/passwd file is modified. In our example the user mault is created with the login directory of /user/dba/mault. The commands to create this directory are

```
$ mkdir /user/dba/mault
$ chgrp dba /user/dba/mault
$ chown mault /user/dba/mault
```

The first two commands, **mkdir** and **chgrp**, can be executed before the /etc/passwd file has been modified. The last command, **chown**, must be executed after the **/etc/passwd** command is modified because user mault doesn't exist until the /etc/passwd file says he does. Don't, under any circumstances, use the **chown mault /user/dba/mault/.*** command because this gives mault ownership of not only all subfiles under his directory but everything under /dba as well. This is because ".*" is also equivalent to "..".

6.3.2 Making Users' Lives Easier

Just in case your memory is as short as mine, here are the things you need to do to make users' lives easier:

1. Copy in the startup files (.profile (C shell), .csh (C Shell), .login (K shell), and so forth, depending on the shell).

2. Set an initial password.

3. Grant them access to an alternate group by editing the group file (/etc/group).

4. If on BSD, authorize their use of the ingres database.

5. If using a dual OS machine, such as a dual ATT/BSD-capable one, set their universe.

Now let's examine these steps and see what is required for each.

Copying in the Startup Files Depending on your system and its setup, there are several startup files that should be copied into a new user's login directory. These fall into two categories. The Command-shell-specific files are

.login   This is the setup script for users in the C shell, /bin/csh. It is used to set and export environmental variables and to set such things as terminal type.

.cshrc   This is the file for the C shell that sets variables for sub-shell commands, path for searches, command aliases, and the value for the umask. It also sets up for history and savehist.

.logout   This is also used by the C shell. It clears your terminal screen, prints reminders, and does some generally useless things like printing a good-bye message or a usually useless quote or fortune.

.profile   This is used by the Bourne shell, /bin/sh, to do the same things that the .login and .cshrc files do in the C shell.

The generic files are

.exrc   This is used by the /usr/ucb/vi (the vi editor) to set up certain options used by the editor.

.emacs_pro   This sets command options and key bindings used by the emacs editor.

.dbxinit   This sets aliases for the debugger used by the **/usr/ucb/dbx** command.

.mailrc   This sets mail aliases and mail parameters used by the **/usr/ucb/mail** command.

.newsrc   This sets the user's newsgroups of interest.

I suggest that you create a set of the files you use on your system to be used as templates for new users. With a set of templates, all that is required for a new user is copying the files into the new user, changing the ownership and mode of the files, and making some minor changes to the files (which, if they are standard, can be automated). Create a set of directories in which to store these files, such as /user/newuser/templates/csh, /user/newuser/templates/sh, /user/newuser/templates/ksh, and so forth. To copy the files into the new user, mault, who uses the Bourne shell, the procedure would be

```
$ cp /user/newuser/templates/sh/.[a-z]* /user/dba/mault
$ chmod 644 /user/dba/mault/.[a-z]*
$ chown mault /user/dba/mault/.[a-z]*
$ chgrp mault /user/dba/mault/.[a-z]*
```

One thing to notice about these commands is how we avoid the ".*" trap (".*" being equivalent to ".."). We use the **.[a-z]*** string to tell the commands to effect only files that begin with "." followed by a–z and then anything after the initial a–z. This prevents us from effecting ".." (i.e., /user/dba).

Setting an Initial Password   If you recall, we set the password in the /etc/passwd file to "*". This allows the user to get into the system without setting a password—not a good idea. Therefore, as system administrator you should set the initial password from the superuser account using the **passwd** command. This command has the basic format:

```
passwd [-ni] [-xi] [-l] [-wi] user
```

where

-**n** specifies the minimum time a password must be used before it can be changed, in hours (used from superuser only).

-**x** specifies the maximum time in days a password can be in effect before it must be changed (used from superuser only).

-**w** specifies the warning period in days for required password changes.

i specifies the value the parameter is set to; i is an integer value.

-**l** specifies that the user is locked and can't be used until the **passwd** command is reissued against it.

user specifies the username for which the password is to be changed or for which the default minimum and maximum change limits are to be set.

So, for our example user mault we can set the initial password with the command

```
$ passwd -n5 -x60 -w5 mault
passwd: changing password for mault
Old password:
New password: ChgThis
Re-enter new password: ChgThis
$
```

We have set mault's password to "ChgThis." Remember, UNIX is case-sensitive, so the password has to be entered exactly the same each time—"cHgtHis," "ChgThis," "CHGTHIS," and "chgthis" are all different passwords. In addition, passwords on most systems are limited to a maximum of eight characters, so "ChangeThis" and "ChangeThat" would both turn into "ChangeTh."

Granting Access to Alternate Groups In most environments a user may need access to several groups' files. Especially in development environments a user may need to access several projects. Under old versions of UNIX this meant either different users for different projects or use of the **chgrp** command. Under modern UNIX releases such as BSD the user can belong to several groups (eight or more) at the same time without having to do a thing. This is accomplished via the /etc/groups file.

To edit the /etc/groups file, you need to know what fields it contains. These fields are

1. Group name

2. Encrypted password (never used)

3. GID number

4. Comma-separated list of members

The general format of an entry in the /etc/groups file is

```
dba:*:10:oracle,root,mault
```

In this example, dba is the group name, there is no password, 10 is the GID, and the users in the group are "oracle," "root," and "mault." On modern implementations such as BSD the group name can be any length; on ATT SVR4 it is limited to eight characters. Strictly speaking, we didn't have to add mault to the dba group in the /etc/group file, since the entry in the /etc/passwd file automatically grants membership in the group dba to mault. However, we need to ensure that the entries in the /etc/groups file reflect actual system user status. If we want to add mault to another group or set of groups, we simply append his user name to the list of names for each group in which he is to have membership.

We can add groups by adding a line to the /etc/group file. GIDs must be unique, as must group names. As a reminder, GIDs range from 0 to 32,767, with 0 reserved for the root or superuser group and 1 usually restricted to the daemon group.

Authorizing Use of the ingres Database On BSD systems the ingres database is provided as a part of the system release. In order to use ingres, the user must be granted access; accomplished by editing the /usr/ingres/files/users file. The entries in the /usr/ingres/files/users file resemble those in the /etc/passwd file. The entries contain:

1. User name

2. A two-letter access control string (it must be unique—see your system documentation for use)

3. UID

4. GID

5. ingres permissions vector (see your system documentation for use)

6,7. Not usually used

8. Path to the ingres system startup file (usually a copy is placed in the user's home directory)

To use ingres users must also have the directory /usr/ingres/bin in their search path set in the .login or .profile files. An example entry for our mault user would be:

```
mault:a1:100:10:000001:::/user/dba/mault/.ingres::
```

In this example user mault is given general access (000001), and he must have the **.ingres** ingres startup file copied into his directory.

SVR4 doesn't use ingres, so this is not required for SVR4 or its variants. It is only used for BSD and its clones, such as HP-UX.

Setting a User's Universe Some computers, such as the Pyramid, Masscomp, Sequent, and Apollo systems, are capable of running two operating systems. Generally, this is a dual BSD/SVR4 setup. In this case you must tell the system to which "universe" the user belongs, via an entry in the /etc/u_universe. This file has a very simple format:

```
user:universe
```

So, if our example user mault was on one of these systems and we wished him to log in to the BSD universe, the entry in the /etc/u_universe file would be mault:bsd.

Each user has only one entry in this file. Under these systems each user must be added to the file.

6.4 MAKING YOUR LIFE EASIER

All of us want our lives made simple. Under UNIX the administrator's job can be made easier by the following actions if they are done during user setup:

1. Set the user's mail home.
2. Enter the user's information into the user database.
3. Enter the user's information into the local phonebook.
4. Set BSD disk quotas (if on BSD).
5. Record accounting information.

For our final section in manually adding users, let's examine these actions.

6.4.1 Setting the User's Mail Home

The user's mail home is the system to which all of his or her mail is sent. This mail home is set up in the /usr/lib/aliases file. The /usr/lib/aliases file is set up on each machine the user has a login on, and it redirects mail to his or her mail home. The entries in this file are of a simple format:

```
user: address-or-alias: user
```

In the first entry, user:address, the user's mail home is set. This entry is usually of the format

```
mault: mault@snoopy
```

where snoopy is the mail home node for mault. The second entry is used to establish any alias the user may have. For example, if mail addressed to mikeault should also go to mault, then the entry becomes

```
mikeault: mault
```

These entries should be the same for all nodes upon which the user has an account and which have connections to the mail home node.

6.4.2   Entering the User's Information into the User Database and Phonebook

For ease in locating a user, a user database should be created and maintained. This isn't a requirement, but it makes your life easier. This database is created from the GECOS field in the /etc/passwd via the **cut** command.

```
$ cut -d : -f 1,5 /etc/passwd > /usr/local/pub/phonelist
```

This command must be executed from the root or superuser account. Once the file is created its mode should be altered to allow everyone to read it:

```
$ chmod 744 /usr/local/pub/phonelist
```

Each user can maintain a private list of phone numbers as well. If you standardize on a filename such as .phonelist, then a simple command can be created that allows a search of both files (the local-user-maintained file and the global file) . Under the C shell this command can be as easy as

```
grep -i $1 ~/.phonelist /usr/local/pub/phonelist
```

The **$1** allows the first argument passed to the command to be processed. This command is placed in a file and the file is made executable. When the file is executed with an argument passed into it, it uses the argument to search the files. The argument may be the user name, first name, last name, phone number, building—in short, anything stored in the first field (username) in /etc/passwd or anything stored in the fifth field (GECOS). The **cut** command can also cut out the user's login directory or shell if desired. Generally, you won't want anything but fields 1 and 5.

6.4.3   Setting BSD Disk Quotas

Under the BSD version of UNIX you have the option of limiting a user's disk usage by setting disk quotas. In Chapter 2, on kernel reconfiguration I discussed how this option was configured. Now let's look at what needs to be done to set a new user's quota if you are using the disk quota option.

The BSD system provides the **edquota** command to set quotas. The general format for this command is

```
edquota -p proto-user new-user
edquota -t
```

In the first format above the -p option tells **edquota** to copy the quotas of the user specified as proto-user into the user specified as new-user. Once the quotas are copied, they are placed in a temporary file and the editor of choice (the default is vi) is invoked on the temporary file. The format for lines in this file is similar to

```
fs /mnt blocks(soft=100, hard=120) inodes (soft = 0, hard
   = 0)
fs /blocks (soft=1000, hard = 1200) inodes (soft=200,
   hard=200)
```

A setting of zero (0) disables quotas for that item. To change an item, just change its line. Before invoking quotas on an existing user you should be sure to run the quotacheck() procedure in order to get current statistics on that user. The **edquota** command utilizes the following files:

/etc/checklist—This gives **edquota** the current file systems.

/etc/mnttab—This gives **edquota** the information on mounted file systems.

directory/quotas—This contains the quota statistics for the file system. *directory* is specified to be the root of the file system specified to mount().

The -t option allows you to edit the time limits for each file system. Time limits are set for systems, not users. The format for this type of edquota file is

```
fs /mnt blocks time limit = 10.00 days, files time limit =
   20.00 days
fs / blocks time limit = 0(default), files time limit = 0
   (default)
```

Once the edquota program has been run, user setup is complete. The use of prototype users is encouraged, since this gives you a set of basic quotas to use when creating users. It removes the onus of having to remember what limits you want to set for each user type.

6.5   AN EXAMPLE PROCEDURE FOR ADDING USERS TO A UNIX SYSTEM

In Figure 6.1 we see a procedure written for the Bourne shell that allows addition of a new user to a SVR4 system. This script gets all of the required information, edits it into the /etc/passwd file, sets up password aging if required (via a call to a second script, /etc/agepw), and copies in the required startup file. The script could be enhanced to do more checking for whether or not the user already exists, that the group exists, and other nice-to-haves. Another nice add-on would be a case-esac construct that changes the files copied into the user according to the shell that you choose for him or her. For BSD the script would also have to handle the setting of disk quotas, if they are enabled, and access to the ingres database if required.

6.6   USER SECURITY

We have already discussed setting a user's mode and setting the value of his or her umask variable. These two issues deal with protection of the user's files and allowing the user access to them. Another issue is access outside of the user's usual domain. Again, we discussed this when we discussed how file modes are set and how a user can be assigned to more than one group. So, other than file access issues, what else needs to be taken into account for user security?

6.6.1   Monitoring Security

How many times has someone attempted to log in from a remote source unsuccessfully? How many times has a person logged in during other than normal working hours? Has anyone tried to become root who shouldn't have? These are all questions that deal with user,

```
#!/bin/sh
#adduser shell script ... bypasses most of the
# agony the sysadm (SysVr4) route makes you go through
#jhn 06jan87, mra 24jan95
#used numbers for other directories than /usr, thus udir settings
case `uname` in
        3b2b)
                echo "put user where? 2,3,or 4 [default is /usr] \c"
                read thedir
                case $thedir in
                        2) udir=2;;
                        3) udir=3;;
                        4) udir=4;;
                        "") udir="";;
                        *) echo "valid responses are <cr>, 2, 3, or 4. Bye...";
                           exit;;
                esac ;;
        3b2a) udir="";;
esac #end case uname
udir=usr${udir}
echo "putting them in /$udir
        please wait ... looking for next avail userno"
group=100
#
# find the next userid in /etc/passwd
#
nextuser=`/usr/bin/awk -F: '$3+0>num+0 {num=$3+0}
END {print 1+num}' /etc/passwd
#nextuser=`expr $nextuser + 1`
echo next available userno is $nextuser
#
# Build GECOS entry
#
while : ; do
echo "enter fullname \c"
read fullname
```

FIGURE 6.1 Example of a user addition script.

```
case $fullname in
        "") echo "null user fullname not allowed"; exit 1;;
esac
#
# get user name
#
echo "enter loginname \c"
read login
case $login in
        "") echo "null user name not allowed"; exit 1;;
esac
echo "enter usernumber [$nextuser] \c"
read user
case $user in
        "") user=$nextuser;echo "using $user";;
esac
nextuser=`expr $user + 1`
#
# Now get group number
#
loop=true
while :
do
        echo "Enter group (? for cat /etc/group) [$group] \c"
        read xroup
        case $xroup in
                \?) cat /etc/group;;
                "") break;;
                *) group=$xroup;break;;
        esac
done
case $group in
        "") echo null group not allowed ... bye; exit 1;;
esac
#
```

FIGURE 6.1 Continued.

```
# Add entry to file
#
/usr/bin/awk -F: '$1=='\"$login\"' || $3=='\"$user\"' {print}' /etc/passwd\
        >/tmp/au$$
already=""
#
# check if either the user name or login name is used
#
if test -s /tmp/au$$
then
        /bin/cat /tmp/au$$
        echo "login=$login or user=$user in use ..."
        rm -f /tmp/au$$
        already=1
fi
#
# Check if directory exists
#
if test -d /${udir}/$login
then
        echo "/${udir}/$login already exists ... !"
        rm -f /tmp/au$$
        already=1
fi
case $already in
        "")
        /bin/mkdir /${udir}/$login
        echo "$login::$user:$group:$fullname:/${udir}/$login:"
        echo "ok? [y] \c"
        read doit
        case $doit in
                n) /bin/rmdir /${udir}/$login; exit 1;;
        esac
        /bin/chmod u+w /etc/passwd
        echo "$login::$user:$group:$fullname:/${udir}/$login:">>/etc/passwd
```

FIGURE 6.1   Continued.

```
sync
/bin/chmod u+w /etc/passwd
tail -2 /etc/passwd
#
# Set file protections for the user
#
/bin/chown $user /${udir}/$login
/bin/chgrp $group /${udir}/$login
/bin/chmod 755 /${udir}/$login
#
# copy in the .profile file
#
/bin/cp /etc/stdprofile /${udir}/$login/.profile
#
# change ownership of .profile file
#
/bin/chown $user /${udir}/$login/.profile
/bin/chgrp sys /${udir}/$login/.profile
/bin/chmod gu+w /${udir}/$login/.profile
#
# Set a umask if needed
#
case $umsk in
        "") echo "Enter umask for user [22]: \c"
        read umsk
                    case $umsk in
                    "") umsk=22;;
                    esac
        ;;
esac
echo "umask $umsk">>/${udir}/$login/.profile
#
# Get default shell
#
echo "Users menu-shell? [n]: \c"
```

FIGURE 6.1 Continued.

```
        read yesno
        case $yesno in
                y) echo "/usr/uncw/msh" >> /${udir}/$login/.profile;;
                *) echo "No menu-shell selected";;
        esac
        #
        # Set a password...I would say a must do...
        #
        echo "Set password? [y]: \c"
        read yesno
        case $yesno in
                y|"") /bin/passwd $login;;
                *) echo "no password set for $login";;
        esac
        rm -f /tmp/au$$
        #
        # initialize password aging. On BSD this is done with the
        # passwd command itself. here the command is
        # /etc/agepw which runs a short procedure to do the passwd call
        #
        echo "put password aging in effect? [y]: \c"
        read yesno
        case $yesno in
                y|"") /etc/agepw $login;;
                n) echo password aging not set for $login;;
        esac
;;
esac    #end of case $already==""
echo '***** done *****
        want to add another user? [y] \c'
read domore
case $domore in
        n) exit;;
esac
done
```

FIGURE 6.1   Continued.

and system, security issues. In this section we will look at these questions and their answers.

Monitoring for Break-Ins One key indicator of an attempted break-in to your system is repeated attempts to log in from a remote source that are unsuccessful (multiple attempts from internal sources should also be considered cause for investigation, but aren't usually as important). Unfortunately, with most UNIX versions there is no password invalidation after x number of attempts to log in. On systems such as mainframes and VAX/VMS you can set up a maximum number of login attempts before a user is disabled, set days and hours when accounts are inactive, and specify numerous other security-related parameters. Except in the most advanced systems, most versions of UNIX don't have sophisticated security control on logins. Almost all break-in attempts employ a recursive program that tries password after password until it finds one that fits. Obviously, a recursive password program won't work if the user account is disabled after just a few attempts.

If auditing has been started on your system, there will be a file that keeps track of attempts to become the superuser. This file is usually located in /usr/adm/sulog and is a log of all uses of the **su** command or of logins as root. An example excerpt from this file is shown in Figure 6.2.

The /usr/adm/sulog file has the following fields: command, date-time, + (success) − (failure), terminal, and user using the command. From our excerpt in Figure 6.2 we can see that user nm90388 failed twice to log in in as root from his or her user. If we have no clue who nm90388 is, we should probably finger him and then ask him why he is using the superuser account.

Password Protection The importance of password protection cannot be emphasized enough. It does no good to have the most involved security system imaginable in place if users post their passwords on their terminals or leave their terminals logged in overnight or even while on a coffee break.

```
# cat /usr/adm/sulog
SU 01/12 15:19 - ttyp8 nm90388-root
SU 01/12 15:19 + ttyp8 nm90388-root
SU 01/12 15:27 - ttyp8 nm90388-root
SU 01/12 15:27 + ttyp8 nm90388-root
SU 01/12 23:00 + tty?? root-oracle
SU 01/13 01:55 + tty?? root-oracle
SU 01/13 07:45 + ttyp9 nm90388-root
SU 01/13 08:03 + tty?? root-gisc
SU 01/13 08:03 + tty?? root-gisc
SU 01/13 08:26 + ttyp7 nm90388-nm02767
SU 01/13 23:00 + tty?? root-oracle
SU 01/14 01:55 + tty?? root-oracle
SU 01/14 23:00 + tty?? root-oracle
```

FIGURE 6.2   Excerpt from the /usr/adm/sulog file.

A favorite means of getting passwords is to place a "Trojan Horse" (TH) program on a terminal that has been left logged in. The TH mimics a standard UNIX login prompt, making the user think he or she was logged out while on break. It then captures the user's login name and password and passes them back into the system after sending the security data to the creator of the TH. Some TH programs will even delete themselves, leaving no trace of their pilferage. Most users won't even realize they have been compromised if the creator of the TH is clever enough. It only takes a few lines of code to create one that will do the job quite well—a period of time well within a coffee or cigarette break.

There are numerous security-checking programs available commercially or via the Internet. They attempt to crack your passwords and tell you which may be too easily guessed. One small thing to remember is that these cracking programs are in the public domain—not only can you get them, so can hackers.

Idle Processes To prevent an idle, logged-in terminal from posing a security problem, there are several C routines available on CompuServe and the Internet that will watch for idle processes, warn users that they have been idle too long, and, if no action is taken, log them out. I highly suggest that these be used. I came in from a four-day holiday once to find that the backups had hung on Friday evening because someone had left her terminal logged into a sensitive database. Since the database couldn't shut down, the script that ran the backup couldn't get beyond that point because it waited for the shutdown to continue with the backup. If I had had one of these programs at that time, it would have saved me some "carpet" time (you know, when you are "called on the carpet" for a problem).

How can we prevent recursive login attempts on a UNIX box? Unfortunately, there is no standard answer. Solutions range from restricting access to your system to within the company or site boundaries (no phone-in access) to purchasing a security shell or writing your own. I have located several security add-ons on the Internet and CompuServe with just a cursory search, I'm sure numerous others are available as well. Just be sure that you completely understand what a downloaded program is doing before you compile it and run it on your system—it might be a Trojan Horse, rabbit, or virus carrier. I suggest not running precompiled programs but only those that you have compiled. Essentially, these programs take the place of the login program and add security-related features such as multiple login attempt detection, login time restrictions, and so forth.

We can monitor for attempted break-ins and attempts (and successes) at violating security. Security monitoring is accomplished through the use of the authcap database on SVR4 systems and via the files maintained by the audit system in the /.secure/etc/audnames file on BSD systems. The authcap database files are used by the **auditcmd** and **authck** commands on SVR4 systems. Under BSD (HP-UX implementation) there are several audit commands available: **audsys**, **audusr**, **audomon**, **audevent**, and **audisp**. Under AIX several commands are available as well: **audit**, **auditb**, **auditpr**, **auditselect**, **auditstream**, and **auditcat**. A typical procedure for conducting a security audit on HP-UX consists of the commands given below

First, let's check the last 10 user logins:

```
# last -10 ——> for some implementations the "n" is
  omitted
root      pty/ttyp6    Sun Jan 29 10:27 still logged in
root      pty/ttyp6    Sat Jan 28 13:22 - 13:37 (00:15)
oracle    pty/ttyp6    Sat Jan 28 13:22 - 13:22 (00:00)
root      pty/ttyp6    Sat Jan 28 13:07 - 13:21 (00:14)
oracle    pty/ttyp6    Sat Jan 28 13:07 - 13:07 (00:00)
root      pty/ttyp6    Sat Jan 28 13:00 - 13:06 (00:06)
root      ftp          Fri Jan 27 15:40 - 15:41 (00:01)
root      ftp          Fri Jan 27 14:51 - 14:53 (00:01)
root      pty/ttypd    Fri Jan 27 14:34 - 15:42 (01:07)
root      pty/ttypd    Fri Jan 27 14:28 - 14:33 (00:04)
```

These records show the user, terminal, or process; date; time interval, and duration of the logins.

Next, we check to see who has tried to become superuser:

```
# cat /usr/adm/sulog

SU 01/12 15:19 - ttyp8 nm90388-root
SU 01/12 15:19 + ttyp8 nm90388-root
SU 01/12 15:27 - ttyp8 nm90388-root
SU 01/12 15:27 + ttyp8 nm90388-root
SU 01/12 23:00 + tty?? root-oracle
SU 01/13 01:55 + tty?? root-oracle
SU 01/13 07:45 + ttyp9 nm90388-root
SU 01/13 08:03 + tty?? root-gisc
SU 01/13 08:03 + tty?? root-gisc
SU 01/13 08:26 + ttyp7 nm90388-nm02767
SU 01/13 23:00 + tty?? root-oracle
SU 01/14 01:55 + tty?? root-oracle
SU 01/14 23:00 + tty?? root-oracle
```

Finally, if auditing is turned on, we review the audited items:

```
# audisp -t 0125080095 -s 0129160095 /.secure/.etc/current
All users are selected.
All events are selected.
All ttys are selected.
Selecting successful & failed events.
start time :
Jan 25 08:00:00 1995
stop time :
Jan 29 16:00:00 1995
TIME            PID E EVENT PPID  AID RUID RGID  EUID  EGID TTY
1:
  950129 12:03:00 14277 S  9218   14276  201   0   200   0     200  ttyp6
  [ Event=login; User=oracle; Real Grp=dba; Eff.Grp=dba; ]
  SELF-AUDITING TEXT: User= oracle uid=201 audid=201 Successful login

  950129 12:03:00 14277 S  23    14276  201  201   200  201    200  ttyp6
  [ Event=setuid; User=oracle; Real Grp=dba; Eff.Grp=dba; ]
  RETURN_VALUE 1 = 0;
  PARAM #1 (int) = 201

  950129 12:03:00 14282 S   126 14277 201 201 200 201 6 ttyp6
  [ Event=setresuid; User=oracle; Real Grp=dba; Eff.Grp=mail; ]
     RETURN_VALUE 1 = 0;
     PARAM #1 (int) = -1
     PARAM #2 (int) = 201
     PARAM #3 (int) = 1

  950129 12:03:00 14282 F   10    14277   201   201    200   201      6     ttyp6
  [ Event=unlink; User=oracle; Real Grp=dba; Eff.Grp=mail; ]
     RETURN_VALUE 1 = -1;
     PARAM #1 (file path) = 1 (cnode);
                 0x40000005 (dev);
```

```
                   2 (inode);
                   (path) = /tmp/maa14282


950129 12:03:00 14282 S    10   14277   201   201   200   201      6    ttyp6
[ Event=unlink; User=oracle; Real Grp=dba; Eff.Grp=mail; ]
    RETURN_VALUE 1 = 0;
    PARAM #1 (file path) = 1 (cnode);
                   0x40000003 (dev);
                   6878 (inode);
        (path) = /usr/mail/oracle.lock


950129 12:03:00 14282 S    10   14277   201   201   200   201      6    ttyp6
[ Event=unlink; User=oracle; Real Grp=dba; Eff.Grp=mail; ]
    RETURN_VALUE 1 = 0;
    PARAM #1 (file path) = 1 (cnode);
                   0x40000005 (dev);
                   227 (inode);
        (path) = /tmp/maa14282


950129 12:03:00 14282 F    10   14277   201   201  200   201      6    ttyp6
[ Event=unlink; User=oracle; Real Grp=dba; Eff.Grp=mail; ]
    RETURN_VALUE 1 = -1;
    PARAM #1 (file path) = 1 (cnode);
        0x40000005 (dev);
      2 (inode);
        (path) = /tmp/marXXXXXX


950129 12:03:00 14283 S    12   14277   201   201   200   201     200    ttyp6
[ Event=chdir; User=oracle; Real Grp=dba; Eff.Grp=dba; ]
    RETURN_VALUE 1 = 0;
    PARAM #1 (file path) = 1 (cnode);
                   0x40000003 (dev);
                   6766 (inode);
        (path) = /usr/news
```

```
2:
    950129 12:03:40 14301 S    80  14277   201   201   200    0      200    ttyp6
    [ Event=setgroups; User=oracle; Real Grp=dba; Eff.Grp=dba; ]
        RETURN_VALUE 1 = 0;
        PARAM #1 (int) = 10
        PARAM #2 (int array) = 0 1 2 3 4 5 6 7 20 200

    950129 12:03:40 14301 S    46  14277   201   201   3      0      3      ttyp6
    [ Event=setgid; User=oracle; Real Grp=sys; Eff.Grp=sys; ]
        RETURN_VALUE 1 = 0;
        PARAM #1 (int) = 3

    950129 12:03:40 14301 S    23  14277   201   0     3      0      3      ttyp6
    [ Event=setuid; User=oracle; Real Grp=sys; Eff.Grp=sys; ]
        RETURN_VALUE 1 = 0;
        PARAM #1 (int) = 0
3:
    950129 12:04:21 14303 S  9218  14302   0     0     3      0      3      ttyp6
    [ Event=login; User=root; Real Grp=sys; Eff.Grp=sys; ]
    SELF-AUDITING TEXT: User= root uid=0 audid=0 Successful login

    950129 12:04:21 14303 S    23  14302   0     0     3      0      3      ttyp6
    [ Event=setuid; User=root Real Grp=sys; Eff.Grp=sys; ]
        RETURN_VALUE 1 = 0;
        PARAM #1 (int) = 0

    950129 12:04:21 14308 S   126  14303   0     0     3      0      6      ttyp6
    [ Event=setresuid; User=root; Real Grp=sys; Eff.Grp=mail; ]
        RETURN_VALUE 1 = 0;
        PARAM #1 (int) = -1
        PARAM #2 (int) = 0
        PARAM #3 (int) = 1
```

In the above records we see a date/time stamp, process id, success/failure flag (S or F), event number, parent process PID, audit ID number, actual user id, actual user group id, effective user id, effective group id, and the user's TTY number. The next line gives a summary, in English, of what was going on, and the following parameters show different variables that were used during the process. The above formats are from an HP-UX system; your audit record may look different. Generally, system calls will be available that show the structure of these records; on HP-UX the man page for audit(5) has this information. The numbers to the side of the entries show some general areas you might want to look at more closely, user logins, and attempts to be superuser.

To start monitoring user logins, access mode changes, and administration command usage for users root, oracle, and mault on the HP-UX system without using SAM, use the following commands:

```
# mkdir /.secure
# mkdir /.secure/etc
# audsys -n -c /.secure/etc/current -s 1024 -x
   /.secure/etc/next -z 1024>start_audit.log
# audevent -e login -PF
# audevent -e modaccess -PF
# audevent -e admin -PF
# audusr -a oracle root mault
```

To look at the audit records generated on the HP-UX system you use the **audisp** command. To take a look at what mault has been doing since we started auditing (and he logged off and on) we issue the command

```
# audisp -u mault /.secure/etc/current
```

If we want just to see mault's login and logout information the command is

```
# audisp -u mault -e login /.secure/etc/current
```

The commands vary from UNIX implementation to UNIX implementation. For example, under SVR4 the audit subsystem is controlled through calls to **auditcmd**. I suggest that you curl up with your security manual or take a quick tour through your man pages before trying to audit.

6.7   REMOVAL OF USERS

Removal of user accounts is much more than just removing their entry from /etc/passwd. Before a user can be removed a complete audit of all files he or she own needs to be done, also, assignment of these files to new users, archive, or removal must take place. Once the user's files have been disposed of, what about such things as mail accounts, group assignments, database authorizations, and quota assignments? All of these user-related issues must be dealt with when a user is removed.

Again, as with the process of adding users, your system may have a utility like smit on AIX or SAM on HP-UX that allows configuration, modification, and removal of users. If not, there is a template script for removing users shown in Figure 6.3. There are numerous sources for scripts of this nature if this one isn't complex enough for your needs. This script just does the removal of the user from the /etc/passwd file; it is left to the system administrator to edit the other files such as /etc/group, /usr/mail/aliases, the entry in edquota, and the ingres database authorization files.

In this chapter we examined adding users, monitoring through the audit system, and removal of user accounts under UNIX. Be sure that you read your system manuals completely and look at the man pages for your system before you add users, start auditing, or remove users.

```
#! ruser shell script for Bourne shell
runner = 'whoami'
udir = /usr
mdir = /usr/spool/mail
pdir = /etc/passwd
#!
#! Get the user name to be removed
#!
if [ $runner = "root" ]
then
echo "\nUser name to be deleted: \c"
read username
If [ -n "$username" ]
then
        echo "User to be deleted is: $username \n"
else
        echo "No user specified. Re-run program.\n"
        exit 1
fi
x=`/usr/bin/awk -F: '$username=='\"$username\"' {print $6}' $pdir `
case $x in
/||/etc|/bin|/usr/bin|/usr/uncw|/lib|/usr/lib|/usr/spool ) \
        echo "rm -r $x would be considered raeson for termination";exit 1;;
        "") echo no such user...bye; exit 1;;
        /usr* ) ;;
        *) echo "wtf?? x=$x"; exit 1;;
esac
echo "about to rm -r $x ok [y] \c"
read ans
case $ans in
        "") rm -rf $x;;
        y) rm -rf $x;;
        n) exit;;
```

FIGURE 6.3 Example script to remove a user.

```
        *) echo "invalid response ... $x not removed";exit;;
esac
grep -v $username $pdir > /tmp/kusr$$
/usr/bin/awk -F: '$1!='\"$username\"' {print }' $pdir >/tmp/kusr$$
diff $pdir /tmp/kusr$$
echo "ok? [y] \c"
read ans
case $ans in
        n) exit;;
        y)
                /bin/rm -f $mdir/$username;
                cp /tmp/kusr$$ $pdir ;
                /bin/rm /tmp/kusr$$;
                /bin/rm -f $udir/$username/.profile;
                /bin/rm -f $udir/$username/.login;
                /bin/rm -f $udir/$username/.cshrc;
                /bin/rm -f $udir/$username/.logout;
                /bin/rm -f $udir/$username/.exrc;
                /bin/rm -f $udir/$username/.exrc;
                /bin/rm -f $udir/$username;
                echo "\n $username has been removed.\n";;
        *) echo "invalid response interpreted as \"no\" ";exit;;
esac
else
        echo "Cannot execute - not a root user!\n"
        echo "Check your permissions!\n"
fi
```

FIGURE 6.3 Continued.

UNIX
Communications

7

E-mail is here to stay. Originally seen as "nerd-mail," it has now penetrated into virtually every nook and cranny of the modern office environment. Indeed, e-mail has even pushed its way into our homes via the first installments of the information superhighway: CompuServe, Delphi, America Online, and even the Internet or any of the thousands of smaller computer networks and BBS systems.

E-mail is nothing more than an elaborate user-to-user communication process. With the first use of ARPNET and the beginnings of the Internet, it was realized that owing to the large number of machines and their different means of communication, some method of tying all this mess together was required. Not only was there a need to communicate from machine to machine, but most systems didn't even provide user-to-user communications that were efficient and useful.

Like other multiuser operating systems, UNIX allows users to communicate with each other and with other machines over networks or modems. The most used communication protocol is TCPIP, and the most used communications program is sendmail. The send-mail program uses the simple mail transfer protocol (SMTP) and is present on all UNIX machines in one form or another.

There are MTA and MUA programs involved with communications between users. MTAs, short for mail transport agents, are programs like **sendmail**. MUAs, short for mail user agents, are programs like /etc/mail. MTA programs allow the transfer of mail between users and systems, while MUA programs allow the creation, reading, and deletion of mail messages.

There are also several other programs, such as wall, write, and uucp, that provide user communications. In this book we will spend a majority of our time on the sendmail program and just brush lightly against the others.

7.1   THE SENDMAIL PROGRAM

The sendmail program was written by Eric Allman at UC Berkeley. He first called it delivermail, and it was shipped in 1979 with BSD 4.0 and 4.1. In the beginning configuration data was linked into the program, reducing the program's flexibility. delivermail was converted to use an external configuration file and renamed sendmail with BSD 4.1c. The sendmail program has gone through numerous revisions and updates and is, at the time of this writing, at version 8.x, or V8 for short. Lennart Lovstrand of University of Linkoping, Sweden, has developed IDA enhancements to sendmail. Neil Rickert of Northern Illinois University and Paul Pomes of the University of Illinois took over the IDA version and now maintain it.

A number of sendmail clones have been developed; some are reasonable and some are trash. Whenever possible use the original sendmail program. These clones may or may not offer full compatibility for configuration file or alias file options and probably won't have the full capabilities of sendmail.

The configuration file, /etc/sendmail.cf, is the heart of the sendmail program. It is safe to say that without this file the entire sendmail system would collapse. Since this file is so important, we will cover it first.

7.1.1   The sendmail Configuration File

One of the minor annoyances of the sendmail configuration file is that it is read when sendmail is started and only then. For any configuration file changes to take effect, the sendmail process must be killed and restarted. Locations for the sendfile queue directory, host file, and alias files are stored in the configuration file, as are the sendmail options and the text conversion rules that allow an address string specified by one type of communications protocol to be understood by another. In addition, mail agents, delivery priorities, trusted users, and macros are defined within the configuration file (see Figure 7.1).

As you can see from the figure, the configuration file looks quite complex. Well, in this case looks aren't deceiving; it is. Also notice that the file is broken into discrete sections. These sections deal with the different aspects of the sendmail system that need configuration.

This particular file was derived from the default file provided by Hewlett-Packard for its HP-UX computers. The comment sections (ten pages' worth) and extra, commented-out options have been removed, and the line comments have been appended to the end of the command lines wherever possible. Note that for pre-V8 versions of sendmail there are only a few commands that can have comments appended, so don't run over to your system and start butchering your sendfile configuration file. The original, unmodified size of the file was 24 pages, which was reduced to 4 pages by these steps. We will try to look at each section of this file and cast some light into the dark corners. It is hoped that this section will give you a better understanding of this file and its contents and, above all, when and how to change them.

```
###        Localizable Options      ###
OL10                  # logging level
OI                    # defer messages to [IPC] mailers if the nameserver is
                      # not running
Odbackground          # delivery mode
Oep                   # error reporting mode
Or5m                  # read timeout
OT3d                  # queue timeout interval
Ox8                   # load average at which low priority messages are queued
                      # rather than delivered
OX12                  # load average at which daemon refuses to accept
                      # connections
OPPostmaster          # postmaster address which will receive headers of
                      # undeliverable messages
###        Other Options        ###
OQ/usr/spool/mqueue   # queue directory
Of                    # Save those UN*X From_ lines
OA/usr/lib/aliases    # location of alias file
OF0600                # temporary file mode
Ou1                   # default UID
Og1                   # default GID
OH/usr/lib/sendmail.hf # location of help file
Oo                    # recognize old style as well as new style lists in
                      # headers
OS/usr/lib/sendmail.st # statistics file
Oa5                   # wait up to 5 minutes for completion of alias db
                      # initialization
Os                    # queue up everything before starting transmission
Om                    # send to me, too if in alias expansion
Oq10000               # if the load average exceeds the x option limit, divide
                      # the q option value by the difference (plus one) between
                      # the current load average and the x option limit to find
                      # the maximum priority value (i.e. minimum priority) of
                      # messages to send immediately.
```

FIGURE 7.1 Example sendmail configuration file.

```
Oy1000                    # value added to message priority per recipient
Oz1800                    # message precedence factor
OZ9000                    # value added to message priority per queue run
###         Configuration-Specific Macro and Class Definitions      ###
DY                        # site hiding: local sender identified as user@my_site
                          # instead of user@my_host
Cw                        # class w defines aliases for the local host
DL                        # UUCP relay for unresolved ! addresses (via UUCP)
DW                        # UUCP relay for unresolved ! addresses (via SMTP)
DS                        # SMTP relay for unresolved @ addresses
DX                        # dumb (not RFC 822 compatible) UUCP hosts
DP/usr/bin/uupath    # pathalias external nameserver program
###         Configuration Version         ###
DV16.2
###         Required Macro Definitions        ###
Dj$w                              # official domain name of this host for SMTP
DnMAILER-DAEMON                   # my name
DlFrom $g $d                      # UNIX header format
Do.:%@!^=/[]|                     # delimiter (operator) characters
Dq$?x$x <$g>$|$g$.                # format of a total name
De$j HP Sendmail ($v/$V) ready at $b  # SMTP banner
###         Message Precedences         ###
Pfirst-class=0
Pspecial-delivery=100
Pjunk=-100
###         Trusted Users        ###
Troot
Tdaemon
Tuucp
Tx400
###         Header Field Formats        ###
HReceived: $?sfrom $s $.by $w$?r with $r$.
     ($v/$V) id $i; $b
HResent-Date: $a
```

FIGURE 7.1 Continued.

```
HDate: $a
HResent-From: $q
H?F?From: $q
H?x?Full-Name: $x
H?P?Return-Path: <$g>
HSubject:
#####        Address Rewriting Rulesets        #####
S1      ### Ruleset 1 - Sender Field Pre-rewriting     ###
#rhr              lhr                    comment
R$+               $:$>6$1                strip my_host and canonicalize
R$*<@$+>$*        $@$1<@$2>$3            already has (remote) domain
R$+/$*/$*/$*/$*   $:$1/$2/$3/$4/$5<@$w>  @my_domain on local X.400 sender
S2      ### Ruleset 2 - Recipient Field Pre-rewriting  ###
R$+               $:$>6$1                strip my_host and canonicalize
R$*<@$+>$*        $@$1<@$2>$3            already has (remote) domain
R$+/$*/$*/$*/$*   $:$1/$2/$3/$4/$5<@$w>  @my_domain on local X.400 recpt
S3      ### Ruleset 3 - Address Internalization        ###
# handle "From:<>" special case
R<>               $@$n                   null address => MAILER-DAEMON
# basic textual canonicalization
R$*<$*<$+>$*>$*   $1<$2$3$4>$5           strip <> from inside
R$*<$+>$*         $2                     strip phrase and <>
R$+ at $+         $1@$2                  RFC 733 at => RFC 822 @
# source route <@a,@b,@c:user@d> syntax to internal form <@a>:@b:@c:user@d
R@$+,$+           @$1:$2                 change all , to :
R@$+.UUCP:$+      $@<@$1.UUX>:$2         .UUCP pseudo-domain in route
R@$+:$+           $@<@$1>:$2             focus on next hop
# The @ delimiter takes precedence. Leave this alone.
R$+@$+            $:$1<@$2>              focus on domain
R$+<$+@$+>        $1$2<@$3>              move gaze right
R$+<@$+.UUCP>     $@$1<@$2.UUX>          .UUCP pseudo-domain
R$+<@$+>          $@$1<@$2>              already in internal form
# The ! delimiter.
R$+^$+            $1!$2                  convert obsolete ^ to !
```

FIGURE 7.1 Continued.

```
R$+!$+              $@$2<@$1.UUX>                host!user => user<@host.UUX>
# % is a low precedence @.
R$+%$+              $:$1<%$2>                     focus on domain
R$+<$+%$+>          $1$2<%$3>                     move gaze right
R$+<%$+>            $1<@$2>                       user%host => user@host
R$+<@$+.UUCP>       $@$1<@$2.UUX>                 .UUCP pseudo-domain
# miscellaneous cleanup
R$+@               $@$1                          user@ => user
R$+%               $@$1                          user% => user
S4      ### Ruleset 4 - Final Output Post-rewriting      ###
R$+<@>             $1                            null domain (special cases)
# UUCP must always be presented as host!user
R$+<@$+.UUX>        $@$2!$1                       user<@host.UUX> => host!user
# UUCP hop in source route
R<@$+.UUX>:$+       <@$1.UUCP>:$2                 .UUX in source route => .UUCP
R<@$+>:$+.UUX$+     <@$1>:$2.UUCP$3               .UUX in source route => .UUCP
R$*<$+>$*           $1$2$3                        remove internal form <> (defocus)
# don't change %s or @s in mixed addresses
R$+!$+@$+           $@$1!$2@$3                    don't interpret it any further
R$+!$+%$+           $@$1!$2%$3                    don't interpret it any further
# restore source route to external form
R@$+:$+:$+          @$1,$2:$3                     all but last : => ,
R@$+               $@<@$1>                       add <> to protect the ,s
# should be exactly one @ in user@domain style address
R$+%$+              $1@$2                         all % => @
R$+@$+@$+           $1%$2@$3                      all but last @ => %
S0      ### Ruleset 0 - {Delivery_Agent, Host, User} Resolution ###
# recognize local host or canonicalize
R$+                $:$>6$1                       anything to ruleset 6 once
# resolve domain-literals (numeric internet addresses) not canonicalized above
R$*<@[$+]>          $#tcp$@[$2]$:$1@[$2]          user@internet address
R<@[$+]>:$*         $#tcp$@[$1]$:@[$1]:$2         internet address in source route
# resolve mail to dumb UUCP hosts
R$+<@$=G.UUX>       $#dumbuucp$@$2$:$1            user@dumb_host.UUX
```

FIGURE 7.1 Continued.

```
# resolve mail to other known UUCP hosts
R$+<@$=U.UUX>           $#uucp$@$2$:$1               user@host.UUX
R<@$=U.UUX>:$+          $#uucp$@$1$:$2               @host.UUX in source route
# other UUCP addresses are in error
R$*<@$+.UUX>$*          $#error$:unable to route to UUCP host name $2
# try to connect to any host for user@domain
R$+<@$+>               $#tcp$@$2$:$1<@$2>           user@domain
# try to connect to any host for source route
R<@$+>:$+              $#tcp$@$1$:<@$1>:$2          source route
# pass unresolved SMTP addresses to the SMTP relay (don't relay source routes)
R$*<@$+>$*             $#error$:unable to route to domain $2
                                                    other SMTP addresses are in error
# file names, programs, and :include: must resolve to local mailer;
# explicitly distinguish these from X.400 and OpenMail syntax
R/$*                   $#local$:/$1                 to absolute file path name
R|$*                   $#local$:|$1                 to a program
R:include:$*           $#local$::include:$1         to :include: list
# by default, reject X.400 address as error
R$+/$*/$*/$*/$*        $#error$:X\.400 delivery agent not configured
# by default, reject OpenMail address as error
R$+/$*                 $#error$:OpenMail delivery agent not configured
# other addresses must resolve to local mailer in order for mail to Full.Name,
# command line aliases, and quoted user names (\user) to be delivered.
# remaining names must be local
R$+                   $#local$:$1                  name
#####          Special Rulesets           #####
S5     ### Ruleset 5 - Pathalias Nameserver         ###
R$+                   $:$<P$1                      uupath pathalias routing
R$+                   $:$>3$1                      re-internalize
S6     ### Ruleset 6 - Local Host Recognition       ###
R$*<@$*.>$*            $1<@$2>$3                    strip trailing . as per RFC 822
# strip local host
R$+<@$w>              $>3$1                        strip my_host and re-internalize
R<@$w>:$+             $>3$1                        strip my_host and re-internalize
```

FIGURE 7.1 Continued.

```
# recognize local host in UUCP syntax
R$+<@$k.UUX>            $:$1<@$w>                       my_host in UUCP syntax
# Recognize mail from uucp for x400 user on this system
R<@$k.UUX>:$+           $:<@$w>:$1                      my_host.UUCP in source route
R$*<@$+.UUX>$*          $@$1<@$2.UUX>$3                 don't canonicalize host.UUX
# canonicalize host and possibly recurse
R$*<@$+>$*              $:$1<@$[$2$]>$3                 user@host or source route
R$*<@$=w>$*             $:$>6$1<@$w>$3                  recurse if still to my_host
#####    Mailer (Delivery Agent) Definitions    #####
###           local and program mailers         ###
Mlocal, P=/bin/rmail, F=DFMPlms, S=10, R=20, A=rmail -d $u
Mprog, P=/bin/sh, F=DFMPlshu, S=10,  R=20, A=sh -c $u
S10
R$*<@$+.UUX>            $@$1<@$2.UUX>                   don't modify UUCP address
R$*<@$+>$*              $@$1<@$2>$3                     already has domain
R$+                     $:$1<@$w>                       add local domain to user
S20
R$*<@$+.UUX>            $@$1<@$2.UUX>                   don't modify UUCP address
R$*<@$+>$*              $@$1<@$2>$3                     already has domain
R$+                     $:$1<@$w>                       add local domain to user
###          SMTP TCP/IP mailer             ###
Mtcp, P=[IPC], F=CDFMXmu, S=11, R=21, E=\r\n, A=IPC $h
S11
R$*<@$+.UUX>            $@$2!$1<@$w>                    add local domain to UUCP address
R<@$+>:$*               $@<@$w>:@$1:$2                  add local domain to source route
R$+<@$+>                $@$1<@$2>                       already has domain
R$+                     $:$1<@$?Y$Y$|$w$.>              add local domain
S21
R$*<@$+>$*              $@$1<@$2>$3                     already has domain
R$+                     $:$1<@$w>                       add local domain
###          UUCP mailer             ###
Muucp, P=/usr/bin/uux,  F=DFMUshu, S=13, R=23, A=uux - $h!rmail ($u)
S13
R$+<@$+.UUX>            $@$2!$1<@$k.UUX>                host!user => my_host!host!user
```

FIGURE 7.1 Continued.

```
R$+@$+<@$+>              $1%$2<@$3>                  all but last @ => %
# enable uucp recipient to reply to remote x400 sender
# R$*/$*<@$+>  $@hpx400!$1/$2%$3<@$k.UUX>       user@host => my_host!hpx400!user%host
R$+<@$+>                 $@$1%$2<@$k.UUX>           user@host => my_host!user%host
R<@$+>:$+                $@<@$k.UUCP>:@$1:$2        prepend @my_host.UUCP to route
# enable uucp recipient to reply to local x400 sender
# R$*/$*        $@hpx400!$1/$2<@$k.UUX>   user => my_host!hpx400!user
R$+                      $@$1<@$k.UUX>             user => my_host!user
S23
###    UUCP for hosts running non-RFC 822 mailers (Dumb UUCP)    ###
Mdumbuucp, P=/usr/bin/uux, F=DMUshux,    R=23,  A=uux - $h!rmail ($u)
###        X.400 mailer        ###
Mx400, P=/usr/lib/x400/x4mailer, F=CDMFmn, S=14, R=24, A=x4mailer -f $g $u
S14
S24
###         OpenMail mailers        ###
Mopenmail, P=/usr/openmail/bin/UNIX.in, F=DFLMXmnu, S=15, R=25, A=UNIX.in
S15
S25
Momxport, P=/usr/openmail/bin/xport.in, F=LMn, A=xport.in $u
Momx400, P=/usr/openmail/bin/x400.out, F=LMn, A=x400.out $u
```

FIGURE 7.1 Continued.

The Command Prefix   Each line in the configuration file performs a single command and begins with a single letter code that tells send-file what the purpose of the line is. Lines that begin with a pound sign (#—American usage) are comments. Before V8 comments could only be on a line by themselves or after the **S**, **P**, and **R** command lines; for V8 and later versions they can follow any command. The other types of line prefixes are shown in Figure 7.2.

     The "O" command prefix indicates that an option prefix will follow. The option prefixes are listed in Figure 7.3.

Prefix Letter	Meaning
C	Specify class macro
D	Specify macro
F	Specify pipe or file class macro
H	Header definition
K	Indicates keyed database*
M	Specify mail delivery agent
O	Specify option (option codes in Figure 4.3)
P	Specify priorities for mail delivery
R	The line is a writing rule
S	Start of a rule-set
T	Shows user to be a trusted user
V	Configuration file version* (will be 5 for V8)
<space>	Continuation line
<tab>	Continuation line
<blank>	Comment
#	Comment
<anything else>	Error

*Version 8 only.

FIGURE 7.2 Configuration file command prefixes.

You can see that there are numerous options and that some are only applicable to certain versions of UNIX, as shown in Figure 7.3. Of course, with each new version or clone there may be more or fewer options. You should always refer to your system-specific documentation before changing or using any option, since at best a wrong option will be ignored and at worst it could scramble the receipt and/or the delivery of mail messages on your system.

Options Usage in the File The configuration file in Figure 7.1 begins with the options sections. As I said above, the option lines are recognizable because they begin with the command line prefix "O." Figure 7.4 is the options section from the configuration file in Figure 7.1.

Option	Format	Meaning
7	Boolean	Force 7-bit input[1]
a	Number	Wait for rebuild of alias file
A	Text	Location of alias source file and db file
b	Number	Specify maximum free blocks in queue[1]
b	Number	Maximum recipients[2]
B	Text	Unquoted string replacement character
c	Boolean	Ignore expensive delivery agents
C	Number	Force queue checkpoint[1]
d	Text	Specify delivery mode
D	Boolean	Rebuild the aliases db automatically
E	Text	Error message header[1]
e	Text	Error-handling mode
f	Boolean	Save **FROM** lines
F	Octal	File protection mask for temporary files
g	Number	Group id for delivery agents
G	Boolean	Match GECOS field to receptor
h	Number	Maximum hop count
H	Text	Location of help file
i	Boolean	Disregard leading message dots
I	Boolean	Queue messages where connection was refused
I	Text	Use DNS lookups[1]
j	Boolean	Show MIME format errors[1]
J	Text	Forward search path[1]
k	Number	Number of SMTP connections to keep
K	Time	Timeout for multiple SMTP connect
K	Text	Associate key with database[3]
l	Boolean	Use **Errors to:** for errors[1]
L	Number	Logging level setpoint
m	Boolean	Send to sender (me)
M	Text	Define a macro's command-line value
n	Boolean	Check right side alias validity[1]
o	Boolean	Allow space-delimited recipient lists

FIGURE 7.3 The sendmail option codes.

Option	Format	Meaning
O	Text	Set daemon network options[1]
p	Text	Set privacy of daemon (SMTP)[1]
P	Text	Send extra copies of postmaster mail here (string)
p	Number	Refuse connection if too many processes[4]
q	Number	High-load queueing multiplier factor
Q	Text	Queue directory location
r	Time	Timeout setting (SMTP reads)
r	Text	Timeout setting for SMTP
R	Boolean	Stop route address pruning[1]
R	Text	NFS-mounted spool directory routing[2]
s	Boolean	Queue everything for safety
S	Text	Statistics file
t	Text	Set timezone[5]
T	Time	Queue lifetime in days
u	Number	Use user id of mailer
U	Text	User database specification[1]
v	Boolean	Verbose mode
V	Text	MX fallback host[1]
w	Boolean	Use A for ambiguous MX[1]
x	Number	During high-load conditions queue only
X	Number	During high-load conditions refuse SMTP connections
Y	Boolean	Queue files processed individually on non-Sun systems
Y	Text	NIS alias map name[2]
y	Number	Messages with large recipient lists penalized
z	Number	Priority increment multiplier
Z	Number	Per-job increment priority
/	Boolean	Split header/envelope rewriting[3]

[1]Version 8 only.
[2]SunOS only.
[3]IDA only.
[4]NeXT only.
[5]SysV.

FIGURE 7.3   Continued.

```
###          Localizable Options          ###
OL10                    # logging level
OI                      # defer messages to [IPC] mailers if the nameserver is not
                        # running
Odbackground           # delivery mode
Oep                    # error reporting mode
Or5m                   # read timeout
OT3d                   # queue timeout interval
Ox8                    # load average at which low priority messages are queued
                       # rather than delivered
OX12                   # load average at which daemon refuses to accept
                       # connections
OPPostmaster           # postmaster address which will receive headers of
                       # undeliverable messages
###          Other Options          ###
OQ/usr/spool/mqueue    # queue directory
Of                     # Save those UN*X From_ lines
OA/usr/lib/aliases     # location of alias file
OF0600                 # temporary file mode
Ou1                    # default UID
Og1                    # default GID
OH/usr/lib/sendmail.hf # location of help file
Oo                     # recognize old style as well as new style lists inheaders
OS/usr/lib/sendmail.st # statistics file
Oa5                    # wait up to 5 minutes for completion of alias db
                       # initialization
Os                     # queue up everything before starting transmission
Om                     # send to me, too if in alias expansion
Oq10000                # if the load average exceeds the x option limit, divide
                       # the q option value by the difference (plus one) between
                       # the current load average and the x option limit to find
                       # the maximum priority value (i.e., minimum priority) of
                       # messages to send immediately
Oy1000                 # value added to message priority per recipient
Oz1800                 # message precedence factor
OZ9000                 # value added to message priority per queue run
```

FIGURE 7.4 The options section of the example configuration file.

We might as well dive right in. The first option, OL10, sets a logging level of 10. For early versions of sendmail the maximum logging level was 22, with 11–22 used for debugging information. With version 8 the highest logging level is now 98, with 11–98 reserved for debugging. Each subsequent level, starting with 0, includes those below it. Thus the **OL10** command sets us at logging level 1–10 inclusive. Figure 7.5 shows what the pre-V8 and V8 logging levels mean.

As you can see from the figure, you can't simply use a pre-V8 configuration file OL option level. There are significant changes between pre-V8 and V8 meanings. Each type of logging activity may go to a different location as specified in the /etc/syslog.conf file on most systems. Figure 7.6 shows the various standard locations for non-V8 and V8 logging levels.

Level	Pre-V8	V8
0	No-logging	No-logging.
1	Major problems only	System failures and security issues.
2	Record message collections and failed deliveries	Communications failures.
3	Record successful deliveries on addresses.	Bad format.
4	Record abnormally deferred deliveries	Bad qf filenames, minor errors.
5	Record normal queue deliveries	Record each message received.
6	Record noncritical errors	Record SMPT VRFY return to sender.
7	Unused	Record delivery failures.
8	Unused	Record successful deliveries.
9	Record queue-id to message id mappings	Record temporarily deferred mail.
10	Unused	Record each key as looked up in the database and each result.
11–22	Debugging—you must have the source code to use these	Same, only through 98 vice 22.

FIGURE 7.5   Logging levels for sendmail.

Level	Pre-V8 Location	V8 Location
0	None	None
1	LOG_CRIT or LOG_ALERT	Same
2	LOG_NOTICE	LOG_CRIT
3–4	LOG_NOTICE	Same
5	LOG_NOTICE	LOG_INFO
6	LOG_NOTICE	LOG_INFO
7–8	None	LOG_INFO
9	LOG_INFO	Same
10	None	LOG_INFO
11–22	LOG_DEBUG	Through 98 LOG_DEBUG

FIGURE 7.6 Logging level notice locations.

With a logging level of 10 we are covering all of the errors over which we have control. We need to watch the various locations as specified in the /etc/syslog.conf file. In addition to the locations shown in Figure 7.6, important errors are also posted to the console.

The next option, **OI**, forces non-V8 systems to use the domain naming system (DNS) to convert hostnames to IP addresses, and it forces requeue if the name can't be converted. Under V8 **OI** takes on the additional meaning that it can be used to tune DNS lookups. It makes no sense to declare this option unless you are connected to the Internet and/or are using DNS. This option can take an argument in either pre-V8 or V8 configurations. For pre-V8 configurations the argument is Boolean; for V8 it will be a space followed by a string that specifies tuning options. The old Boolean argument can be specified for compatibility, but with V8 it is ignored.

The available tuning options for the **OI** command are AAONLY and DNSRCH, as shown in Figure 7.7. Each of these can be prefaced with a "+" or a "−" to turn the option on or off, respectively.

The default tuning options are for DNSRCH, DEFNAMES, and RECURSE to be enabled and for all other tuning options to be disabled.

Tuning Option	Meaning
AAONLY	Authoritative answers only
DNSRCH	Search domain path

FIGURE 7.7 OI command options.

The next line specifies the **Odbackground** option. This option, Od with a modifier, is used to specify how a message is to be delivered—in this case, in the "background." The other modes are "interactive" and "query-only." Under Version 8 this command forces the alias database to be rebuilt if "true" follows the command. In V8 this is a Boolean argument of either "true" or "false" and defaults to true.

The next line, **Oep**, specifies how errors are to be handled. There are several arguments that can be used with **Oe** which are shown in Figure 7.8.

The next command line, **Or5m**, specifies the amount of time the sendmail program will wait if an SMTP connection fails. In other words, if sendmail attempts connection to another host and for some

Argument	Meaning
p	Prints all error messages; this is the default mode.
m	Mails an error notification to the sender regardless of what is going on. This should only be used from the command line or with automated programs where there is no human monitoring.
q	"Quiet" mode; it doesn't report any errors. Not a good mode to be in.
e	Similar to m mode. This argument forces sendmail to exit with a zero error code.
w	Forces the writing of errors to the user's terminal if he or she is logged in. If the user isn't logged in, a mail message is sent containing the error message.

FIGURE 7.8 **Oe** command arguments.

reason loses connection, this is how long it will wait until it disconnects. In this case the setting is for five minutes. Under version 8 there are additional arguments that allow you to specify the type of wait and the time period. Some of these wait types are **initial**, **helo**, **mail**, **rcpt**, **datainit**, **datablock**, **datafinal**, **rset**, **quit**, **misc**, **command**, and **ident**. The additional arguments are specified as a comma-separated list after the command. An equal sign is used to tell sendmail the value for each of them. For example, an **Orinitial=5m,mail=5m** would tell a version-8 sendmail to wait five minutes for the initial greeting message and to wait five minutes for the other host to return a "sender ok" message in response to a mail command that it sends.

The next line, **OT3d**, tells sendmail to allow up to three days for messages to be cleared from the queue. If a message reaches this age, it is deleted without being sent and a "bounce" is returned to the sender.

The next line, **Ox8**, specifies that sendmail queue and not deliver low-priority mail during high-load periods. The sendmail program uses the value specified and the value for the Oq option command to calculate the cutoff priority value. Eight is the default value.

The **OX12** command line specifies the load level at which sendmail will refuse all further connections. This value correlates to the number of requests queued in the last minute. Generally, this load level must be higher than that specified in the x option, since this is a more serious level of action. Under Version 8 exceeding the limit causes mail to be queued instead of delivered.

The **OPPostmaster** command tells sendmail the address to which all failed mail will be sent. This is usually an alias to a regular user name. The postmaster argument is not case-sensitive.

As you can see, the comment lines in the file accurately explain what each command is doing. Since this is not a book on sendmail, let's get on with some other parts of the configuration file.

Macro and Class Definitions As in other applications a macro in sendmail allows you to specify a series of commands or operations that are to be executed each time the macro is invoked. Classes are groupings of related items such as macros or names.

Look at Figure 7.9. You can see that the next section we will be dealing with is the section that declares macros and classes. Macros are simply shorthand versions of commands that sendmail will use for various things; classes are groups or arrays of string values. Declared macros are prefaced with a D, while classes are prefaced with a C. In addition to declared macros there are preassigned macros—each of the arguments shown in Figure 7.9 that begin with a "$" is preassigned. Figure 7.10 shows the major macros and how they are defined.

As we did with the options section, we will examine a few examples from the macro and classes section to help you understand how to read the sendmail.cf file.

```
###      Configuration-Specific Macro and Class Definitions    ###
DY                 # site hiding: local sender identified as user@my_site instead
                   # of user@my_host
Cw                 # class w defines aliases for the local host
DL                 # UUCP relay for unresolved ! addresses (via UUCP)
DW                 # UUCP relay for unresolved ! addresses (via SMTP)
DS                 # SMTP relay for unresolved @ addresses
DX                 # dumb (not RFC 822 compatible) UUCP hosts
DP/usr/bin/uupath  # pathalias external nameserver program
###          Configuration Version           ###
DV16.2
###          Required Macro Definitions       ###
Dj$w               # official domain name of this host for SMTP
DnMAILER-DAEMON#  my name
DlFrom $g $d       # UNIX header format
Do.:%@!^=/[]|      # delimiter (operator) characters
Dq$?x$x <$g>$|$g$. # format of a total name
De$j HP Sendmail ($v/$V) ready at $b      # SMTP banner
```

FIGURE 7.9 The macro and class definition section of the sendmail.cf file.

Macro	Definition
$_	Host and user validated under RFC-1413 for version 8*
$a	RFC822 formatted origin date
$c	Hop count
$d	For IDA, the origin date formatted in ctime(3) format
$e	Greeting message
$w	Canonical name for the host*
$v	sendmail program version*
$f	Sender's address
$g	Sender's address in relation to receiver
$h	Host name of recipient
$b	RFC822 formatted date*
$i	Identifier for the queue
$j	Official canonical name for our host
$m	DNS domain name for version 8*
$m	SunOS NIS domain name*
$m	IDA original user address
$n	Error message sender
$o	Token separator characters
$p	Process id of sendmail process
$k	IDA and Version 8 uucp node name*
$q	Default format of the sender's address
$r	IDA and Version 8 protocol used
$s	IDA and Version 8 sender's host name
$t	Current time in seconds
$u	Recipient's name
$x	Full name of the sender
$y	Basename(1) of the controlling tty
$z	Recipient's home directory

*A predefined macro.

FIGURE 7.10 Macro symbol definition for sendmail.

You will notice that the file defines the **e**, **j**, **l**, **n**, **o** and **q** macros. These macros must be defined in any configuration file for the file to work properly. In addition, there are several format characters that you must know in order to be able to make sense of the entries. The format characters are shown in Figure 7.11.

Also, in pre-V8 releases the first comma and anything that follows it is stripped out unless you escape it or quote it. You should only use uppercase letters to specify user-defined macros. If you inadvertently specify a lowercase improperly, you can get results far from what you expected.

Macros are expanded by a "$" (dollar sign) placed in front of them in text listings. This will cause a recursive expansion beginning with the leftmost macro that may be a part of a larger macro. Under IDA and Version 8 the combination of characters "$&" turns off recursive expansion. Under IDA only the combination of "$!" forces the rewrite of an address into the RFC822 standard format.

Macros may also require the use of conditional statements. Rather than use traditional "if-then-else" statements sendmail uses "$?" for if, "$|" for else, and "$." for end-if. Under version 8 conditionals can be nested; this is not the case with versions prior to version 8.

You will need to be careful if you define your own macros. Several problems can occur, such as looping caused by improper recursion (this can cause sendmail to go off into never-never land). Also, strange problems can result if macros are redefined while sendmail

Character	Meaning
\b	Insert a backspace here.
\f	Insert a formfeed here.
\n	Insert a newline here.
\r	Insert a carriage return here.
\\	Keep one backslash here.

FIGURE 7.11 Format characters for macros.

is executing. Bearing all this in mind, let's look at a few of the macro definitions from our example file.

The first command in this section, **DY**, specifies that the name of the mail server be substituted for the actual user's host name. This hides the user's node and makes all mail appear to come from the mail server node.

The next command, **Cw**, defines a class, w, which is the class that refers to the host and its possible aliases if additional arguments are present. In this case since just the w is specified, only the default host name will be used.

The **DL**, **DW**, **DS**, and **DX** macros are used to resolve old or badly formatted uucp and SMTP addresses.

The **DP/usr/bin/uupath** command defines /user/bin/uupath to the **P** macro. The **P** macro is used to specify the path to the external name server program. In this case the uupath program is used to resolve names that are external to the current host.

The **DV16.2** macro sets the sendmail configuration file version to 16.2.

The **Dj$w** macro defines the macro **j**, which is the fully canonical name macro, to the value w (remember, the "$" tells sendmail to translate the w, which is the official name for the host).

The next command, **DnMAILER-DAEMON**, defines the **n** macro to the value **MAILER-DAEMON**. The **n** is a predefined macro that specifies the name of the mailer process.

The **DlFrom $g $d** command assigns to the macro **l** (lowercase "L") the value "From" concatenated with the sender's name (**$g**) and the date (**$d**); this is the UNIX "from" header assignment.

The **Do.:%@!^=/[]|** command assigns to the **o** macro the value **.:%@!^=/[]|**. These are the valid token separator values. The **[]** symbol is actually **[** and **]** not a box. sendmail combines these token separators with the \r and \n (carriage return and new line specifiers). Space and tab character definitions are also, by default, token separators but aren't included in this process.

The **Dq$?x$x <$g>$|g.** command defines the macro **q** to be **$?**(If) **x$x**(the full name of the sender is undefined) **<$g>**(use the value of the **g** macro (the sender's relative address) surrounded by brackets) **$|**(else) use **$g** (just the value of g) **$.**(end if).

The final macro definition command, **De$j HP Sendmail ($v/$V) ready at $b**, defines the SMTP greeting message **e** to the value of **j** (**$j**), which is the official canonical name for the server appended to the string **HP Sendmail** (appended to the sendmail version, **$v/$V**, appended to the string) **ready at**, appended to the date in RFC822 format, **$b**.

Message Precedence The next section of the configuration file sets the precedence for how different classes of messages are handled. Look at Figure 7.12. First notice that each precedence begins with a P followed by a type specification. We see three message types: first-class, special-delivery, and junk. This precedence value is used to determine how the message is handled during high-load conditions. For example, if in your message you specified **Precedence: junk**, your message would begin with a class value of −100. This class value is then placed in the equation **priority = number_of_bytes - (class * z) + (number_of_recipients * y)**, where z is the multiplier for priority increments and y is the penalty value for large recipient lists.

So, from our configuration file option section:

```
Oy1000    # value added to message priority per recipient
Oz1800    # message precedence factor
```

For a 500-byte record with three recipients our priority for junk mail would be

500 − (−100 * 1800) + (3 * 1000) or 500 −(−180000) + 3000 = 183500

```
###            Message Precedences            ###
Pfirst-class=0
Pspecial-delivery=100
Pjunk=-100
```

FIGURE 7.12 Sendmail message precedences.

For first-class the calculation would become

$$500 - (0 * 1800) + (3 * 1000) = 3500$$

And for special-delivery:

$$500 - (100 * 1800) + (3 * 1000) = 500 - 180000 + 3000 = -176500$$

The smaller the precedence, the more likely it will be processed on a busy system.

Trusted Users Trusted users apply to pre-version-7 sendmail. A trusted user can use the -f option to respecify the sender name of a message. This was required for some situations in uucp where the sender address would be interpreted as uucp. The conf.h file for sendmail has the MAXTRUST specification that sets the maximum number of sendmail trusted users at compile time. You can't exceed this value, and you will receive an error for each line over this value that tries to use the T option.

As you can see from Figure 7.13 we have four trusted users specified: root, daemon, uucp, and x400.

Header Specifications You have control over how your mail headers appear through the use of the header specifications in the configuration file. Figure 7.14 shows the header specifications from the example file.

```
####               Trusted Users               ####
Troot
Tdaemon
Tuucp
Tx400
```

FIGURE 7.13 Trusted user section of the configuration file.

```
###                   Header Field Formats                 ###
HReceived: $?sfrom $s $.by $w$?r with $r$.
        ($v/$V) id $i; $b
HResent-Date: $a
HDate: $a
HResent-From: $q
H?F?From: $q
H?x?Full-Name: $x
H?P?Return-Path: <$g>
HSubject:
```

FIGURE 7.14 Example header specification section from the sendmail.cf file.

The configuration file header section commands tell sendmail
how to format the header of incoming messages. The header can be
as simple as a from/to line or as complex as the complete route,
date, time, and all other information you wish to include. I prefer a
simple header. I don't really care how many places my mail has to
go to get to me as long as it gets to me!

The first command in this section:

```
HReceived: $?sfrom $s $.by $w$?r with $r$.
              ($v/$V) id $i; $b
```

formats the received line of the header. The **$?s** states that if the
value of s is defined, make it **from $s**. The **s** macro is set to the name
of the sender's host machine. As you recall from previous sections,
the **$.** is the end-if symbol. The string **by $w** sets the next part of the
received line to **by** followed by the value of the **w** macro, which is
the name of this machine. Next we have another condition statement,
$?r with r., which translates into "if **r** has a value, append the
string **with $r** (the translated value of **r**)." The **r** macro is the proto-
col type. The next line, **($v/$V) id $i; $b**, specifies the sendmail version (**($v/$V)**), the queue (**$i**), and the date (**$b**). So for a mail
message from user "smith" on node "gamma," ending an smtp mes-

sage to user "jones" on node "delta" using queue "alpha" on November 4, 1994, the line would cause the following to be printed:

```
Received from gamma by delta with smtp
(16.2) alpha; 11/4/1994
```

The next command, **HResent-Date: $a**, sets as the next line of the header the words **Resent-Date:**, followed by the value of the **a** macro. The **a** macro is the origin date of the mail message; however, this date is reset each time there is an error, such as a delay and resend due to a downed host machine.

Other header options can be added as needed or desired.

Rule-Sets The next section of the configuration file deals with rule-sets. Rule-sets tell sendmail how to translate other mail utilities' addresses into sendmail addresses, how to transform addresses for needs other than those related to sendmail, how to select the right mail agent, and how to translate sendmail addresses into other mail utility addresses. Each rule-set is used to translate a different part of an address, such as the "header" or "envelope."

Rule-sets generally are numbered beginning with zero. The standard rule-sets are zero through four, and specific needs are addressed by rule-sets higher than ten. The beginning of a rule-set is always shown by the **S#** command, where the **#** sign stands for a particular number that designates the rule-set being delineated. If the **#** (number) is missing or if an alpha character is placed here instead, the rules that follow are placed in the zero rule-set. In version 8 there is a warning for non-numeric specified **S** commands. Normally, the value assigned to a rule-set cannot exceed that set by the MAXRWSETS parameter in the sendmail link file (conf.h) that holds the sendmail internal configuration parameters. Each rule begins with an R, and the S and R options can be used several times. Multiple declarations of the same value of S will add the rules after each declaration to the existing rule-set. The value for the **S** argument can also be made in hexadecimal or octal, but why would you want to do this?

Rule-sets are applied to addresses in a specific order depending on the type of address. In each case processing starts with rule-set 3. A sender address will flow through rule-set 3 to rule-set 1 and finally through rule-set 4. A recipient address will flow through rule-set 3 to rule-set 2 and then on to rule-set 4. In version 8 there are additional R= and S= rule-sets for use in processing the envelope and header sections of an address. Under IDA the uucp form of mail addresses can be handled by separate rule-sets enabled by setting the / option to true.

Under version 8 additional processing is carried out on the recipient address by rule-set 5 if the address is unchanged when it completes processing through alias files and such. This is usually the case when, for example, a mail filewall machine is used between the mail receipt node and the Internet.

Let's look at some common rules and how they are translated, in Figure 7.15. A quick glance shows that rule-sets 1 and 2 are identical. At first the myriad letters, numbers, and symbols that make up a rule seem a bit daunting. Notice how the rules have been formatted. First, of course, the **R** to show a rule or **S** to show the beginning of a rule-set. Next we have what is known as the lefthand rule, the text immediately following the **R**, and then one or more tabs and then the righthand rule, and finally a comment explaining the rule (which is, of course, optional, although sadists who leave them out should be forced to code in COBOL). The confusion should be reduced somewhat if you remember how sendmail tokenizes. Recall the **Do.:%@!^=/[]** command we discussed in the section on declared macros? This **o** macro is how sendmail knows what characters are used as token separators. Thus **aaa.bbb@ccc** becomes five tokens: **aaa**, **.**, **bbb**, **@**, and finally **ccc**. Another point to remember is that the space is always a token separator. The **$** character is an operator that tells sendmail to perform an action such as a token replacement.

```
S1          ### Ruleset 1 - Sender Field Pre-rewriting        ###
R$+              $:$>6$1                      strip my_host and canonicalize
R$*<@$+>$*       $@$1<@$2>$3                  already has (remote) domain
R$+/$*/$*/$*/$*  $:$1/$2/$3/$4/$5<@$w>        @my_domain on local X.400 sender
S2          ### Ruleset 2 - Recipient Field Pre-rewriting      ###
R$+              $:$>6$1                      strip my_host and canonicalize
R$*<@$+>$*       $@$1<@$2>$3                  already has (remote) domain
R$+/$*/$*/$*/$*  $:$1/$2/$3/$4/$5<@$w>        @my_domain on local X.400 recpt
S3          ### Ruleset 3 - Address Internalization        ###
R<>              $@$n                         null address => MAILER-DAEMON
R$*<$*<$+>$*>$*  $1<$2$3$4>$5                 strip <> from inside
R$*<$+>$*        $2                           strip phrase and <>
R$+ at $+        $1@$2                        RFC 733 at => RFC 822 @
R@$+,$+          @$1:$2                       change all , to :
R@$+.UUCP:$+     $@<@$1.UUX>:$2               .UUCP pseudo-domain in route
R@$+:$+          $@<@$1>:$2                   focus on next hop
R$+@$+           $:$1<@$2>                    focus on domain
R$+<$+@$+>       $1$2<@$3>                    move gaze right
R$+<@$+.UUCP>    $@$1<@$2.UUX>                .UUCP pseudo-domain
R$+<@$+>         $@$1<@$2>                    already in internal form
R$+^$+           $1!$2                        convert obsolete ^ to !
R$+!$+           $@$2<@$1.UUX>                host!user => user<@host.UUX>
R$+%$+           $:$1<%$2>                    focus on domain
R$+<$+%$+>       $1$2<%$3>                    move gaze right
R$+<%$+>         $1<@$2>                      user%host => user@host
R$+<@$+.UUCP>    $@$1<@$2.UUX>                .UUCP pseudo-domain
R$+@            $@$1                         user@ => user
R$+%            $@$1                         user% => user
S4          ### Ruleset 4 - Final Output Post-rewriting      ###
R$+<@>           $1                           null domain (special cases)
R$+<@$+.UUX>     $@$2!$1                      user<@host.UUX> => host!user
```

FIGURE 7.15 Example rule-sets from the configuration file.

```
R<@$+.UUX>:$+          <@$1.UUCP>:$2           .UUX in source route => .UUCP
R<@$+>:$+.UUX$+        <@$1>:$2.UUCP$3         .UUX in source route => .UUCP
R$*<$+>$*              $1$2$3                  remove internal form <> (defocus)
R$+!$+@$+              $@$1!$2@$3              don't interpret it any further
R$+!$+%$+              $@$1!$2%$3              don't interpret it any further
R@$+:$+:$+             @$1,$2:$3               all but last : => ,
R@$+                   $@<@$1>                 add <> to protect the ,s
R$+%$+                 $1@$2                   all % => @
R$+@$+@$+              $1%$2@$3                all but last @ => %
S0         ### Ruleset 0 - {Delivery_Agent, Host, User}        Resolution ###
R$+                    $:$>6$1                 anything to ruleset 6 once
R$*<@[$+]>             $#tcp$@[$2]$:$1@[$2]    user@internet address
R<@[$+]>:$*            $#tcp$@[$1]$:@[$1]:$2   internet address in source route
R$+<@$=G.UUX>          $#dumbuucp$@$2$:$1      user@dumb_host.UUX
R$+<@$=U.UUX>          $#uucp$@$2$:$1          user@host.UUX
R<@$=U.UUX>:$+         $#uucp$@$1$:$2          @host.UUX in source route
R$*<@$+.UUX>$*         $#error$:unable to route to UUCP host name $2
R$+<@$+>               $#tcp$@$2$:$1<@$2>      user@domain
R<@$+>:$+              $#tcp$@$1$:<@$1>:$2     source route
R$*<@$+>$*             $#error$:unable to route to domain $2
                                               other SMTP addresses are in error
R/$*                   $#local$:/$1            to absolute file path name
R|$*                   $#local$:|$1            to a program
R:include:$*           $#local$::include:$1    to :include: list
R$+/$*/$*/$*/$*        $#error$:X\.400 delivery agent not configured
R$+/$*                 $#error$:OpenMail delivery agent not configured
R$+                    $#local$:$1             name
#####      Special Rulesets      #####
S5         ### Ruleset 5 - Pathalias Nameserver      ###
R$+                    $:$<P$1                 uupath pathalias routing
R$+                    $:$>3$1                 re-internalize
```

FIGURE 7.15 Continued.

There are also internally defined token separators that are found in the file parseaddr.c. These are **()<>,;\"\r\n**, which also provide token separation for sendmail. The separated tokens are written into a workspace, where sendmail uses the rule-sets to process them. As long as a rule applies, it is used to modify the address. This is known as rule recursion and is both a blessing and a curse. Once a rule can no longer be applied, control is passed to the next rule in the set until there are no more rules to apply or another **S** command is reached. In this way rules perform like a "while" loop.

The **$** symbol has different meanings depending upon on what it is paired with. Figure 7.16 shows these pairings and their meanings.

Combination	Side	Meaning
$*	LHS	Match zero or more tokens (anything).
$+	LHS	Match one or more tokens.
$-	LHS	Match exactly one token.
$@	LHS	(V8) match zero tokens (nothing).
$=	LHS	Match any in class.
$~	LHS	Match any not in class.
$#	RHS	Rule-set zero only—delivery agent.
$@	RHS	Rule-set zero only—recipient host.
$:	RHS	Rule-set zero only—recipient user.
$x (x is a digit)	RHS	Copy token x.
$:	RHS	Rewrite once (must be specified first in RHS).
$@	RHS	Rewrite and return.
$>x	RHS	Rewrite through rule-set specified by x (should be followed by a space).
$#		Specify delivery agent.
$[$]		Canonicalize the hostname.
$($)		For IDA and V8 do a database lookup.
${ $}		For SunOS do an NIS lookup.

FIGURE 7.16 Meanings for the **$** operator in rule-sets.

Some Things to Remember

■ Sendmail will do minimum matching in LHS rules. It will add tokens one by one until it gets a match if multiple match tokens such as **$*** are used.

■ The **$x** RHS rules for writing apply to the order of tokens as matched by the LHS rule, not the actual individual tokens in the address. The values 1–9 are the only valid values for x.

■ If an RHS rule contains the **$@** operator, processing will stop with that rule if the rule is used.

■ Use of Windows-based editors, especially during copy from window a to window b, can result in the tabs being converted to spaces within the rule-sets. It will look the same, but will not work.

■ Watch use of the **$*** operator—it can lead to endless loops.

■ Always test new rule-sets (We will cover this shortly).

■ If the LHS or RHS becomes NULL, the sendmail routine will crash with a core dump.

■ If the **$>** operator points to a nonexistent rule-set number that is less than zero or greater than MAXRWSETS, sendmail may crash at unexpected times with a core dump.

■ All versions before V-8 process the envelope sender incorrectly by calling-rule set 2 and the recipient R=.

■ Watch the use of letters and numbers in rule declarations. On some terminals l ("ell") looks like 1 (one) and O ("oh") looks like 0 (zero). Miss-specifying a rule-set number can cause assignment of the rules to rule-set 0 when you meant rule-set 1 and to rule-set 1 when you meant 10, and so on.

Well, enough of this blithering. Let's get down to business and examine a couple of the rules to see how all this works. We will start with the first rule in rule-sets 1 and 2.

```
R$+      $:$>6$1
```

The first operator (and the only one!) in the LHS is $+. As you will recall from Figure 7.16, this means to match one or more tokens. So, if our address is **clyde@wacocraft.com**, the first token is **clyde**, which is moved into the workspace and then compared to the RHS. In this case we have the **$:** operator that says "Do this once" and then feeds us to rule-set 6 (not shown in the example but present in the listing of the entire file). Rule-set 6 will rewrite the address if it finds specific items such as "<" or ".". Since **clyde** doesn't have any of this, it falls through the rule. Because mail was told via the $: operator to do this only once, we now go on to the next rule.

```
R$*<@$+>$*     $@$1<@$2>$3
```

This LHS rule breaks down into $*, <@, $+, >, and $*. Essentially this is saying, "Find everything up to the first occurrence of <@ and place it in token 1; next, take everything up to the first occurrence of > and place it in token 2, and then take everything else and place it into token 3."

The RHS rule breaks down into $@, which means that if this rule works, rewrite the address and leave the rule-set. That is, this rule is the last one that should be used to rewrite the address if it works. The next command, **$1**, places the value of the LHS token 1 into the workspace as the first token followed by a "<" and an @ symbol. Next, the value of the LHS token 2 is written followed by a ">" symbol. Lastly, everything that is LHS token 3 is written in, completing the address. As was stated before, if this rule is used, control is passed to the next rule-set and the third rule isn't applied.

The third rule:

```
R$+/$*/$*/$*/$*     $:$1/$2/$3/$4/$5<@$w>
```

takes a forward-slash-separated list of names and, using the "process once" operator **$:**, simply appends the node name in the following fashion: <@node>. Once this rule is applied, control is passed to the next rule-set with no further processing.

To complete our discussion of rule-sets we will look at the first two rules in rule-set 3:

```
R<>                  $@$n
R$*<$*<$+>$*>$*       $1<$2$3$4>$5
```

The first rule, **R<> $@$n**, simply refers all empty addresses (<> is an empty address) to the value of **$n**, which if you will look back at the definitions of the declared macros, you can see is set to **MAILER-DAEMON**. If you get the message "can't parse myself," the macro has not been set properly. This rule is used to provide a "from" identifier to the process to which the error message is returned.

The second rule, **R$*<$*<$+>$*>$* $1<$2$3$4>$5**, removes any extra sets of brackets. It does this by taking any tokens up to the first < and placing them in LHS token 1, taking any tokens up to the second < and placing them in LHS token 2, placing any tokens up to the first > in LHS token 3, placing anything up to the second > in token LHS token 4, and then placing anything after the last > in LHS token 5. The RHS rule then writes the value of LHS token 1, a <, the values of LHS tokens 2, 3, and 4, a >, and the value of LHS token 5.

As you can see, if you take it slow and remember what are separators, what are operators, and so forth, decoding rule-sets can be accomplished with only minor pain. But what if you want to add your own rules to a rule-set? How can you be sure that you don't corrupt the thing beyond redemption? By using the -bt and -d options to the command line running of sendmail and re-setting queues, you can get sendmail to show you exactly how it will use, or, misuse, your rule.

Testing New Rules If you add new rules to your rule-sets and don't test them, you are a fool. I'm sorry if that hurts your feelings, but it is the truth. Even a simple-seeming rule such as **R$*   <$1>** will wreak havoc with your system. See if you can figure out what this rule will do to your workspace. I'll tell you at the end of the section. Here is another thought problem: What will the rule **R$* $1** do? (Think recursion.) IDA and V8 limit the corrosiveness of such rules, but don't eliminate it all together. Let's look at the command to test a rule-set.

If you are using a normal user for testing, as you should be (remember, only use root or the superuser when absolutely needed), you will have to reset your queue by using the -oQdir command line option. In this command "dir" should be replaced with the location for the queue.

I also suggest that you copy your old sendmail.cf to a safe location and only test on a modified copy. This gives you a fallback position in case your changes cause a system crash and file corruption.

Now that the warnings are finished, the format for running sendmail in the rule test mode is

```
% /usr/lib/sendmail -bt
```

This will place sendmail in rule-set test mode and allow command-line input. Generally, sendmail will prompt you for the rule-set and address to be tested. On old versions it will automatically run the address through rule-set 3. To disable this, place the following rule as the first one for rule-set 3:

```
R$*     $@$1
```

If your version tells you that rule-set 3 hasn't been automatically invoked, then this action isn't needed. For heaven's sake, don't forget to take out this rule once you've completed testing! In most cases you will want the rule-set 3 preprocessing, so this can be disregarded.

On older versions only one rule-set at a time can be tested. In newer versions you can specify multiple rule-sets as a comma-separated list, with no spaces.

For additional levels of detail the -d option for sendmail can also be used during testing. This option is the debugging switch and will give you great and gory detail about how the rule is being processed. The -d option has numerous arguments, and you need to consult your system's documentation for their meanings. On most systems there are over 60 different -d options, so I won't go into them here because they are probably different on your system.

In any case, use of the -bt and -d options will show you how your rule is being processed and will show you the before and after workspace. For a detailed discussion of the -bt and -d options, I refer you to *sendmail*, by Bryan Costales, Eric Allman, and Neil Rickert (O'Reilly and Associates, 1993).

I promised to tell you what that rule would do to you. Instead of just taking everything in the workspace and placing a set of angle brackets around it, it takes everything (including the new angle brackets) and places another set around it, and again, and again, and so on, until you have filled the entire workspace, at which time sendmail will probably crash with a core dump. The second rule goes off in an infinite loop. IDA and V8 will warn you that this is happening, but won't stop it.

Mail Delivery Agents   The final part of the configuration file example deals with mail delivery agents. Look at the sendmail.cf listing in Figure 7.17. Each of the lines that begin with **M** designates a mail delivery agent. Mail delivery agents differ, sometimes by quite a large margin, so sendmail needs to be told a great deal of information about each one used. The **M** command is the way to do this.

Figure 7.17 shows the **M** command lines extracted from the sendmail.cf file. This file has eight mail delivery agents specified. Notice the top two lines in the figure. The specifications for the local and prog mail delivery agents must always be present or sendmail will issue a warning and continue to run. You might also notice that each line has the **P** and **A** equates present. The **P** and **A** equates are the only required equates; all others are optional. In all, there are 11 equates that can be specified (more or less,

```
Mlocal,  P=/bin/rmail,  F=DFMPlms, S=10, R=20, A=rmail -d $u
Mprog,   P=/bin/sh, F=DFMPlshu, S=10,  R=20, A=sh -c $u
Mtcp, P=[IPC],  F=CDFMXmu, S=11, R=21, E=\r\n, A=IPC $h
Muucp, P=/usr/bin/uux,  F=DFMUshu, S=13, R=23, A=uux - $h!rmail ($u)
Mdumbuucp, P=/usr/bin/uux, F=DMUshux,      R=23,  A=uux - $h!rmail ($u)
Mx400, P=/usr/lib/x400/x4mailer, F=CDMFmn, S=14, R=24, A=x4mailer -f $g $u
Mopenmail, P=/usr/openmail/bin/UNIX.in, F=DFLMXmnu, S=15, R=25, A=UNIX.in
Momxport, P=/usr/openmail/bin/xport.in, F=LMn, A=xport.in $uMomx400,
P=/usr/openmail/bin/x400.out, F=LMn, A=x400.out $u
```

FIGURE 7.17   Mail delivery agents specified in sendmail.cf.

depending on the version of sendmail you are using). These are shown in Figure 7.18.

The general format of the **M** command line is

```
Mname, equate, equate, equate
```

The NAME value is an internal sendmail variable, and the equates are whatever is required for the mail delivery agent to function properly. The equate list is comma-separated and may contain spaces for clarity. The comma after the NAME variable isn't required, but can result in problems on some sendmail versions (like SunOS 4.1.2) if left out.

Using Figures 7.18 and 7.19, you should be able to make sense of the **M** lines shown in Figure 7.17. Before modifying any of your existing **M** configuration file lines, or adding additional lines, read your documentation thoroughly.

7.1.2   The sendmail Command-Line Options

So far we have delved deeply into the sendmail configuration file and its many mysteries. Now we are ready to go on to sendmail itself

Equate	Name	Definition
A=	Argv	Command-line arguments for the specific delivery agent (must be last equate specified; the argument list goes from the "=" to the EOL; macros are expanded as required).
C=	Charset	IDA option to allow specification of non-ASCII character set.
D=	Directory	V8 equate to specify execution directories (path1:path2...).
E=	EOL	String that defines the end-of-line condition (usually \n or \r\n).
F=	Flags	Delivery agent's behavior flags. (Up to 32 are available depending upon your version of sendmail; check your documentation. Figure 7.19 shows those used in the example.)
L=	Linelimit	IDA and V8 line length limit.
M=	Maximum	Maximum length in bytes for the message.
P=	Path	Directory path to the MDA program location (can be either a path or [IPC] or [LPC]).
R=	Recipient	Specifies the recipient address rewriting rule-set number (for IDA and V8 two sets can be specified: envelope/header).
S=	Sender	Specifies the sender address rewriting rule-set number (for IDA and V8 two sets can be specified: envelope/header).
X=	Xescape	IDA default escape character.

FIGURE 7.18 Mail delivery agent command-line equates.

and its numerous command-line options. Normally, sendmail will be started when the system is booted and it will take care of itself. However, sometimes we may need to run the sendmail program from the command line, and in these situations we must know what command-line options are available. Remember, while I will try to discuss as many options as are currently available, the options

Flag	Meaning
C	Add the @domain to recipient addresses.
D	Require Date: in header.
F	Require From: in header.
M	Require Message-ID: in header.
P	Require Return-Path: in header.
U	Use UNIX-style for From: line.
X	Require RFC821 hidden dot.
h	Keep uppercase for host name.
l (ell)	Specify local (final) delivery agent.
m	Agent allows multiple recipients.
n	Don't use UNIX-Style From: line.
s	Strip quotation marks.
u	Keep uppercase for username.

FIGURE 7.19 Flags used in mail delivery agent specifications in example.

change from release to release and by the flavor of UNIX you use, so be sure to review your system's documentation before blindly going where no one has gone before.

At times there may be aliases pointing to sendmail. These aliases perform different functions and are usually named for those functions. Examples are **mailq** (show queue contents), **bsmtp** (for IDA run in batched SMTP mode), and **newaliases** (rebuild the aliases file). These aliases actually run sendmail using one of the command-line arguments we will be discussing.

The actual sendmail program may exist in different locations and by different names. The executable image of sendmail may reside in /usr/etc, /usr/sbin, or /etc. On most systems the program is located in the /usr/lib directory. If your documentation isn't clear on the location, try looking in the /etc/init.d file for SVR4 or in the /etc/rc files for BSD UNIX.

The format for use of sendmail in command-line mode is

```
% /usr/lib/sendmail command addresses
```

The arguments must be in this order. The **command** argument is one of the many switches available, and **addresses** is a list of possible recipients and is optional. Figure 7.20 lists the switches, their meanings, and their applicable sendmail version.

Switch	Meaning	sendmail Version
-B	Message body type	Version 8 only
-b	Operating mode	All
-C	Configuration file location	All (Prescanned)
-d	Set debugging mode	All (Prescanned)
-F	Full name of sender	All
-f	Address of sender	All
-h	Hop count (initial)	All
-I	Same as -bi	All
-M	Process queue by id	IDA and SunOS
-m	Set the "me-too" option	All
-n	No aliasing	All
-o	Set an option from command line	All
-p	Set host and protocol	V8
-q	Force queue processing	All (Prescanned)
-R	Process queue by recipient	IDA
-r	Same as -f	All
-S	Process queue by sender	IDA
-t	Retrieve message recipients from header	All
-v	Verbose mode (tell me everything)	All
-Z	Freeze file location	IDA (Prescanned)

FIGURE 7.20 Command-line switches for sendmail.

Switches such as -b and -d also have arguments. In the case of -b the arguments tell sendmail in what mode to operate—for example, the -bt switch option that allows testing, which we have already discussed. Figure 7.21 shows the different modes for sendmail. Switch -d has 60 main arguments, each of which has the possibility for several subarguments. The arguments for the -d (debug) switch take the form of xx.xx where the x's are numbers. Currently there are 0–60 main argument categories, and each may have levels. Multiple categories may be specified as a comma-separated list or a range. The level is an integer in the range of 0 to 127. Output from the -d switch can be quite complex, and you should probably avoid it unless you have the sendmail manual and code list at hand.

When sendmail is started the command line switches are prescanned; then several actions occur. These are

1. Thawing the frozen (a preparsed disk resident file) configuration file, if it exists.

2. Initializing environmental variables.

-b Mode	Meaning	sendmail Version
-bb	Batched SMTP mode	IDA (Sometimes known as bsmtp)
-bd	daemon mode	All (Sometimes known as smtpd)
-bi	Initialize alias mode	All (Sometimes known as newaliases)
-bm	Act as mail sender	All
-bp	Print mail queue	All (Sometimes known as mailq)
-bs	Use standard input for SMTP	All
-bt	Run in test mode, resolve addresses only	All
-bv	Verify, don't collect or deliver	All
-bz	Freeze configuration file	All but V8 (prescanned)

FIGURE 7.21 **-b** switch mode settings.

3. Initializing macros (internal predefined macros, not declared macros).

4. Processing non-prescanned switches.

5. Processing the configuration file.

6. Processing the recipient list, if it is present. If it is not needed; ignore it, if it is needed, whine.

Once these actions complete, sendmail processes your requests and generates results as required.

I will once again refer you to your system documentation, or read *sendmail* by Costales, Allman, and Rickert for further reading on the sendmail program. Their text is 792 pages of great information— much more than I can hope to give, or even want to give, here. After all, this is not a sendmail book but a book on UNIX administration.

7.2   THE UUCP PROGRAM

The UNIX-to-UNIX copy program (uucp) was first developed in 1976 by Mike Lesk at AT&T Bell Laboratories. It was first distributed in 1977 in UNIX version 7 as version 2 uucp and several updates have been made since then, with multiple updates per flavor. Thus not all uucp commands and options listed in this section will be appropriate for your version. I suggest that you check the man pages and your system documentation before making any changes.

As if the situation wasn't complex enough, in 1983 an entirely new version of uucp was put out by Peter Honeyman, David A. Nowitz, and Brian E. Redman. Appropriately, this new version is known as the HoneyDanBer version, or simply as the HDB, or "Basic Networking Utilities," (BNU), version. BNU is supposedly backward compatible with version 2, but occasionally some odd things will pop up. As this is usually different version to version, it would be nearly impossible to give you a quantitative guide on how to get around any of the problems. Post your problem on the Internet or under the CompuServe UNIXFORUM, and nine out of ten times someone will be able to give you a workaround.

7.2.1 Configuration of uucp

As with sendmail, the most important facet of uucp management lies with maintaining its configuration files. Unlike sendmail, which has at most two files, uucp can have six or more. How these files are named depends on whether your uucp is based on version 2 uucp or BNU. Figure 7.22 shows how these uucp release configuration files compare. The uucp system was designed to operate over the telephone system, and recent additions allow its use over most networks as well. Some systems such as AIX and HP-UX have automated the setup of uucp in their smit and SAM utilities. BNU also has an automated shell script called uucpmgmt located in the packagemgmt management script menu. The XENIX implementation has the uuinstall script for this purpose.

Version 2 Filename	BNU Filename	Type	Purpose
L-devices	Dialers, Devices	Config	Specifies types of available modems.
L-dialcodes	Dialcodes	Config	Specifies number and access codes database.
L.aliases	None	Config	Deals with hosts that have multiple names (BSD only).
L.cmds	Permissions	Config	Commands that uuxqt can use.
L.sys	Systems	Config	Lists uucp nodes, login scripts.
USERFILE	Permissions	Config	Lists accesses available to remote sites.

FIGURE 7.22 uucp Files, programs and commands, and purposes.

Version 2 Filename	BNU Filename	Type	Purpose
none	grades	Config	Sets up the job grades and multiple queues.
none	Config	Config	Override file for some uucp parameters.
none	Limits	Config	Sets up usage limits to prevent uucp from taking over the system.
SQFILE	None	Config	Keeps track of the number of connects.
FWDFILE	Permissions	Config	Keeps track of what systems yours will forward to.
ORIGFILE	Permissions	Config	Keeps track of users who can forward through your system.
none	Sysfiles	Config	Allows multiple sets of configuration files to be used.
uucico	uucico	Program	Performs intermachine communications.
uuclean	uuclean	Program	Cleans up spool directory.
uuxqt	uuxqt	Program	Remote command server.
acucntrl	uugetty	Program	Controls modem serial ports.
uucp	uucp	Command	Command that uses uucico.
uux	uux	Command	Command that uses uuxqt.
uusend	uusend	Command	Command used to send files to an indirect host.
uusedn	uusedn	Command	Command to send a single file only to an indirect host.
uuto	uuto	Command	Command to send a file to a system.
uupick	uupick	Command	Command to get a file sent to you.
	uucheck	Command	Command to verify that uucp is set up.
ERRLOG	ERRLOG	Logfile	Program error logger.
LOGFILE	LOGFILE	Logfile	General message logger.
SYSLOG	SYSLOG	Logfile	System-level error logs.

FIGURE 7.22 Continued.

7.2.2   **The uucp Directories**

The files shown in Figure 7.22 will reside in /usr/lib/uucp. In addition to the directory that holds the programs and configuration files there should also be a /usr/spool/uucp directory set up for the files sent by uucp to be queued into. The final directory that should be present on properly configured uucp systems is the /usr/spool/uucppublic, which is a directory set up with universal read/write permissions so that all users can transfer files there for further processing by uucp. This directory provides a place where a user can transfer a file to, modify the mode of the file, and then transfer it into his or her home directory. This prevents the file from being transferred directly into a user file with a bad or improper mode. All files handled by uucp are assigned to the ownership of the uucp user on most systems. Finally, most of the user-level commands will reside in /usr/bin for the uucp system. Generally, these commands will consist of a file containing a uucp, uucico, or uuxqt command with or without options.

Some uucp implementations will have more program files; however, it is virtually unheard of for them to have less. Most of the time users will not use uucp directly. The uucp programs are used by mail and other network programs.

7.2.3   **General Procedure for Initial uucp Setup**

The uucp setup consists of two distinct parts. The first deals with one-time setup steps; the second, with repetitive setup tasks. Since it is always better to start at the beginning, let's examine the one-time setup tasks first.

One-Time uucp Setup Tasks   The one-time tasks strictly involve the configuration of uucp. In general these tasks are

1. Locating/installing the uucp software.

2. Creating the uucp login account and giving correct mode (permissions) to the files.

3. Connecting modem(s) (physically).

4. Describing the modem(s) to uucp in the configuration files.

5. Establishing the best phone service (usually low-cost).

6. Entering telephone access codes in the L-dialcodes or Dialcodes files.

7. Establishing an initial connection.

8. Reconfiguring the mail system to use uucp.

9. Testing uucp mail connections.

10. Publishing your uucp connection data.

These steps can be quite complex. Let's examine each in a general way (after all, this isn't a book on uucp!) and discuss what should be accomplished.

Locating the uucp Installation   First you will need to find out if uucp is even installed. On some systems it is installed as a matter of course; on others it is a separate configuration option. The first step is to locate the /etc/lib/uucp directory. Chances are, if this directory isn't present, uucp isn't installed. If no files other than uucico, uucp, and uuxqt are present, uucp is probably installed but you have no example configuration files. In this case, be sure to review any documentation, including the man pages, before proceeding with the implementation.

Creating the uucp Login   The next step is to create the uucp account. This account may already be set up as a part of the installation process. If so, you may need to use this account to edit any of the configuration files. On some systems you should use the root account to edit the configuration files. I suggest you check your documentation to be sure. Generally speaking, the uucp user is used on newer versions of uucp, while root is used for old XENIX or BSD versions. If you look at the /etc/passwd file and there is only a single-line entry for uucp or uucpadm, such as **uucp::5:1::/usr/lib/uucp:**, then your system probably hasn't been configured yet. Two logins for uucp are usually created: the first is used by uucico for all activities; it performs a set-userid from whatever user invokes it into the uucp user id. The second should be a general-use user and will normally have "uucp" in its name, although it may be just the name of the remote system allowed to use it, such as "italy." The second user will generally look like this:

```
xuucp::6:1::/usr/spool/uucppublic:/usr/lib/uucp/uucico.
```

This sets the user xuucp to use the directory /usr/spool/uucppublic and gives the user /usr/lib/uucp/uucico as a shell. Of course, once **uucico** is invoked it immediately sets the user id to uucp, so no group id setting is really required for the other uucp logins. Thus for this configuration, remote users log in under the xuucp user.

For security reasons each remote system should have its own account. These accounts can be set up identically to the xuucp account, except with different names. As shipped, the uucp account(s) may have no passwords set; in this case you should use the **passwd** command to set passwords as soon as possible.

The uucp directories and files need to have certain modes or protections set. Generally speaking, the configuration files should have **-rw-r——** (mode 640), uucico should have **——s—s——x** (mode 6001), as should uuclean, and program uuxqt should have **——s—x——** (mode 2010). The /usr/spool/uucp directory should have **drwxr-xr-x** (mode 761). On some installations there may be log files. These will normally have permissions set properly when they are created. The /usr/spool/uucppublic directory should have **drwxrwxrwx** (mode 777) set.

Installation of Modems for uucp Once the uucp user(s) are set up and the file and directory modes are set, you are ready to install modems. Most modems will come with installation guides and connection cables. Modems connect to serial lines, usually with RS-232 protocol cables. If you must manufacture a connection cable, most often pins 2 and 3 will have to be switched on one end if you are using a straight-through cable to start with. Switching pins 2 and 3 on one end produces a null-modem cable. Null-modem adapters that will perform this for you are available from most computer stores.

Once the physical connection is made between the computer and modem(s), each modem must be connected to an analog telephone line. (Be careful—some modern offices may have digital communications systems, and modems don't work on them. You may have to have the telecommunications group run in lines if your office has digital instead of analog lines.) After each modem is connected to both the computer and phone line, you have to tell the uucp and UNIX system about it. If you are using network connections, a simple connection between the computer and network is required.

To tell UNIX about the modem, you must create or copy a device file into the /dev directory. This device file must have a protection mode of 664 on most systems. If you have to create a new device file, the general specifications for a modem for the **mknod** command are: c, specifying a character-type device, and the major and minor port numbers. For example, to create a modem device file on port 9 the command is

```
$ mknode modem1 c 0 9
```

If your system allows modem ports to be designated other than as cu-type devices, it is handy to define them using descriptors such as those shown in the above example. This allows the modem to be moved from port to port with only a minor change. For example, if you want to change modem1 from port 9 to port 2, the series of commands is

```
$rm /dev/modem1
$ mknode modem1 c 0 2
```

Once the device file is set up, the physical installation is complete. However, UNIX and uucp still don't know about the modem. In order for the system to recognize the modem and be able to use it properly, you must edit the uucp and UNIX configuration files.

Describing the Modem to the uucp System and UNIX The next task is to describe the modem or connection to uucp and UNIX. This is accomplished by configuring the appropriate files—L-devices for version 2, Devices and Dialers for BNU, /etc/inittab on SVR4, and /etc/ttys for BSD. The /etc/inittab and /etc/ttys files usually have one line per serial port. On older versions of UNIX a modem requires two lines: one for outgoing and one for incoming calls. If your system has the acucntrl or uugetty programs, then you only require one.

The format for the lines in the /etc/inittab file is

```
id:level:type:process device_file baudrate
```

So, a device installed at port id 5, running during modes 2 and 3, that should allow bidirectional communication, and using BNU with device file /dev/modem1 at 9600 baud, would have the following line in the /etc/inittab file:

```
005:23:respawn:/etc/uugetty modem1 9600
```

If instead you want the line to be for dialout purposes only, use **off** instead of **respawn**. If you place an **-r** before the device file specification, the process will wait for the calling process to issue a character. This prevents the death of a thousand cuts, an ancient torture by which the victim was repeatedly given small cuts until he bled to death. If you don't prevent the process from responding immediately, each system will reissue the "login:" prompt until its repeated small cuts into your resources bring your system (and maybe the other one as well) to its knees. The first system to do an explicit write will be the call initiator and the other system will be the listener. This parameter is ignored for outgoing calls.

On some versions of UNIX, such as SunOS, the device number is used to govern whether or not a device is a modem type (i.e., whether it responds only on carrier detect or always responds.) On SunOS the two types of terminal connection are specified by "tty" and "cua" followed by a number. If the device file's device number is in the range of 0–127, the device is a carrier detect line (one that will only respond when a carrier signal is detected), if the device number is in the range of 128–255, the line will respond even if no carrier is detected (cua may be used only with 128–255; tty, only with 0–127). On SunOS 0–127 and 128–255 correspond to the same devices, 0 to 128, 127 to 255, and so on. This means that if cua0 is open, tty0 cannot be.

The general procedure for creating a bidirectional port on SunOS is similar to the following:

1. Issue the command

   ```
   $ ln /dev/ttya /dev/ttyd0
   ```

   which links the port ttya to a specific device file ttyd0.

2. Issue the command

   ```
   mknod /dev/cua0 c 12 128
   ```

   which creates the device file cua0 and gives it a device number of 128.

3. Insert the following line in the /etc/ttytab:

   ```
   ttyd0 "usr/etc/getty" d2400" unknown on
   ```

   which tells SunOS that logins are enabled for ttyda.

4. Issue the command

   ```
   $ ttysoftcar n /dev/cua0
   ```

   which disables the SunOS "software carrier detect" for the dialout port cua0.

After this procedure has been carried out, ttyd0 should be used for incoming calls and cua0 for outgoing calls. This means that people calling you will have to place the port designation ttyd0 in their configurations, while you will use the cua0 designation to call them.

Once the physical connection and configuration into UNIX have been set up, you have to configure the uucp link into the uucp configuration files. Essentially this is a five-part procedure:

1. Set up the physical connection.

2. Give your systems unique names. This is accomplished with one of these commands: **setuname**, **uname**, or **hostname**, depending on the type of UNIX you are using.

3. Edit the appropriate configuration files to give the uucico program data on systems that you wish to connect to. For V2, edit L.Sys; for BNU, Systems. These files contain system names, devices, telephone numbers, and the appropriate login sequence.

4. Edit the appropriate configuration files and specify further connection data such as speed and type of link—for V2, L-Devices; for BNU, Devices.

5. Test the link.

The uucp systems support several communications protocols. You specify the type of communications protocol to use in the L.Sys or Systems file. The general format of a line from these files is

```
system schedule(/grade - optional) device_type,protocol
   speed phone chat_script
```

where

> **system** is the system name to be called.
>
> **schedule** is the allowed calling schedule, usually a time range in 24-hour format; multiple time designations can be used via comma-separated specifications.

grade is the grade or level of communication. BNU and BSD versions of uucp allow this optional parameter. The grade is set to 0–9, A–Z, or a–z, with 0 being the highest possible grade and z the lowest.

device_type is the terminal port designation such as tty0 or cua0. Under BNU this will point to a device driver file. Generally, this is set to ACU under version 2. It may also be set to DIR or TCP if the connection is made over a TCPIP line.

protocol is a single protocol designator or, under BNU, a list specified in the order of preference. The available protocols are

> g—64-bit, checksum on each packet, automatic retransmit of bad packets. This is the oldest of the protocols and is used for transmissions on low-quality lines.

> f—BSD only, 256-bit, checksum for the entire file. If used with 7-bit encapsulation, this may increase file length.

> t—BSD only, 1,024-byte packet lengths, 8-bit data path.

> x—BNU only, used under X.25 protocols.

> e—BNU only, known as BNU error-free protocol.

phone is the phone number used for calling the system. Some special-use characters can provide pauses and do other special functions. These vary from system to system. Some versions allow specifications of modem control codes. Review your system documentation for your version's limitations. Special characters available on most versions include "=" or "–" for a pause, and special modem control characters as used by supported modems.

chat-script is used to specify special connection requirements that the called system must see if it is to allow you to log in. Such things as break signals, questions and responses, and so forth, can be placed in a chat-script. In most cases you can get the chat-script by calling the system manager for the system you are connecting with. You can also find it by looking at the published address data if it is available. The general format for a chat-script consists of expected scripts, sends, and subexpects.

There are also special characters that may be specified; see Figure 7.23 for a list of them. A simple chat-script might look like

```
ogin:--ogin: nuucp sword: nuucp_pass
```

where **ogin:** represents the last characters in the **login:** string sent by the system being called.

— specifies that if you don't find **ogin:**, send multiple break signals and look at **ogin:** again. Once you get it send the user

Escape Sequence	Meaning to uucp
" " (space)	Expect a null string.
EOT	Send an end-of-transmission.
BREAK	Send a BREAK character.
-	Send a BREAK character.
\\	Send a "\".
\OOO	Send the octal digit OOO as its corresponding ASCII character.
\b	On BSD send a BREAK; on others send a backspace character.
\c	Supress a newline.
\d	1-second delay.
\K	BNU "insert a BREAK".
\n	Linefeed/newline.
\N	BNU—send a null.
\0 (zero)	Other than BNU—send a null.
\p	BNU—pause for a bit (less than a second).
\r	Carriage return.
\s	Send a space.
\t	Send a tab on all except BSD 4.3.

FIGURE 7.23 Chat-script special characters.

name **nuucp** and then expect the string **password:** as shown by the last part of the string **sword:**. Once you get **sword:** send the user nuucp's password **nuucp_pass**.

Once the L.Sys or Systems file is configured you will need to configure the L-Devices file for version 2 or the Devices file for BNU. These files contain the actual dialing sequences for the specific types of modem on your system. There may also be files such as modem-cap or acucap that perform similar functions. Since the format of these files is difficult at best, take a look at your system documentation before trying to modify them. BNU also includes the file Dialers that describes the modem dialing sequences. If you have an old-style file, you can build the dialing instructions directly into your chat-script. For example, adding the code: **" " ATZ OK ATDTnumber CONNECT speed**, where **number** is the number to dial and **speed** is the speed of the expected connection, will permit the use of a Hayes compatible modem without resort to the special files.

The L.Devices or Devices file has the same general format:

```
type device call_unit speed
```

where

> **type** is the type of device. Generally, this will be ACU for Automatic Call Unit, but can also be DIR for a direct link. BSD also supports the types DK (AT&T Datakit network), MICOM (for a MICOM switch), PAD (for an X.25 PAD connection), PCP (for a GTE-Telenet PC Pursuit connection), SYTEK (for a SYTEK high-speed modem), and TCP for a TCP/IP connection.
>
> **device** is the name of the device file to be used.
>
> **call_unit** is used only on older versions of uucp that still expect a special callout unit that dials the number for the modem. For most modern systems this is replaced with a dash (-) or a zero (0) to nullify the parameter.
>
> **speed** is the baud rate of the modem link.

The L-Dialcodes or Dialcodes file can be used to provide a short-hand method of specification for common prefixes used for calling multiple sites. For example, if you are located at the University of Mugwamp, you dial 8 to get an internal line, the general prefix for the University is 333, and several machines are spread throughout campus that communicate via uucp, you can place a line like

```
uom 8=333
```

into the file and then, instead of having to specify the 8=333 each time a university machine is configured into your network, you would just place **uom** in place of the prefix. Of course, this is a much-simplified example, and generally you would use these files for much longer or use complex series of codes where there might be several dozen systems using the same prefix.

Another file that can be considered a part of this configuration is the BSD file L.aliases. This file allows multiple names to be specified for a single node in your network. L.aliases is handy when you have to rename systems but don't want to search through all of the uucp configuration files for each time the node name is used. The L.aliases file is simply a list of name pairs with the new name specified first followed by a space or tab and the old name.

Checking the Connection Face it, none of us is perfect. I strongly suggest that you check your connections and not just "think" that they are correct. There are multiple ways of doing this. You can manually connect, using the **cu** on SVR4 non-version 7 or BSD, or **tip** on BSD, and note the actual sequences used, comparing them manually to what you have in the script, or you can use the **uucico** **-x** command to show the results of the chat-script as it is executed (the -x option places **uucico** into debug.) An additional source of debugging is the log scripts that **uucico** keeps. Along with the above methods, BNU provides a shell program, Uutry, that allows a level-5 debugging of BNU links.

Once the connection has been established and tested the final steps involve telling the mail system how to use uucp and publishing your connection information so that others can reach you or "hop" through you to other sites.

Telling the sendmail System about uucp Telling your mail system about uucp is important so that mail will know how to forward information received via uucp transfers, and notifications about uucp transfers, to the appropriate users. In addition, uucp needs to be told how to forward and who is allowed to forward mail. This is accomplished in sendmail by appropriate use of sendmail.cf as covered in previous sections. For other mail systems you will have to review the documentation. The uucp configuration files that handle its end of this bargain vary from a single file under BNU, Permissions, to several files under other incarnations of uucp—USERFILE, ORIGFILE , and FWDFILE. In addition, the type of commands that other systems can fob off on you via uuxqt is controlled via the L.cmds file. Refer to the documentation for your system for the proper way to format entries in the files your system uses.

Telling Other Systems about Yours (Publishing) If you expect to be able to communicate with other systems, you should expect that they will want to communicate with you. In order to make this possible, and to keep from having to answer several phone calls weekly about uucp connections, you need to tell the world about your installation. This is called publishing your uucp information. Generally, the uucp mapping project will eventually find you and send you an electronic form to fill out about your site. Once this form is completed you **uucp** it to **rutgers!uucpmap**.

Further Reading on uucp As I said before, this isn't a book on uucp. There are many fine sources of uucp information, including the system documentation for your version. I might also suggest the following references:

UNIX System Administration Handbook, Evi Nemeth, Garth Snyder, and Scott Seebass, PTR Prentice-Hall, 1989.

Managing uucp and Usenet, Tim O'Reilly and Grace Todino, O'Reilly and Associates, 1994.

Open Computing—Best UNIX Tips Ever, Kenneth H. Rosen, Richard R. Rosinski, and Douglas A. Host, Osborne-McGraw-Hill, 1994.

7.3 OTHER MEANS OF USER COMMUNICATION

So far we have discussed sendmail and uucp. Both of these systems are quite important to UNIX managers, but they deal mostly with communication next door or around the world. What about when you just want to talk to the next cubicle over? UNIX provides user-to-user communications in the form of the **mail**, **xmail**, **talk**, **ytalk**, and **wall** commands. Some of these, like **mail**, use the existing protocols installed on the machine, such as sendmail, while others simply provide for process-to-process communication.

The use of these commands is not really a management issue. Once you have established the users and links by use of sendmail or some other system, these commands can be used. Use your system documentation and your man pages to find out more information for your specific commands.

Terminal and Peripheral Administration

How you manage terminals and peripherals will determine how your user community views you. The terminals and peripherals are the users' way in and out of the system. If the way is smooth and easy, they will think favorably of you; if the way is hard and full of pitfalls, they will say unkind things about you. Again, this falls under the heading of staying invisible, which you can't do if users have to constantly ask you to configure terminals, peripherals, and what have you, for them. This is one area where being a little proactive can help you quite a bit.

When I speak of managing terminals and peripherals, I don't mean hooking up terminals and PCs or changing the paper in the laser printer, although if yours is a small shop you will probably be doing these things. The management that I am referring to involves ensuring that the system is properly configured to handle the terminals (proper escape sequencing, backspacing, erasing, using arrow keys, etc.) and that the peripherals perform as they are expected to—for example, proper font setup for the laser printers. The following sections will help you to be proactive.

8.1 CHARACTER-BASED TERMINALS

Character-based terminals such as the VT100 are the old workhorses of the industry, and virtually all systems support them. Other character-based terminals are TTY, ANSI, VT52, and so forth. These terminals handle characters and some simple (line) graphics, but don't deal with bitmaps, or complex or color graphics. The major part of managing character-based terminals is making sure that the system knows their peculiarities. Depending on the system there are a number of files that deal with terminal definition; usually the file will be /etc/termcap.

On BSD systems the files used for configuration are /etc/ttys, /etc/ttytype, and /etc/gettytab. On ATT systems the files are /etc/inittab, /etc/gettydefs, and /etc/gettytab. These tables are used to tell the system what terminals are connected, the speed at which the terminal communicates, and other basic information. In addition, the system needs to also know how the terminal handles interrupts, escape sequences, and other communications-related signals; this is handled through the termcap or terminfo file.

In most modern offices a system will be configured with one of the new network protocols such as Ethernet or Token-Ring. If your office is still in the dark ages, you may also have to deal with RS-232C connections. With Ethernet you will usually have the main connection or connections into each UNIX platform; these connections go to hubs or routers to which the terminals and peripherals connect. This set of main connections and hubs or routers is called the backbone, since when you diagram them they resemble a backbone, with the ribs forming the connections to the terminals and peripherals.

Figure 8.1 depicts basic network diagrams.

8.1.1 Configuration of termcap

It is to be hoped that you will never need to edit termcap. When a new terminal comes, it is usually provided with some means of installing the terminal definition in the termcap file. The /etc/term-

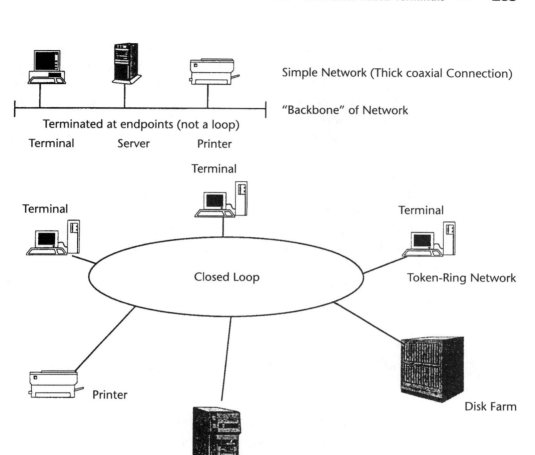

Simple Network (Thick coaxial Connection)

"Backbone" of Network

Terminated at endpoints (not a loop)

Terminal   Server   Printer

Terminal

Terminal

Terminal

Closed Loop

Token-Ring Network

Printer

Disk Farm

Server

Under either scheme, multiple sets of backbones, rings, or a combination of both can be used through the use of repeaters. Each component on the network is known as a node and must have a unique address. Usually with UNIX the communication protocol is TCP/IP. Each branch off of the network can lead to a concentrator which can split the signal out to multiple devices.

FIGURE 8.1 Example network topologies.

cap file on most new systems contains definitions of over 480 different terminal types, so unless you just invented a new terminal, yours will probably be in there. You specify the terminal type by its name, so for VT100 it will be VT100, or vt100. The termcap file uses multiple aliases for terminals to handle case differences. Terminals that have the same definition are listed together. The ATT 4425 and ATT 5425 terminals have identical definitions, so instead of having two definitions, one is used for both terminals.

If you ever have to enter a configuration in termcap, you can usually find an example in the documentation that comes with the terminal. If not, put out a call over the Internet or in one of the CompuServe forums that deal with UNIX, such as UNIXFORUM, SCOForum, SUNSoftforum, and the like. Usually someone out there will already have done it and will be willing to ship you the definition, or at least point you in the right direction. Figure 8.2 shows an example

```
#
#     This entry is for the Wyse 50 terminal, 132 columns.
#
#
w2|wyse50-132|Wyse model 50 - 132 columns:\
    :am:bs:co#132:li#24:cm=\Ea%i%dR%dC:cl=\E*:cd=\Ey:ce=\Et:\
    :is=\El\E"\E`;:\
    :if=/usr/lib/tabset/stdcrt:\
    :al=\EE:dl=\ER:im=\Eq:ei=\Er:dc=\EW:\
    :ho=^^:nd=^L:bt=\EI:pt:\
    :so=\E):se=\E(:sg#0:\
    :us=\EG8:ue=\EG0:ug#1:\
    :up=^K:do=^V:\
    :kb=^H:ku=^K:kd=^V:kl=^H:kr=^L:kh=^^:\
    :ko=ic,dc,al,dl,cl,ce:\
    :hs:ts=\Ef:fs=\r:ds=\Ef\r:
```

FIGURE 8.2 Example termcap entry.

termcap entry, which was pulled from an example file downloaded from CompuServe in the library section of the UNIXFORUM. A search on the word "termcap" brought up several files including various utilities.

As an example of what can be done with termcap, Figure 8.3 is a C routine that allows a clear screen to be done for any terminal with a definition in the termcap file (assuming that the clear screen option is available for the terminal).

8.1.2   Use of stty

The stty program allows the general user to reset certain terminal attributes. I suggest that you check the man pages for your system for all of the available options, since they are numerous and they change depending on the release and version of UNIX. Let's look at some general examples of the use of stty.

There are times when a user will abnormally exit from a program such as vi that does odd things to the default terminal definition. If this happens, use the **stty sane** command to reset the terminal based on the termcap definition. Another way to do this is to use the **reset** command on BSD systems. Sometimes the terminal will get so crazy that enter produces a control m. In this case enter a ctrl-J, enter either **stty sane** or **reset**, and then enter another ctrl-J.

Under BSD the following string might be good to place in the generic login script:

```
stty new crt cr0 intr ^C kill ^U erase ^H -tabs
```

This has the effect of specifying the new BSD terminal driver; **crt** sets the proper modes for a crt (such as crterase, crtkill, or ctlecho), and **cr0** tells the system not to put any delays in the output due to carriage returns. The **-tabs** disables tabs (some terminals have a

```
/****
        clear screen
***/
#include <stdio.h>
#include <sgtty.h>
int outc();
main()
{
        char terminfo[1024]; /* terminal information buffer */
        static char tbuf[100]; /* hold cls string */
        char *getenv(),*tname,*p, *tgetstr();
        tname = getenv("TERM");
        switch (tgetent(terminfo,tname) )
                {
                case -1: printf("\nCannot open termcap file.\n");
                        exit(1);
                        break;
                case 0: printf("\n%s is not in termcap file.\n",tname);
                        exit(1);
                        break;
                }
        p = tbuf;
        tputs(tgetstr("cl",&p),1,outc);
}
outc(c)
char c;
        {
        putchar(c);
        }
```

FIGURE 8.3 C routine that uses termcap to obtain the clear screen code.

problem with self-managed tabbing), and the other arguments set interrupt, kill, and erase values. Under the Bourne shell the command must be modified to

```
stty new crt intr\^C kill \^U erase |^H -tabs
```

since Bourne treats ∧ like a pipe character. Under ATT UNIX the **new** and **crt** arguments aren't allowed.

If you specify **stty everything**, **stty all**, or **stty -a** (depending on the system), you get a full listing of your terminal definition. If you just use **stty**, you get an abbreviated listing.

The stty command can be used with serial terminals to reset baud rate, parity, and other terminal communication parameters. For example:

```
$ stty 9600 > /dev/ttyi3
```

On BSD stty will reset the terminal communication speed at /dev/ttyi3 to 9600 baud. On ATT systems the command becomes

```
$ stty 9600 < /dev/ttyi3.
```

Not all systems allow rank-and-file users to change terminal characteristics.

There are two general command-line options with stty: -a and -g. The -a option with stty reports on all current option settings. The -g option with stty spits out the current settings in hexadecimal (my favorite format, and I'm sure it is yours as well . . .).

The major use for the **stty -g** option is to place the output in a file that can then be used as a command-line argument for the **stty** command. This allows the user to alter a stty option and then use stty and file to reset the options to their previous settings. The hexadecimal output is more compact and better to use for this function than the output from the -a, which is intended more for human than machine consumption.

8.1.3 Use of tset

The **tset** command is used under BSD-based implementations of UNIX to initialize the terminal driver to a set of codes appropriate for a specific terminal type. You can issue **tset** without any arguments, and it will read whatever the setting of TERM is for the terminal type. If you don't have the TERM variable set in your profile, you can specify the terminal as an argument. If you log in from various terminals, you may wish to add the following line to your startup script for your users:

```
tset -m ?vt100
```

When you log in, you will receive the following prompt:

```
TERM = (vt100)?
```

A press of the **Enter** key accepts the default (vt100), but you can also set it to whatever type you like by entering the appropriate terminal type and pressing **Enter**.

The **stty** command can be used to set baud rate, number of rows, and number of columns. Review your system documentation for all possible options for your flavor.

8.2 X-WINDOWS TERMINALS

X-Windows allows PC, Mac, and workstation devices to be user-friendly interfaces to your system. To a person familiar with Macs or with PCs using the Windows system, the X-Windows environment will be a welcome home compared to the harsh realities of the command line on a UNIX server. Essentially, there will be three types of terminals accessing an X-Windows system: intelligent workstations, dumb X-terminals, and microcomputers using an X-Windows emulator. In most environments, I'll wager, most access will be through a PC or PC clone using an X-Windows emulator.

Numerous manufacturers provide X-Windows emulation products, among them Hummingbird-Exceed-W, DEC-Excursion, PC-Xview, and Reflections. All of these are companies and products that support emulation in the X-Windows environment. What can X offer me, you ask? A simplified user environment that is friendly and easy to use. The X-Windows system supports complex onscreen graphics, use of mice, digitizers, hot-screens, and all of the fun toys that the masses have come to associate with computing. With enhanced usability comes enhanced productivity. The editors and tools provided in the X-Windows environment are lightyears ahead of vi, grep, and other common user tools under plain-Jane UNIX.

X-Windows operates in the client/server configuration mode. The terminals, be they workstations, X-terminals, or Macs, are the clients, and the UNIX box they connect to is the server. Workstations and X-terminals will provide localized X-Windows processing; that is, they perform the graphic manipulations required to do X-Windows without producing a burden for the server. PCs and Macs, depending on the emulator or X-Windows package, may or may not offload the processing. X-Windows requires a high-speed link; and anyone who has ever tried X-Windows over a modem can tell you it is not fun. Generally, X-Windows requires network speeds that are up to ten times what a modem can support with current technology. X-Windows is strictly a network application.

X-Windows will run over most major networks, such as DEC-NET, TCPIP, NOVELL, or Net-Bios. Generally speaking, the network will be transparent to the users.

X-Windows systems have sorted out to two major standards—Motif and Open Look. Depending on your UNIX system, you may support one or both of these. Check with your vendor.

The X-Windows system requires special software on both the server and client boxes (unless the client is an X-terminal). This software contains the Xlib libraries, the Xt intrinsics, and usually vendor-specific toolkits that allow development within the specific X-Windows environment. This isn't an X-Windows developer's book, so we won't be discussing these development tools in detail. Numerous books are available for X-Windows developers, and I will leave that complex material to them.

So, what do you as the UNIX system administrator need to do with X-Windows? Let's find out.

8.2.1 The X-Windows Display Manager

The X-Windows display manager, usually called xdm, manages X clients whether they are local or remote. The xdm program provides all of the services of the init, getty, and login processes. Depending on your system xdm may have numerous options, and you should consult your man pages for a complete listing. Your system should also come with documentation on your particular version of X-Windows. Read and understand the sections dealing with administration before attempting to use your supplied xdm.

Some common xdm options are shown in Figure 8.4

The DisplayManager parameters allow control of the xdm. These parameters are located in the configuration file. If a resource is applicable to a specific terminal, then the terminal specification will be in the parameter name; otherwise, the parameter applies to all sessions and terminals. Generally speaking, the file provided with your system will be sufficient for your use. If you need to alter this configuration, there will usually be a configuration tool supplied. If a configuration application isn't available, read your documentation completely before attempting to modify the configuration files. A poorly running X-Windows environment will usually be better than no X-Windows environment at all.

There are usually two scripts run at root and user levels: The first is run at root and establishes the authenticity of the user session; the second is run by the user and declares the proper setup of the

Option	Purpose
-config	Specifies the configuration file. This can be used to hold all of the rest of the options listed below if desired, which makes the command line easier to deal with.
-daemon	Defaults to TRUE. This places the xdm process in the background in a hibernation state until it is invoked by an X-Windows client. I don't suggest altering this parameter.
-debug	Specifies a debug level and forces the server to run synchronously. Unless you are troubleshooting an application, leave this alone. Consult your documentation for proper debugging steps using debug level.
-error	Specifies the location for the error log.
-nodeamon	Sets the DisplayManager.daemonMode to FALSE.
-resources	Specifies the xrdb resource file used by the xrdb widgets.
-server	Specifies the value for the DisplayManager.servers resource.
-xrm	Allows specification of a special resource.

FIGURE 8.4   Common xdm options.

environment for running the X-Windows system. These scripts are generally called Xstartup on the root end and Xsession on the user end. Consult your X-Windows documentation for the proper naming and contents of these scripts on your system. Once a user logs out a third script, Xreset is run by root to eliminate any residual X-Windows settings and definitions.

8.2.2   The Motif and Open Look Window Managers

The Motif window manager and the Open Look window manager programs are X11 clients providing window and session management functions. The **mwm** command has two options, one to specify the display to use and one to specify the resource string. The display is usually the node address for the terminal using X-Windows. Each window manager will provide the following basic window services, contained in a title bar:

A title area usually containing the session name or program name.

A Minimize button to minimize the screen to an icon.

A Maximize button to make the window fill the screen.

A window menu button or bar.

These features allow a window to be controlled.

Depending on its use, a window may also contain icons. These are small graphics that represent a program, application, or another window with additional icons. The usual method to access an icon is to select it using the mouse cursor and click on the lefthand mouse button. This activates the icon or feature.

8.2.3   The Configuration of Clients

Usually clients start the X-Windows system by use of the **xinit** command. This command has the format

```
xinit [[client] options [- [server] [display] options]
```

The **xinit** command can be used to start up over 28 different X-Windows client services. Consult your system documentation for the appropriate services and clients for your system

It is suggested that you load some of the more useful services into a generic startup file for your users. This will allow them to access the X-Windows system without having to be an X-Systems expert. Some X-Windows systems allow the startup of an X-Windows manager service that allows users to select which services to run via a point-and-click interface.

8.2.4   Using Graphics Services

Graphics services allow a user or the administrator to dump bitmap files of the X-Windows session to a printer or to a file for later viewing. These services are usually called xpr for printing, xwd for dumping a window to a file, and xwud for displaying the dumped files. Most modern X-Windows systems provide an automated interface to these services via a menu called from the window menu bar at the top of the screen. Consult your X-Windows documentation for the details of using these commands manually.

8.2.5   Using Viewable Services

Viewable services allow users to see a displayed clock, check if they have mail, or display man pages properly formatted for X-Windows display. Again, on most modern X-Windows systems these services have been automated and are either user-selectable from a menu or automatically displayed. Check your X-Windows documentation to see how these options are switched on for your version.

The viewable services can be manually called via these commands:

xbiff   Displays a nifty mailbox icon. If the flag is down, there is no mail; if the flag is up, there is mail.

xclock   Displays a clock (usually you can specify analog or digital).

xload   Displays a histogram of your processes system load.

xsetroot   Allows respecification of window display attributes such as background.

8.2.6   Management of Fonts

For the unenlightened, fonts are typefaces and graphic characters. The font in this book is ITC Garamond. The size of the font is determined by points—the more points, the bigger the characters. Fonts can also have slant and aspect ratio as well as bold or normal aspects. In X-Windows there are numerous fonts, which at certain times you may be required to load or update for your X-Windows version. A new application may require special fonts. These may be located on the host, or they may have to be loaded onto each of the client boxes, or both. Generally, loading fonts is covered in the system installation document. The application documents will also be a source for information on font requirements.

To find the windows active on the server, the **xlswins** command can be used. This command has the format

```
xlswins [-options...] [windowid...]
```

where the options are

- display	Name the display name to list the fonts for.
-l	Generate a long list of fonts for each window.
-format radix	Specify hex, octal, or decimal as the display format for the window id.
-indent n	Specify that n number of spaces will be indented for each level of the window tree. The default is 2.

To find the fonts available for X-Windows' clients on the server, the xlsfonts command can be used. The command has the following format:

```
xlsfonts [-options...] -fn pattern
```

where the options are

-fn pattern	Specify the font name pattern to match.
-display host:dpy	Specify the host that you want the list for.
-l	Generate the long list for each font; don't use this one unless you've got all day.

-m	Specify that the long list should include the min and max boundaries for each font listed.
-C	Allow multiple column listing; use this or -n 0.
-1 (one, not "ell")	Specify a single column list—same as saying n 1.
-w width	Specify the column width of the printout. This defaults to 79.
-n col	Tell how many columns to put in the printout.

8.3   PRINTERS

Putting all the information in the world into your system won't do much good if there isn't a way of getting it out. In spite of what the "paperless" office pundits would have us believe, nothing quite beats a hard copy—it gives us a feeling of permanence. It is difficult to alter the contents of a printed page and not have it detectable. In contrast, a computer record can be altered without a trace in most files if a person knows what he or she is doing. Before a truly paperless office can exist, computer security will have to improve by several orders of magnitude. In order to get this hard copy, some form of printer—archaic dot-matrix, daisy-wheel, or state-of-the-art color laser—must be used. This section will give you some pointers on how to set up your system to use these hard-copy devices.

8.3.1   Using Printer Type Devices

In these days of high-speed, quiet, laser and inkjet printers the old standard line printer is fast becoming a thing of the past. However, before we relegate all of these trusty, noisy, slow printers to the junk heap, we need to recognize that there are some tasks they do better than the new high-tech ones. For example, you can't run the system console out to a laser printer very well. Laser printers operate in the page mode. That is, each print signal sent causes a page to be printed;

in most cases, log output will be spooled until an end of file is generated and then it will be sent to a laser printer for just this reason.

Given that line printers aren't completely dead yet, a few words on how to set up and configure them are still in order. Line printers are usually dot-matrix or daisy-wheel types that use an inked ribbon to print on paper. In a dot-matrix, circuits control solenoids that shoot small pins out at high speed when activated; these pins act just like the keys in an old typewriter (an early form of word processor, just after the pen)—they strike the inked ribbon and transfer a dot of ink to the page. Properly grouped by the firmware and software in the printer and computer, they create letters, graphic symbols, and other recognizable images on paper.

A daisy-wheel takes all of the keys from a typewriter for a specific font and places them on flexible strips of plastic or metal all joined to a central wheel (hence the name "daisy-wheel"). The small flexible strips are rotated via the wheel until the proper one is in place, and then a solenoid is activated that causes the strip's head to strike the inked ribbon and transfer the image on the strip's face to the paper.

A full-fledged line or page printer may employ a full series of wire sets and solenoids to transfer an entire line, or even an entire page, of print at one time. In many cases a line or page printer can be very fast—faster than any laser printer. Unfortunately, it doesn't always handle multiple fonts or complex graphics very well.

Line printers can be either serial or parallel devices. Generally, the slow-speed, single-character-at-a-time versions are serial and the higher-speed line and page printers are almost always parallel. A serial line usually has only pins 2, 3 and 7 for an RS232C standard connector. A printer may require more pins to be wired, so check the documentation for your printer if this doesn't work. Usually a serial printer will also have a small panel of dip-switches (try saying that five times real fast, but not out loud) that set character set, parity, stop bits, data bits, and communication baud rate. A setting of 8 data, 1 stop and no parity, and the fastest speed available is normally a good guideline. Since the dip switches are usually different for each printer, you are on your own if there are no indications or documentation available for yours.

Generally, a parallel interface has no settings unless there is a selectable character set. Most of the time it is just plug it in and go.

If you must set up a connection to a network, the modern printers will likely have a network interface port for this purpose and either a set of dip switches or a control panel that is used to set the address. For older printers an interface box can usually be purchased for this purpose.

Printers under SVR4   Once the printer is physically attached via a serial, parallel, or network connection, you have to identify it to your system. This is accomplished through the **lpadmin** command under SVR4. The command is the same for most other UNIX versions, but some of the options may be different; therefore, as with all of the other commands I have mentioned, be sure to consult your man pages for any techno-gotchas that your version may have lying in wait.

Before **lpadmin** can be used to add or modify printers, most UNIX versions require that the print daemon controlled by lpsched be stopped. This is accomplished via the **lpshut** command. All of the **lp**-type commands are located in the /usr/lib subdirectory on most systems. To restart the stopped daemon, just issue the **/usr/lib/lpsched** command to start it, copy the old **/usr/spool/lp/log** to **/usr/spool/lp/oldlog**, and start a new file. The log contains a single line for each job that contains the printer name or alias, the user, the printer class, and the date of the job.

Just in case a crash shuts down the system without stopping lpsched and its associated daemon (crashes are so rude that way), you should add the following lines to your /etc/rc or other applicable startup file:

```
rm -f /usr/spool/lp/SCHEDLOCK
/usr/lib/lpsched
echo "Print daemon started"
```

You see, if lpsched and its associated daemon aren't stopped via **lpshut**, the **/usr/spool/lp/SCHEDLOCK** file isn't removed, resulting in lpsched not being able to start (it first checks if the file is present; if it is, it won't start, preventing multiple copies of the lpsched daemon from botching the print queues). Thus the first line in the above script removes the file if it is present and doesn't do anything if it isn't. The next line starts the lpsched process and its daemon, and the last line is just a little note to you to tell you what is going on and can be omitted if desired.

Once lpsched is shut down, you can use **lpadmin** to add, drop, or reconfigure printers. One standard command format for lpadmin is

```
/usr/lib/lpadmin -p|-xprintername -d -vdevicefile [-epr |
    -mmod | -iinterface] [-c|-rclass...] [{-l | -h}]
```

where

> **printername** is the name of the file, which can't be longer than 14 alphanumeric characters.
>
> **devicefile** is the name of the character special device file associated with the printer, such as /dev/pr3 or /dev/tty05.
>
> **-e**, **-m**, or **-i** specifies the printer interface program the queuing system should use. The interface is a formatting routine for the printer and is usually a script file. The -e option specifies a named file for a specific printer; however, more than one printer may use the same file. The -m option specifies a particular model; these files are usually kept in /usr/spool/lp/model directory. The -i option specifies an interface file stored in the /usr/spool/interface/printername directory.
>
> **-c|-rclass** specifies a particular class of printer. For example, all laser printers could be class laser; all line printers, class lp. If the class doesn't exist, it is created; if it does exist and the last printer is deleted from it (using **lpadmin -r**) it is deleted.

-x removes a printer.

-l specifies the printer as a login-type device. A login-type device is disabled by lpsched when lpsched is started. The -h option tells the system that the printer is "hardwired" and shouldn't be disabled. A printer can be enabled or disabled using the **enable** or **disable** commands.

-v tells the system to append the output to the specified printer to the special named file.

-d tells the system to make this printer the default system printer.

A second format for /usr/lib/lpadmin is

```
lpadmin -x printer -p printer options
```

where the options are

[-Fcontinue | beginning | wait] [-cclass] [-Dcomment] [-eprinter] [-f allow:forms | deny:forms] -h | -l

[-iinterface] [-Icontent-list] [-M -f form | -Sprint-wheel] [-mmodel] [-ooption] [R machine-list]

[-rclass] [-Slist] [-Tprinter-type] [-u allow:users | deny:users] [-U dialup-info] [-v device]

[-A alerttype]

We've already seen the definitions for -c, -e, -m, -h, -l, -i, -r, x, p, and, -v, so let's look at the new definitions for this version of the command:

-F sets the failsafe mode; "continue" sets the mode to continue printing on the same page after recovery, "beginning" resets to the start of the current document on a new page, and "wait" waits for the operator to restart printing.

Examples:

-D displays the comment field in the printer description if it is requested.

-d [dest] specifies that dest is the new default destination for lp commands.

-I tells the system that only documents exhibiting this content type are allowed here. Check your system's man pages for how to implement. A good example would be a printer used strictly to print a specific form, checks, or the like.

-M is the mount option and with the -f option is used to set a specific set of parameters dealing with page size, orientation, layout, and fonts to a printer. This combination is known as a form type. With the -S option it is used to load a specific printwheel on a daisywheel printer or to load a specific font for a multifont printer.

-R is used to provide a list of remote systems that can print to this printer.

-S establishes a list of available printwheels or fonts for the printer.

-T assigns a specific printer type to this printer. This must be specified for certain printer control options to work.

-u allows or denies the provided list of users access to this printer.

-U sets certain dialing information (for remote printers).

-A sets the alert type and with the -W n option (n is an integer) sends the system administrator a message for errors depending the specified alert type. The alert types are:

> **mail**—Send alert by mail.

> **write**—Send message to the terminal where the administrator is logged in.

> **quiet**—Don't send any more messages about this condition to me.

none—Don't bother me until I send you this command with mail or write for this printer.

shell—A shell command that will be executed for each alert.

list—Send the alert to standard output (can be used to send to a printer).

-W n—Set the number of times an alert is given; 0, the default, sends one message per alert condition.

-o printing option allows a specific printing option, such as character per inch (cpi), lines per inch (lpi), length, and width, to be specified.

The following command tells the system that the printer hp1 is connected to device file /dev/tty07, and to print to it using the interface file for an HP Laserjet and to place it in the class of laser.

```
$ /usr/lib/lpadmin -php1 -v/dev/tty07 -
  m/usr/spool/lp/model/hpjet -claser
```

The following command tells the system to remove the printer hp1 from the laser class.

```
$ /usr/lib/lpadmin -php1 -rlaser
```

The following command tells the system to remove the printer hp1 from the system.

```
$ /usr/lib/lpadmin -xhp1
```

Other commands of interest to the system administrator follow.

cancel. This allows a job that is being printed or queued to be printed to be canceled. Each job is assigned a number, and the command is used with a specific job number to cancel that job. The command

```
$ /usr/lib/cancel 756
```

cancels job number 756. In addition, the printer name can be used to cancel the current job for that printer. The **lpstat** command is used to check on queued jobs.

enable and **disable**. These commands are used to stop and start sending jobs to a particular printer. For example:

```
$ /usr/lib/disable hp1 -r"Printer hp1 down to install new
   ocr, back up soon"
```

disables hp1 and doesn't allow any jobs to be sent there. Anyone attempting to send to hp1 receives the message specified after the -r. This command allows hp1 to again accept jobs:

```
$ /usr/lib/enable hp1
```

accept and **reject**. These commands are identical in function to **enable** and **disable** except that they work against either a single printer or an entire class of printers. So, instead of "disable hp1" we say:

```
$ /usr/lib/reject laser -r" All laser printers down to re-
   install font drivers"
```

These commands are for use when a printer is to be out of service for a long period.

lpmove. This command is used to move a queued print job from one printer to another. The format is

```
$ /usr/lib/lpmove prt1[-job1,prt1-job2,...] prt2
```

where

prt1 is the name of the source printer.

[-job1,prt1-job2,...] is a list of jobs that need to be moved (optional).

prt2 is the destination printer.

If prt1 is specified with no job list, all jobs are moved to prt2.

lpstat. This command is used to check on the status of the printer, the print daemon, and the print queue. The command has the following format:

```
/usr/lib/lpstat [-rdst][-cclass][-oarg][-uuser][-
  pprintername][-vprintername][-adestination]
```

where

-r shows the status of the printer daemon.

-d shows the default destination.

-s shows a summary of status information.

-t shows a total list of all status information.

-cclass lists the members in the specified class.

-oarg shows the status for a specified argument—**arg**, which is a printer, jobid, or class.

-uuser shows the status of jobs submitted by a particular user.

-pprintername shows the status of the jobs for the specified printer.

-vprinter lists the character special file associated with the specified printer.

-adestination shows the acceptance status of the destination specified.

Printing under BSD   For a UNIX version with so many nice features it is a shame that printing has to be so difficult. There are two main processes for printing under BSD: /usr/lib/lpd, the printing daemon, and /usr/ucb/lpr, the print process. The **lpr** process queues print requests, and **lpr** prints them. Most other printing routines under BSD function by direct calls to the **lpr** process.

The **lpr** process can be called using several options.

-P printer specifies the printer to be used. If no printer is specified, the value of the environmental variable PRINTER is used, and if that isn't set, the default printer is used.

The **lpd** process uses the file /etc/printcap to determine if a print job is local or has to be sent to a remote printer. Consult your man pages for lpd to see the printcap file layout. Essentially, this file contains file and directory specifications, remote access information, printing filters, communication settings, and page information for the specified printer.

The file **/etc/printcap** is a vital part of the BSD printing environment. If your printer isn't listed here, it doesn't exist. Use your system documentation and the provided documentation to review the format for this file's entries. Review the entries for current printers and use them as templates for new ones. If you are lucky, your system will have an automated administration tool that sets up this file and adds or removes printers from it. If not, the importance of understanding how this file works cannot be overstated. The format of /etc/printcap may vary from one BSD version or implementation to another.

There are several other printer-related commands under BSD. These follow.

lpq views the print queue. Use the -P option to specify a specific printer. The **lpq** command gives you the following information:

printer status (first line), output headings: rank, owner, job, files and total size; one line for each print job. The job column lists the job number that is used with other commands to refer to specific print jobs.

lprm removes a specific print job. The job number shown by the **lpq** command is used to find the job. The command can also take a user name to remove all of the jobs sent by a specific user.

lpc is used by the administrator to make changes to the printers. The program may work just fine, or, if there are problems, it may make them worse. Good luck with its use. This command invokes a process that can then be issued the following commands:

> **help** [command] or **?** [command]—Gets you help with the specified command.
>
> **enable** printername or **disable** printername—Enables or disables the specified printer.
>
> **start** printername or **stop** printername—Starts or stops the named printer. **stop** will allow the current job to finish.
>
> **abort** printername—Same as **stop** but aborts the current job.
>
> **down** printername message or **up** printer—Allows a printer to be taken offline for a long period of time. The message is sent to users who attempt to use the printer. **up** brings the printer back up.
>
> **clean** printername—Clears the print queue for the specified printer. The current job completes.
>
> **topq** printer jobid | username—If a jobid is specified, this moves it to the top of the queue; if a user name is specified, **topq** moves all of that user's jobs to the top of the queue.
>
> **restart** printername—Restarts the printer's print daemon. These things sometimes give up the ghost for unexplained reasons. **lpq** will tell you that there is no daemon present and will still show print jobs if this is the case.
>
> **status** printer—Gives you a four-line status entry for the specified printer. Don't be alarmed if the status tells you no daemon is present; as long as there are no jobs in the printer queue, there will be no daemon activated by **lpd** for a specified printer.

8.4   OTHER PERIPHERALS

Other peripherals may be badge readers, palm readers, plotters, and so forth. Each of these will have documentation that describes how it is physically installed. Once the device is installed, you must inform the system about it, what port it is connected to, and how to talk to it. This is usually done via the **mkdev** command, the format for which is

```
mkdev devicename
```

where

> **devicename** is the name of the device. This name is usually quite specific—mouse, hd, serial, tape, and so forth.

Once the **mkdev** command is issued, the system will prompt you for the information that is needed. If your device documentation specifies the procedure to use, be sure you follow it exactly or unpredictable results may occur.

Before using the **mkdev** command on your system, consult the man pages and any system- or device-specific documentation.

System
Auditing

9

Auditing is a necessary evil that goes with the job of system administrator. It would be wonderful if people did only what they were supposed to, only when they were supposed to, but unfortunately this is not usually the case. Sometimes intentionally, sometimes accidentally, people do things they shouldn't, and you have to catch them before they do harm to the system or its contents. The only way to do this is by auditing the system. How often a system needs to be audited will depend on how it used.

If yours is a high-traffic system with connections to the Internet and numerous call-in lines, you should probably be auditing continuously. In light of recent releases of hacker ware such as the Satan program (a program released for free over the Internet that is supposed to be used by security personnel to test their networks for holes, but works just as well for hackers to check for holes) and the proliferation of Internet users, it is irresponsible not to run auditing on systems that are connected to the Internet.

A high-traffic system with numerous users needs to be audited frequently for inexperienced users. Be proactive and watch for people having trouble logging in or trouble with commands, or people who are just too curious for their own good. (Make the latter assistant system administrators—that will teach them a lesson!)

Finally, a system with a number of dial-in lines is most susceptible to hacking, so auditing for attempted break-ins is very important.

How do system administrators perform this monitoring? This is what we will explore in the next section.

9.1 ADMINISTRATION AND PERFORMANCE OF AUDITS

The heart of the auditing system on most versions of UNIX is the authcap database. This is the place where the system's security features find authentication and identity information for all TCB, Kernel, and user-related security items.

The actual database resides in multiple files. On most systems the files used for authcap reside in /tcb/files/auth and /etc/auth. The /etc/auth directory contains the global system settings in the /system directory. The protected subsystems' data resides in **/etc/auth/subsystems**.

The user's security information is contained in /tcb/files/auth. Users who are secure have their information stored in a subdirectory of /tcb/files/auth that begins with the first letter of the user's user name. For example, if your name was "zeno," your security information would be stored in /tcb/files/auth/z.

Some systems, such as AIX and HP-UX, have direct interfaces to the security monitors via the smit and SAM programs. Other systems, such as Silicon Graphic's IRIX, also provide simple interfaces to security and other system administration features. The command-line programs for IRIX are satconfig, saton, satoff, satstate, satread, sat_eventlostr, and sat_strtoevent (some of these are callable C blocks). Command-line security and administration are rapidly becoming things of the past. However, since we have some old systems out there, we need to cover the manual methods as well. The four major commands used on most systems that have auditing are auditif, auditcmd, authck, and chg_audit.

9.2   AUDITING FACILITIES

Let's look at the auditif, auditcmd, authck, and chg_audit commands to see what they do and how to use them to effectively monitor your system.

9.2.1   Use of the auditif Program

The **auditif** command resides in the /tcb/bin/ subdirectory. It is used to create the /tcb/files/audit/audit_parms file, which is used by the auditcmd program with the -e option to enable auditing.

9.2.2   Use of the auditcmd Program

The auditcmd program resides in /tcb/bin/. The format for the command follows:

```
/tcb/bin/auditcmd [-e] [-d] [-s] [-c] [-m] [-q]
```

where

>   **-e** starts or enables auditing. The **auditif** command must first be run to set up the /tcb/files/audit/audit_parms file.

-s modifies the audit daemon to generate audit records even when the system is being shut down. In fact, until the audit daemon is specifically deactivated it will continue to do its job.

-d is the only way to disable the audit subsystem other than turning off the power to the system.

-m informs the audit daemon that the multiuser mode has been attained. This tells the daemon that the audit files created via **auditif** are available for use.

-c is used to retrieve statistics from the audit files.

-q specifies "quiet" mode.

9.3 USE OF THE AUTHCHK COMMAND

The **authchk** command is used to verify the authentication database. Along with the integrity utility **authchk** is used to ensure that your authentication database and system files haven't been damaged or altered by unauthorized personnel. The format of the **authchk** command is

```
authchk [-p] [-t] [-s] [-f] [-c] [-a] [-v]
```

where

-p checks the password files for consistency. On some systems there are shadow or protected password files as well as the /etc/passwd file. These files should be in sync with each other unless someone has made unauthorized changes.

-t checks the terminal control database to ensure that it hasn't been compromised.

-s checks /etc/auth/subsystemb to ensure that it hasn't been compromised.

-a checks everything (all).

-v places the utility in the verbose mode.

The integrity utility compares file entries against their corresponding entry in the authentication database. If there is a discrepancy, integrity warns you. The integrity utility has the following syntax:

```
/tcb/bin/integrity [-v] [-e] [-m]
```

where

-v lists status for all files, even if there is no problem.

-e (explain) gives what and why when a discrepancy is found.

-m (missing) tells if files are missing (by default, missing files are ignored).

9.4   THE LAST UTILITY

Another useful utility is the last, which displays the most recent logins of users and terminals. The syntax for the **last** command is

```
last [-h] [-n x] [-t terminal] [-w wtmpfile] [username]
```

where

-h tells **last** not to print a header.

-n x tells **last** to only show the last x logins.

-t terminal tells **last** to show only logins from the specified terminal id.

-w wtmpfile specifies that **last** should use the specified file instead of /etc/wtmp. The file specified must have the same format as that of /etc/wtmp.

username tells **last** to show only the logins for the specified user.

9.5   FILES USED BY THE SECURITY UTILITIES

The files used by the security utilities are

/usr/adm/acct	This file is a real disk hog, so be sure to purge it periodically if you use it. It contains the user, command, and usage numbers and is useful for charge-back operations. The file is read with the **lastcomm** and the **/usr/etc/sa** commands. The **/usr/etc/sa** command provides a summary of /usr/adm/acct that is placed in the /usr/adm /savacct file. It is suggested that the /usr/etc/sa routine be run nightly and that the /usr/adm /acct be purged afterward.
/usr/adm/lastlog	This file records the latest login time for each user. Some versions also show the last unsuccessful login attempt. Encourage your users to check these dates every time they log in and report odd dates and times to you (this file is used by the login procedure to display these times; the users don't have to do anything special to get the displays on most systems).
/etc/utmp	This file contains information on users actively logged on to the system.

/etc/wtmp   This file tracks login and logout operations for all users. It should be periodically archived and purged. The file is used by the **last** command.

9.6   USE OF THE CHG_AUDIT COMMAND

The **chg_audit** command is used to enable and disable auditing for the next reboot. The command's syntax is

```
/tcb/lib/chg_audit [on]
```

where **[on]** places the appropriate commands in the /etc/inittab and /etc/conf/cf.d/init.base files to ensure that auditing is started at the next reboot. If no argument is specified, the commands are removed from the files.

System Tuning

10

10.1 WHAT IS SYSTEM TUNING?

UNIX will run right out the box with minimal attention to system tuning. Tuning gives a system the extra bit of performance, that extra oomph that makes users sit up and take notice. In severe cases it can mean the difference between a long weekend or a short Friday night.

Tuning involves monitoring over a period of time to determine what is normal for your system. If you only do a minor amount of monitoring, you may miss key indications. You must monitor at peak usage times; tuning for low usage doesn't buy you anything. As long as you have the memory and disk resources, allocate for peak not average, times. The reason for establishing average usage is to provide a performance baseline so that the results of your tuning can be measured. However, if there is no contention for system resources because of low usage, the effects of tuning may not be apparent until higher usage occurs.

Tuning is the process you use to optimize user and process access to system resources. Ideally, each user or process should get all of the resource it needs. Most users believe it is their right to take

100 percent of whatever resource they feel is necessary. Unfortunately, you as system administrator have to limit user and process access to resources to ensure there are enough resources for everyone to get at least the minimum they need. These are the trade-offs a system manager must make when tuning a UNIX system.

10.2   WHEN IS SYSTEM TUNING NEEDED?

System tuning is needed whenever the system is changed. Changes involve addition of disks, memory, or programs. If you are lucky, the program's documentation will include recommended tuning for your system (usually as values that are added to the existing tuning parameter's values). Unfortunately, most programs don't provide this information, and you can only determine the needed changes through monitoring the system under load.

Generally speaking, you need to do tuning under these conditions:

■ At initial system installation and setup.

■ When system resources such as disks or memory change.

■ When system performance is obviously slow.

■ When excessive errors are generated under normal load conditions.

10.3   WHAT DO YOU TUNE?

UNIX is very tunable. Virtually every aspect of the kernel, disk, memory, and other resources can be tuned. The biggest gain for performance will come from the setup and configuration of your disk systems. The next largest performance gain will be seen from proper allocation of disk swap and page areas, and the next largest after that will be the configuration of memory and kernel parameters.

Each of these areas can suffer from contention for resources, which is what causes systems to perform poorly. The only way to determine if contention is occurring is via monitoring. Some systems such as HP-UX and AIX provide GUI interface tools for system monitoring. Others will require manual monitoring via the available monitoring commands and system reports.

10.4 MONITORING UNIX SYSTEMS

Let's examine as many of these tuning commands as we can, explaining how each is used and giving a quick way to interpret the results. As I said before, monitoring shouldn't be done on a catch-as-catch-can basis. It should be planned and carried out in a very deliberate way so that you get a good cross-section of operating loads for your system. Whenever possible, tune for the maximum load.

10.4.1 Memory Contention

Memory contention is caused by two things: lack of memory and too many users. It happens when too many processes attempt to access a limited memory pool, and this memory battle results in processes being "swapped." Swapping is the way systems deal with memory contention. Essentially, it involves writing a copy of a process's memory onto disk to allow another process to have the memory it needs; once the second process finishes its time slice the first process is brought back from disk. As you can well imagine, this swapping in and out of memory can be quite time-consuming and cause severe performance degradation.

So, how do we deal with memory contention—shoot every third user? Tempting, but not a viable option. We need to better tune the memory we have or add memory. Memory is a cheap resource, so buy more!

Another symptom that says we have memory problems is excessive paging. Paging is when blocks (or pages) of memory are swapped in and out of the process space. Too much swapping indicates that we need to increase the allocated memory to the user processes. Usually there are two types of paging: hard and soft. Hard paging is associated with swapping and involves writing "hard" memory pages to disk; soft paging happens when additional memory is allocated to a process. Of the two, soft paging is preferable but can only occur if additional memory is available.

Let's look at how we can monitor for memory contention.

vmstat (BSD) and sar (SVR4)   Under BSD and BSD derivatives the **vmstat** command allows us to monitor paging and swapping and system statistics. Under SVR4 the **sar** command performs a similar function.

The format for the **vmstat** command is

```
vmstat [-fs][-n namelist][-l lines][interval [count]]
```

where

-f tells you the number of forks performed (processes spawning other processes).

-s gives a detailed (verbose) listing of the number of processes, states, paging, system, and CPU activity.

-n namelist specifies an alternate symbol table to /UNIX.

-l lines tells how often to generate a header. This defaults to s (screen display) with a valid value of 20. If you are piping or redirecting the output to a file for later printout, a larger value such as 63 may be more applicable. You will have to experiment to get the correct pagination for your system.

interval specifies the interval in seconds.

count tells the number of times to run **vmstat**.

If **vmstat** is specified without options, it reports on statistics since boot time, which is not really very useful. It is better to specify that reports be run over an interval for a specific number of reports. This way, deltas can be isolated and problems more readily identified.

The **vmstat** report format shows statistics for three major areas: process, paging, and system.

The process section reports on r, the number of runnable processes in the run queues; b, the number of processes blocked (waiting on resources)—a high number of processes in the b state may mean you need to reconfigure or add to your disks; and w, swapped-out processes—if this is nonzero, you need memory. These are always current statistics.

The paging section reports on

frs	Free swap area space.
dmd	Demand zero and fill pages.
sw	Pages that are swapped.
cch	Pages in cache.
fil	Pages on file.
pft	Protection faults.
frp	Pages freed.
pos or po	Processes swapped satisfactorily.
pif or pi	Pages not swapped satisfactorily.
rso	Regions swapped out.
rsi	Regions swapped in.

The system area reports on

sy	The number of system calls.
cs	The number of context switches.
cpu	The percentage of cpu time spent in various modes: us, user; sy, system, and id, idle (only on certain systems).

Some versions of **vmstat** also give statistics on

avm   The amount of virtual memory available (a useless statistic).

fre   The number of memory pages (usually 512k) on the free list (this should always be nonzero)

de   A severe memory shortage if nonzero (anticipate, short-term memory shortfall).

d0   dn—The number of disk operations per second on the indicated drive.

Always ignore the first report, since it is a cumulative average of statistics since boot time. The subsequent reports are cumulative over the specified interval. It can be annoying to watch **vmstat** or to review lengthy collections of material that has been piped or redirected to a file. You can use a short script, such as the one shown in Figure 10.1, to watch critical parameters and notify you of problems. You will probably have to tailor this script to your system to allow for different positioning of your output fields from **vmstat**. Since swapping is by far the most important item to watch for as it indicates memory shortage that can severely effect performance, this script watches for a nonzero value for this parameter.

One problem with the script in the figure is that awk is a large program and may cause more problems that it solves in a memory-poor environment.

The SVR4 command for gathering these types of statistics is **sar**, which has the format

```
sar [-ubdycwaqvmnprDSACg] [-o file] t [n]
```

or

```
sar [-ubdycwaqvmnprDSACg] [-s time] [-e time] [-i sec] [-f
  file]
```

```
swaps=2       #allow only 2 swaps before notification
timechk=10    #check every 10 seconds (may want to reduce)
vmstat $timechk |awk "
NR==2 {print \$0 }
NR <= 3       {next} # who cares about these (first headers)
NR != 22      {next} # too much data, discard (longer than 22 lines)
/avm/ {next} # intermediate headers, disregard
#count consecutive nonzero page-outs, notify us if more
# than limit are non-zero. $9 indicates the column that
# the page out value is usually in
        { if (\$9 > 0) { npo++ }
          if (npo > $swaps) {print \$0 }       #Prints the line
          if (\$9 == 0) {npo = 0}              #reset if next line 0
        } "
```

FIGURE 10.1   Script to watch for a nonzero value of swapping.

where

    -u reports on cpu utilization:

        %usr—Percent of time in user mode.

        %sys—Percent of time in system mode (when used with -D, this will show usage percentages for remote machines in a networked environment).

        %wio—Percent of time idle waiting for block IO.

        %idle—Percent of time cpu is idle.

    -b reports on buffer activity:

        bread/s—Buffer reads per second.

        bwrit/s—Writes per second to buffers.

        lread/s—Logical object (nonbuffer) reads per second.

        lwrit/s—Logical object (nonbuffer) writes per second.

%cache or %wcache—Cache hit ratios (1-bread/lread) as a percentage.

ppread/s—Physical reads.

pwrit/s—Physical writes.

-D—When used, p statistics also report on remote mounted devices.

-d reports activity for each block device (disks):

%busy or avque—Part of time device was handling requests.

r+w/s, blks/s—Number of transfers in rate/second of 512k blocks.

avwait, avserv—Average wait, in milliseconds, for the device to service requests (This will include seek, rotational latency, and data transfer times for disks).

-n generates reports on name caches. The reports include:

c_hits, cmisses—Number of cache hits and misses.

hit%—Cache hit ratio as a percent (cache efficiency).

-y reports tty device activity such as input character rate; output rate; receive, transmit, and modem interrupt rates.

-c reports on system calls:

scall/s—System calls of all types.

sread/s, swrit/s, fork/s, exec/s—Rates for these types of calls.

rchar/s, wchar/s—Transfer rates for characters during read and write system calls (with -D splits report into remote and local calls).

-w is used to request data on system swapping and switching activity:

swpin/s, swpot/s, bswin/s, bswot/s—512k-byte sections transferred per second for swapin and swapout activities (swpot/s should be zero).

pswch/s—Rate of processes switches.

-a generates statistics on the file access routines:

> iget/s—Inode gets per second.
>
> namei/s—Name-to-inode transfers per second.
>
> dirblk/s—Directory 512k blocks per second.

-q generates statistics on average queue lengths and percentage of time used for queues:

> runq-sz, %runocc—Run queue of processes in memory and ready to run.
>
> swpq-sz, %swpocc—Swap queue of processes swapped out but ready to run.

-v generates status reports for processes, inodes, and file tables:

> text-sz, proc-sz, inode-sz, file-sz, lock-sz—Entries per size for each table.
>
> ov—Overflows that happened between sampling times for each table.

-m generates information on messages and semaphores:

> msg/s—Messages per second.
>
> sema/s—Semaphores per second.

-p generates paging statistics:

> vflt/s—Rate per second for address translation page faults, (this happens when the page being addressed isn't in memory, indicating that a valid or in-use page had to be swapped out—this should be less than 15 for small systems, according to AT&T).
>
> pflt/s—Page faults from illegal activities (protection faults) (not generally useful for tuning).
>
> pgfil/s—vflt/s that were able to be resolved by page-in from the file system.
>
> rclm/s—Rate at which valid pages are being reclaimed from the free list (should be zero).

-r tells you about unused disk blocks and memory:

freemem—Amount of unused pages available for users (if freemem drops below the value of the GPGSLO configuration constant, paging occurs. Paging continues until the value of GPGSHI is exceeded. These are called the low- and high-water marks for memory).

freeswap—Amount of free swap file blocks still available for process swapping.

-D is used with other options to report on file and resource sharing between this and remote systems.

-S reports server and request queue status:

serv/lo-hi—Average number of remove file servers for the system.

request % busy—Percentage of time that receive descripters are in the request queue.

request avh lgth—Average number of requests in the request queue.

-A gives you all statistics.

-C reports on remote file sharing buffer caching:

snd-inv/s—Number of invalidation messages sent by your machine as a server as rate per second.

snd-msg/s—Total outgoing RFS messages as a rate per second.

rec-inv/s—Number of invalidation messages received from remote servers per second.

rcv-msg/s—Number of incoming RFS messages from remote servers as a rate per second.

dis-bread/s—Penalty in missed buffers per second if buffering is turned off.

blk-inv/s—Number of buffers removed from the client machine caches.

-g is used to look at paging behavior:

pgout/s—Number of page-out requests per second for the interval (should be close to, if not at, zero).

ppgout/s—Average number of pages per second that paged out (should be greater than pgout/s).

pgfree/s—Pages per minute returned to the free list by page-stealing daemon (if this shows a lot of page-stealing going on, it may indicate a need for more memory).

pgscan/s—How much memory had to be scanned by the page-stealing daemon to find a stealable page (a value greater than 5 may indicate a memory shortage on some systems).

%s5ipf—Percentage of V5-style filesystems taken off the free list (if greater than 10 percent, reconfigure the kernel with more inodes in older V5-style file systems).

-o, -f are used to indicate output files.

-t [n] specifies interval time in seconds.

-s [time] -e [time] indicate start and end monitoring window times.

-i indicates interval between monitoring times.

Paging and Swapping As you can see from the previous sections, paging and swapping are two of the major indicators of system memory performance. The **sar** and **vmstat** can be used to show paging and swapping activity. The pager makes room in memory by paging individual pages from memory to disk. Paging is preferred over swapping.

The swapper, usually process 0, makes room in memory if things get too crowded by swapping out all of a process's blocks. The number of block swap sets is determined by the parameter MAXSC (the default for this parameter is 1). Processes are candidates for swapping if they have been idle for 20 seconds or more. There is normal swapping and desperation swapping. If desperation swapping occurs, interactive performance will degrade since interactive users usually show the greatest amount of idle time.

The page-in features of the reports are really not very useful statistics, since swap-ins are a normal part of the startup process for any program. If page-outs are excessive, this indicates a memory shortage. Unfortunately, there is no hard and fast number to tell when page-outs are excessive. The best rule of thumb is people complaining about performance. When you see page-outs above a normal value, then page-outs are your problem.

The swap-out statistics tell how much swapping is occurring. Some basic amount of swapping is normal, but if you see an increased amount of swap-out and page-out activity simultaneously, this is an indication of memory shortages.

Conserving Memory As I have said before, memory is cheap, and the best solution to memory problems is to buy more. Unfortunately, we don't always have the budget to get more memory, disks, or other requirements right at the moment. If this is the situation you find yourself in—memory- and money-poor—then you must find ways to conserve memory. This section will delineate some methods you can use to get you over the hump to the next quarter or next year.

There are some basic things that can be done to reduce memory requirements:

■ Sharing text areas.

■ Reducing kernel buffers (see the section on kernel tuning).

■ Reducing kernel tables to required levels (see the section on kernel tuning).

■ Using shared libraries.

■ Restricting the use of the X-Windows system (this is rather draconian, but could be required in severe situations. Moreover, it can convince management that you are serious if they have to relearn the command line).

Shared text areas. Shared text areas are the default on many systems. You have to tell the linker not to link this way. Shared text areas allow each user who calls the same program to share that program's executable image. If you think you have a program or programs that aren't using shared text areas, you can verify this by checking the Makefile for the program and seeing if it was linked with the -N option. If this is the case, relink them with the -n option instead.

Watch the use of the sticky bit. The use of the sticky bit tells UNIX to keep the program in the swap area. While this can reduce startup times for the program, it can eat up swap-area memory. Check your programs and reset the sticky bit on those that aren't used that much.

Use shared libraries—maybe. The SunOS and SVR4 implementations of the shared library concept are very good; other versions may not be. This is a linker option and varies from machine to machine, so check your linker documentation for how to implement shared libraries on yours. A shared library means that only a call to a library is placed in the program code, not the entire library module. This reduces the overall memory requirements on systems that have implemented this feature properly. However, there may be performance penalties of up to 25 percent on some platforms, since the referenced modules have to be obtained instead of being a part of the code itself. The only way to determine if this will benefit your system is to run tests with and without shared libraries.

Encourage good use of memory with programmers. Programmers should use out-of-core matrix solvers when doing matrices and should also use local reference for variables. Out-of-core matrix solvers take less memory, and using local reference for variables instead of allowing them to be spread all over memory speeds execution and thus reduces overall system and memory load. Local reference also allows caching to be used in many cases. Review your man pages for your linker on how to implement these features.

Sizing the cache. On earlier versions of UNIX (pre SVR4) you can reduce memory requirements by reducing the disk cache buffers; however, this will cause performance to suffer. To find the current size of your buffer, check your configuration files (see the section on kernel tuning). Reset the NBUF and S52KNBUF, if they are present, to better values. In most cases resolve any conflict between disk performance and memory in favor of memory; having big pipes go to a little reservoir does little good. On SVR4 set NBUF to between 25 to 100. Since buffers are managed dynamically on SVR4, setting the other parameters may be a waste of time.

In most cases changing the buffer size means that you have to relink the kernel. See Chapter 2 for information on kernel configuration and rebuilding.

STREAMS buffers. Some versions of UNIX use the STREAMS facility, which uses preallocated buffers. Generally speaking, many small buffers, in the 128-byte range, are desirable on X-systems and systems that support a large number of terminals. If you expect large packets on an Ethernet network, you also need a few 2,048-byte buffers. You will have to determine the best mix of buffers for your system. These buffers are usually set with the **NBLKn** parameters where n is the buffer size, so NBLK128 60 would set up sixty 128-byte buffers. Watch **netstat** results and tune appropriately. Check your man pages for the proper setup method on your system. On SVR4 and other current versions, these buffers are dynamically set, so you don't have to worry about them on newer systems. If you aren't sure, check your man pages.

Network buffers. Network buffers are another thing that you can't do much about. However, there is hope. Network buffers under BSD are dynamically allocated but not released until a reboot is performed. I don't suggest that you constantly reboot, but if you know of large network usages, such as backups over a network either from or to your machine, it might be a good idea to reboot the machine after these backups or other network-intensive activity finishes.

You can monitor network buffers on BSD using the **netstat -m** command. It might be advisable to set up a cron job that periodically wakes up, checks **netstat -m**, and then sends you a message if it has increased over a preset threshold (you will have to determine this threshold; it will vary from system to system).

Tuning Paging   First let me reiterate, there are two types of swapping—normal and desperation. Normal swapping is good because it gets inactive pages out of memory so more active processes can use the freed memory. It occurs whenever a process is idle for more than 20 seconds on most systems. Desperation swapping is when active process memory segments are swapped out and only occurs if paging can't reduce memory requirements to a reasonable point.

In order to control the level at which paging, and then desperation swapping, occurs, the **LOTSFREE** and **DESFREE** parameters can be adjusted. These parameters control the point at which normal swapping takes place (**LOTSFREE**) and the point at which desperation swapping starts (**DESFREE**). **LOTSFREE** can be set to a maximum of one-eighth of the available physical memory. **DESFREE** can be set to a maximum of one-sixteenth of available physical memory. In a memory poor environment you should reduce **LOTSFREE** so that normal paging happens sooner, which will allow the swapper to begin swapping before memory becomes critical. This is a no-win solution because you may reduce memory thrashing, but will reduce performance as well.

Another parameter that may help is **HANDSPREAD**. This is the amount of time allowed a memory page before it is paged out of memory. Increasing this parameter may help large programs use memory more efficiently, but may harm small programs' performance.

Managing the Swap Area   On older BSD versions swap areas aren't usually accessible to tuning. BSD swap areas consist of the configured b partition on the drives and are thus hardwired or preconfigured onto the disks themselves. The only way to adjust swapping on BSD is to increase the number of drives with the b partition configured or to reconfigure existing drives to use the b partitions. On newer BSD releases this may not be true, so check your documentation or do a **man -k swapping**.

On SVR4 you can generally reallocate larger swap sizes as needed. The command to do this is

```
# swap -a device start length
```

where

device is the disk drive file.

start is the starting address for the swap area.

length is the length in 512-byte disk blocks.

Check the /etc/partitions file or its equivalent on your system (use **man -k partitions** to identify the location of your partitions file if you don't know it), and find a partition near the size you want to use. Always start with 0 address and take up the entire partition. On SVR4 the **sysadm storage_devices** parameter can be used to identify the available partitions.

Some current systems allow file system paging, permitting you to allocate a swap file instead of a dedicated partition. What this means is that when you need more space you simply drop the existing swap file and create a larger one. The biggest problem with this is that if you create the file on a used disk, the file will be fragmented. You can back up, recreate, and then repopulate the disk to defragment or use a new disk that hasn't been fragmented to get around this annoyance. File system swapping doesn't save space. If you need 200 MB for your swap area now, you still do; you just have the freedom to place it where you want. The commands to utilize this new feature are simple:

```
# mkfile size file
# /usr/etc/swapon file
```

Where **size** is the size of the file in bytes unless k is used to denote kilobytes or m is used for megabytes, and **file** is the full path name of the file to create and use. Never use the -n option or the system will panic and crash when it tries to use the new file.

You will need to monitor how much swap space is being used. Under SVR4 and its derivatives the **swap -l** command is used to find this information. Under BSD the **pstat -s** command is used for showing how swap space is allocated. The **sar -r** command can be used to do long-term monitoring of swap space; the freeswp column indicates the amount of free swap area available. All the reports clearly show the amount of free swap space. Periodic monitoring will show how your swap space is allocated and used. If you are low, allocate more. More is needed if you frequently run with less than 50 percent available. If you never use all you have allocated, think about reducing the size of your swap files or partitions.

Running out of swap space will result in the kernel doing some drastic things, like killing large programs—not a solution I particularly advise you to employ.

10.4.2 Disk Contention

Another type of contention occurs when multiple users attempt to read or write data into the same disk pack. This results in the read head or heads having to move to multiple points on the disk as each user's process is activated in a multiuser environment. In an ideal situation a single drive could be dedicated to a single file or a single user's files, so that between reads there would be minimal repositioning of the read heads. Indeed, in some large database installations entire disks may be taken up by one file or even just a piece of one file, and in these situations you reach the ideal of not having the heads reposition between each read. Unfortunately, most of us have to deal with the problem of disk contention.

By properly planning our disk layouts and balancing the I/O load across the disk farm, we can reduce dick contention. The next few sections discuss monitoring for disk contention and load balancing.

iostat (BSD) and sar -d (SVR4) Disk performance is measured via the **iostat** and **sar -d** commands depending whether you are on a BSD- or SVR4-based system. Both commands produce disk I/O and loading statistics. Let's look at these commands and how to interpret their results.

We will begin with the **iostat** command, which has the format

```
iostat drives [x] t interval c count
```

where:

> **drives** tells **iostat** what drives to monitor.
>
> **x** does extended statistics for all drives (generates one line per disk, which is much easier to evaluate for large disk farms).
>
> **t interval** tells **iostat** what monitoring interval in seconds to use.
>
> **c count** tells **iostat** how many times to run.

The **iostat** command is only available on BSD and BSD-derivative systems. On SVR4 the **sar -d** command is used in a similar manner. If you have several dozen disks, you may want to have several monitoring processes to reduce the information load in any one report. The **iostat** command will provide a report with the following header items:

tin	The number of characters in the input buffer (not used for tuning).
tout	The number of characters waiting in the output buffer (not used for tuning).
bps	The kilobytes transferred to or from the disk in the last interval. This can be used to establish the load level for the disk in comparison to that of the other disks in the farm.

msps or serv   The millisecond seek time for the drive—not a reliable number, so don't use it for tuning.

tps   The average number of transfers per second for the disk. This can be used along with bps to determine load balance and load level for disks in the farm.

cpu   A measure of cpu mode times (us, user; sy, system; wt, wait; id, idle) for the interval; not useful for disk tuning.

The report generated is one line per reading with the disk names as the top header and the statistics for each disk clustered beneath. Ignore the first line, as it is an attempt to summarize all of the activity since time began (i.e., the system was booted). The following lines are summaries for the specified intervals.

Example output (excluding tin, tout, and cpu statistics):

```
% iostat -tc 10 6
...       dk0              dk1              dk2              dk3
... bps tps msps    bps tps msps    bps tps msps    bps tps msps
... 64   6   0.0    10   1   0.0    13   3   0.0    128  10  0.0
....32   4   0.0     2   1   0.0    24   2   0.0    134  11  0.0
....45   5   0.0     8   2   0.0    17   3   0.0    112  10  0.0
....36   3   0.0    10   2   0.0    34   2   0.0    150  12  0.0
....63   6   0.0    10   2   0.0    32   1   0.0    145  10  0.0
....54   5   0.0     9   1   0.0    24   1   0.0    150   9  0.0
```

Notice that dk0 (the system disk) and dk3 are the most heavily loaded. It would be advisable to spread some of their load if possible over the other two available disks.

The **sar -d** command offers the capability to specify the interval and count data like so:

```
sar -d interval count
```

The command produces a report with the following headers:

device   The disk name.

%busy   The percentage of time the device is servicing transfers.

avque   The average number of requests outstanding during the period.

r+w/s   The read and write activity against the disk for the interval.

blks/s   The number of blocks transferred during the period.

avwait   The average wait time in the queue.

avserv   The transfer average completion time.

Let's look at the **sar -d** command's output:

```
% sar -d 5 5
```

```
10:55:10  device %busy  avque  r+w/s  blks/s avwait avserv
(ignore the first set of statistics since these are for
  since the system was last booted)
10:55:15      sd0   6      0.0    15     30     0.0    20.2
         sd1   4      0.0    10     20     0.0    20.1
         sd2   0      0.0     0      0     0.0     0.0
         sd3   8      0.0    20     20     0.0    20.3

10:55:20      sd0   9      0.0    20     20     0.0    20.1
         sd1   4      0.0    10     20     0.0    20.1
         sd2   0      0.0     0      0     0.0     0.0
         sd3  10      0.0    20     20     0.0    20.2
```

As you can see, disk sd2 is not seeing any load, while disks sd0 and sd3 are seeing a majority of the system activity. In this case some of their load should be offloaded to sd2 if possible.

So, what are some ways of balancing the disk load? Here are a few tips:

- Use an in-memory pseudo-disk for the /tmp area if your system supports it.

- Move /usr away from the root disk.

- Put nonsystem executables (locally generated, third party products, etc.) on their own platters.

- Place swap areas across the disk farm if possible. Be sure to place them on your fastest drives.

- Place users and projects evenly across the disk farm. Try to balance the disk activity related to linkers and compilers.

Remember that if you are experiencing any desperation swapping or excessive paging, those issues should be addressed first since they will only make disk load problems worse.

I/O Subsystem The I/O subsystem includes the internal bus, the disk, and terminal interfaces. Essentially, if you tune memory, tune the disk, and apply proper tuning techniques to your network, you have tuned the I/O subsystem.

Striping The topic of disk striping concerns how files are placed on your disk resources. Essentially, there are two types of striping: hardware and software. Hardware striping is determined by how you configure your disk hardware and is very system- and disk-subsystem dependent. Software striping is usually a feature of program systems that use large disk files, such as relational database systems.

Hardware striping treats multiple disk packs as a single large disk. This can also be accomplished through some systems' logical volume managers. In a hardware striped set the actual files are spread evenly across the available platters and data is also spread evenly. With this type of configuration you get very good load balancing for your disks, but if you lose one of the set (except in the case of RAID-type drives), you lose them all. Even so, it looks as if the various RAID configurations and hardware striping are the wave of the future.

Unless you've been living in seclusion from the computer mainstream, you will have heard of the above topics. Let's take a brief look at them and how they affect UNIX.

Disk striping. Disk striping is the process by which multiple smaller disks are made to look like one large disk. This allows extremely large files to occupy one logical device, which makes managing the resource easier since backups only have to address one logical volume instead of several. It also provides the advantage of spreading I/O across several disks. If you need several gigabytes of disk storage for your application, striping may be the way to go.

One disadvantage to striping: If one of the disks in the set crashes, you lose them all.

Disk shadowing. If you have mission-critical applications that you absolutely cannot allow to go down, consider disk shadowing. As its name implies, disk shadowing is the process whereby each disk has a shadow disk to which data is written simultaneously. This redundant storage allows the shadow disk or set of disks to pick up the load in case of a disk crash on the primary disk or disks; thus users never see a crashed disk. Once the disk is brought back on-line, the shadow process brings it back in sync. This also allows for backup, since the shadow set can be broken (i.e., the shadow separated from the primary), a backup taken, and then the set resynchronized.

The main disadvantage to disk shadowing is the cost: For a 2-gigabyte disk farm, you need to purchase 4 gigabytes of disk storage.

RAID (redundant arrays of inexpensive disks). The main strength of RAID technology is its dependability. In a RAID 5 array the data is stored, as are checksums and other information about the contents of each disk in the array. If one disk is lost, the others can use this stored information to re-create the lost data, which makes RAID very attractive. Plus, RAID has the same advantages that shadowing and striping have, at a lower cost. It has been suggested that if the manufacturers would use slightly more expensive disks (RASMED—redundant array of slightly more expensive disks), performance gains could be realized. A RAID system appears as one very large, reliable disk to the CPU. There are several levels of RAID; to date these are

RAID-0—Known as disk striping.

RAID-1—Known as disk shadowing.

RAID-0/1—A combination of RAID-0 and RAID-1.

RAID-2—Data is distributed in extremely small increments across all disks and RAID-2 adds one or more disks that contain a Hamming code for redundancy. RAID-2 is not considered commercially viable because of the added disk requirements (10 to 20 percent must be added to allow for these Hamming disks).

RAID-3—This also distributes data in small increments but adds only one parity disk. The result is good performance for large transfers, but small transfers show poor performance.

RAID-4—In order to overcome the small transfer-performance penalties in RAID-3, RAID-4 uses large data chunks distributed over several disks and a single parity disk. This results in a bottleneck at the parity disk. Because of this performance problem RAID-4 is not considered commercially viable.

RAID-5—This solves the bottleneck by distributing the parity data across the disk array. The major problem is that it requires several write operations to update parity data. The performance hit is only moderate, and the other benefits outweigh this minor problem.

RAID-6—This adds a second redundancy disk that contains error-correction codes. Read performance is good because of load balancing, but write performance suffers because RAID-6 requires more writes than RAID-5 does for data update.

The main drawbacks to RAID are its relative newness, and thus a lack of performance data, and a lack of performance gain.

Software striping is the process by which an application allows its single data files to be spread across multiple drives. One example of this is the ORACLE relational database system. ORACLE overlays the existing file systems with a pseudo-file system of its own. Under this pseudo-file system tables of information are stored in multiple extents. By properly designing an ORACLE system, the extents that make up ORACLE's table structures can be spread across multiple disks. Other applications allow this type of striping as well.

Conservation of Disk Space   Disks are a finite resource. Under some versions of UNIX multiple file versions are allowed, but wherever possible this should be discouraged. An example of when this can become dangerous is under a different operating system—VAX/VMS from Digital Equipment Corporation. VAX/VMS allows virtually unlimited file versions unless you specify otherwise (unlike UNIX, where one version is allowed unless you tell it otherwise). Multiple versions help prevent inadvertent data or program overwrite, since the old version is still available unless purged or deleted, but they encourage disk abuse. In one case I deleted over 100 versions of a 500-block file. It doesn't take too many incidents like this to persuade you to watch how your users are using or abusing disk resources.

Even with version control, clever users may get around this by giving multiple file versions different names "just in case" they need to go back to a previous version. However, they usually forget to delete these just-in-case versions and thus use up disk resources. A command that generates disk usage statistics on SVR4 is **dodisk**. The **dodisk** command is usually run periodically during the day via a cron job, and you can review the results at your leisure (of course).

10.4.3 Miscellaneous Monitoring and Tuning

Some of these topics have been touched on in other chapters, but since people rarely read a book like this cover to cover (a lot of content, not much of a plot), I thought it would be good to pull some of it together here. Originally this section was to be called "Resource Contention" but since this is the topic of the entire chapter, I realized it needed to be changed. We've looked at monitoring CPU, disk, and memory; now let's look at processes. Processes can be three basic types: user, daemon, and cron, and can be active, waiting, or hibernating. We'll look at how these vital parts of the UNIX system are monitored.

ps - all All versions of UNIX seem to have the **ps** command. Process status is important. By examining it you can determine swapping, resource usage, memory usage, memory hogs, and CPU hogs. By identifying these trouble processes you can take steps to correct them (for users try a 2X4—it works wonders sometimes . . . just kidding, of course). The format for the **ps** command is

```
ps [-ea[c]f[c]lw[ww]kv][-t list][-u list][-g list][-s
   device][-n names]
```

where

-**e** prints information about all processes.

-**a** prints information about all processes except those not associated with a terminal and those that are group leaders.

-**f** prints a full listing—usually more than a dozen columns including command information. The [c] modifier for SVR4 shows scheduling class.

-**l** generates a long listing including status, priority, location, and memory usage.

-t list uses the list of terminals provided to generate a status list for just those terminal-related processes. Terminals in the list are enclosed in double quotes and are delimited by commas or spaces.

- p list uses the list of PIDs provided to generate a status for just those PIDs. The PID list is enclosed with double quotes and is comma- or space-delimited.

-u list uses the list of users supplied to generate a status display for just those users. The list is formatted identically to the lists for the -t and -p options.

-g list uses the list of groups provided to generate a status listing for just the members in the groups provided. The list format is identical to that for the -t and -u options.

- s device specifies an alternative swap device when examining core processes.

-n names specifies an alternate name list other than /UNIX.

-w prints 132 columns wide (BSD only).

-ww prints as wide as needed to show all fields (BSD only).

-k looks at kernel crash dumps (BSD only. Use ps -alkx vmUNIX-name core-dump_name).

-v produces a report on virtual memory usage (BSD only).

The format of the **ps** report varies according to the UNIX system you are using. The BSD **ps** columns are

F—Flags about the current state of the process. Check your man pages for the meanings; some typical ones are

0—The process is terminated.

1—The process is a system process and is always in memory.

2—The process is being traced by its parents.

4—The process is being traced by its parents and has been stopped.

8—The process cannot be awakened by a signal.

10—The process is currently loaded into memory.

20—The process cannot be swapped.

USER—The user id that owns this process.

PID—The unique process identifier used by commands like **kill**.

PPID—The parent process identifier.

CP—The scheduler process utilization parameter.

PRI—The priority of the process (low is high priority).

NI—The process's nice number used to calculate priority.

SZ—The process size.

RSS—The resident set size, the actual amount of memory used by the process.

WCHAN—The event the process may be waiting for, if in a wait state.

STAT—The current status of the process; the first letter of the status code is

R—The process is currently runnable.

T—The process is currently stopped.

P—The process is waiting for a page-in.

D—The process is waiting on disk.

S—The process has been sleeping for less than 20 seconds.

I—The process is idle (has been sleeping for more than 20 seconds).

Z—The process has become one of the undead (a zombie)—it has terminated but is still not dead.

The second letter of the status code is

W—The process is swapped.

>—The process has exceeded a memory soft limit.

Blank—Not swapped and hasn't exceeded a memory limit.

The third letter of the status code is

N—The status has been niced (running at a lower priority).

<—The process has been anti-niced (running at a higher priority).

Blank—The process is running at normal priority.

The fourth letter of the status code is

Blank—No special requirements.

S—The process needs sequential memory access.

A—Large memory requirements with random access to memory segments—don't do a normal paging algorithm.

TT—The tty the process is associated with.

TIME—The time the process has been active.

COMMAND—An attempt to give the command the process is using.

Additional fields are reported by other options. The -u option additional fields are

%CPU—The percentage of CPU time the process is using.

%MEM—The percentage of memory the process is using.

START—The time the process started.

And the -v option additional fields are

SL—The amount of time the process has been sleeping.

RE—The amount of time the process has been memory-resident.

PAGEIN—The number of disk actions caused by the process.

LIM—The soft limit on memory used for the process.

The SVR4 **ps** Columns are

F—Flags about the current state of the process. Check your man pages for the meanings; some typical ones are

0—The process is terminated.

1—The process is a system process and is always in memory.

2—The process is being traced by its parents.

4—The process is being traced by its parents and has been stopped.

8—The process cannot be awakened by a signal.

10—The process is currently loaded into memory.

20—The process cannot be swapped.

S—Process state:

O—The process is currently running.

S—The process is sleeping (waiting for an event to finish).

R—The process is runnable.

I—The process is idle.

Z—The process is terminated but still in the process table (ZOMBIE).

T—The process is stopped and being traced by its parent.

X—The process is waiting for more memory.

UID—The identification number for the user who started the process.

PID—The unique id number for the process.

PPID—The parent's process identifier.

C—The estimate of the process's CPU utilization.

PRI—The process's priority, low is high priority scales directly with CPU utilization.

NI—The program's nice number used to calculate priority.

SZ—The amount of virtual memory used by the process.

TTY—The terminal of the process or parent process that started the process.

TIME—The amount of CPU time used by the process.

COMD—The command used by the process.

Interpretation of ps results. The ps output can tell you many things about how processes are using your system. Here are a few things to watch for:

■ If individual users are running many jobs, they may not realize what they are doing. Give them a call and find out if they realize they have so many jobs running. Sometimes poor shell programming practices will cause this.

■ If a seemingly minor job starts consuming large amounts of resources (time, CPU, or memory), it may be stuck in a loop or in some other CPU-intensive operation. Look at using BSD renice (for example, if a process called spot needs to be reduced in priority: **$ renice 4 -p pid**, where **pid** is the pid for the process spot) or at killing the process under SVR4 (since you can't reprioritize SVR4 processes). Before killing a job you might want to get a core dump for the user for troubleshooting purposes (**gcore PID**). For a memory-intensive process, don't renice it, just kill it. Before doing anything radical, call the user and see if he or she can explain what is happening.

pstat (BSD) The **pstat** command is usually available under BSD, but may also be available under some SVR4 implementations. To see if you have it, check the man pages on your system. The **pstat** command is used to report system status information. In general, it gives more detailed information than the **ps** command gives. It gets its information from tables specified by the name list in the /UNIX file, usually /dev/mem and /dev/kmem. The format for the **pstat** command is

```
pstat [-PaifTxts] [-u frame1 frame2] [-n names] [file]
```

where

-P prints the process table for active processes. The formats vary for this report; check your man pages for your system's.

-a is similar to -p, but prints the status for all processes.

-i prints the inode table. The headings are LOC—The core location of the table entry, and FLAGS—state variables:

L—Locked

U—Update time

A—Access time

M—File system mount point

W—Wanted by another process if L flag is also set

T—Text file

C—Changed time

CNT—Number of open files for this inode

DEV—Major and minor device numbers of the file system for this inode

INO—Inode number within the device

MODE—Mode bits (protection code)

NLK—Number of links to this inode

UID—User id of the owner of this inode

SIZ/DEV—Number of bytes of an ordinary device or the major and minor device for a special file

u frame1 frame2—Prints the user process information, as specified by the physical frame numbers specified. These numbers can be obtained from the output of **ps -l**.

f prints the file open table listing:

LOC—The core location for the table entry

FLG—Miscellaneous state variables

R—Open for reading

W—Open for writing

P—Pipe file

CNT—The number of processes that use this file

INO—The inode table entry location for this file

OFFS—The file offset

-T shows the current size and utilization for the kernel table's format:

```
used/full    table
```

Where **used** is the amount of space actually used; **full** is reserved space; and **table** is the name of the kernel table.

-x is a dump of the text table.

-t is a dump of the terminal table.

-s is information on swap space usage.

Idle Time   Many of the commands such as **sar** and **iostat** report on the CPU idle time. The CPU idle time can be used to indicate if you need to upgrade to a faster CPU. If you are running with idle time, you probably don't need to upgrade. Nor do you if you have zero idle time but all of your users' jobs are getting done in an acceptable time. However, if you have zero idle time and the users' jobs aren't completing in time, upgrading the CPU may be the answer. It all depends on system throughput. Generally speaking, a healthy system should show 70 percent user time, 30 percent system time, and 1–2 percent idle time.

The ratios of user to idle/system/idle times will probably vary depending upon how your system is being used. If your system is lightly loaded, the CPU may spend much of its time idle. But if you know that system load is high and still see idle time, this could indicate an I/O bottleneck. You should look to tuning your disks, networks, and other sections of the I/O system.

Daemons The UNIX daemons are background UNIX processes. They are used to do the tedious jobs such as cron and network services. There may be up to 15 network control daemons in addition to the cron daemon and other system-function-related daemons. These daemons are processes and take up memory and resources when operating, just as any other process does. You must allow for these processes when you are tuning and configuring your system.

Once you become familiar with the daemons your system runs and have monitored long enough to know which ones never do anything, you can think about eliminating specific daemons to free up the resources they use. To eliminate a daemon, exorcise it from the startup files by placing a # (pound sign) in front of its entry in the file. These files are usually /etc/rc or /etc/rc.local under BSD and /etc/rc.d under SVR4. The network daemons are invoked by the /etc/inetd.conf file.

To test the results of removing a daemon, comment out its line, reboot, and check performance. Of course, also be prepared for complaints if you eliminate a daemon that is in use, although just not when you looked at it. Some daemons that may be eliminated are listed in Figure 10.2.

top The top program is a public domain utility that can help you to administer a heavily loaded machine. It tells you the top CPU users ranked by raw CPU usage. You can specify the number of processes to display by specifying the **top** command with a number. The top program isn't supplied with most releases, but you can get it from the following ftp sources:

eecs.nwu.edu in /pub/top

ftp.germany.eu.net in /pub/sysadmin/top

CompuServe UNIXFORUM (LINUX version only as of 5/1/95)

daemon Name	Purpose
accounting	Enabled by **accton** command. This enables system-wide accounting. Unless you use accounting why have the overhead?
biod	Allows NFS (networked file systems). If you aren't using NFS you don't need it.
comsat	Prints the mail notification to users; annoying to some, others love it.
lpd or lpshed	Printing daemons. If you don't do printing, exorcise them.
mountd	If you disable biod, diable this; it allows NFS remote mounts on your system.
nfsd	Another NFS daemon.
nntpd	This supports newsgroups. If you don't use newsgroups, axe this one.
quotas	Started by the /etc/rc. file if you have quotas enabled. If you don't use quotas, kill it.
rlogind	If you aren't connected to a network, this isn't used.
routed	If you have only one Ethernet interface and you only connect to the rest of the world through a single router, add "route add default gateway 1" to your /etc/rc.local file and kill this (gateway is the name of the gateway system). You can just kill it if this is an isolated system.
rwhod	If you don't need information about users on other systems, kill this.

FIGURE 10.2 Daemons you might be able to live without.

Further Reading

Nemeth, Evi. *UNIX SYSTEM Administration Handbook*, Prentice-Hall Software Series, Englewood Cliffs, NJ, 1989, ISBN 0-13-933441-6.

Reiss, Levi. *Unix System Administration Guide*, Osborne-McGraw Hill, New York, 1993, ISBN 0-07-881951-2.

Poniatowski, Martin. *The HP-UX Administrator's "HOW TO" Book*, Hewlett-Packard Professional Books, Prentice-Hall, Englewood Cliffs, NJ, 1994, ISBN 0-13-099821-4.

Rosen, Kenneth. *Open Computing Best UNIX Tips Ever*, Osborne-McGraw Hill, New York, 1994, ISBN 0-07-881924-5.

Russel, Charlie and Sharon Crawford. *VOODOO UNIX, Mastery Tips & Masterful Tricks*, Ventana Press, Chapel Hill, NC, 1994, ISBN 1-56604-067-1.

Loukides, Mike. *System Performance Tuning*, O'Reilly & Associates, Sebastopol, CA, 1992, ISBN 0-937175-60-9.

Todino, Grace and Dale Dougherty. *Using UUCP and Usenet*, O'Reilly & Associates, Sebastopol, CA, 1991, ISBN 0-937175-10-2.

O'Reilly, Tim and Grace Todino. *Managing UUCP and Usenet*, O'Reilly & Associates, Sebastopol, CA, 1994, ISBN 0-937175-93-5.

Costales, Bryan, Eric Allman, and Neil Rickert. *sendmail*, O'Reilly & Associates, Sebastopol, CA, 1994, ISBN 1-56592-056-2.

Hunt, Craig. *TCPIP Network Administration*, O'Reilly & Associates, Sebastopol, CA, 1993, ISBN 0-937175-82-X.

Peek, Jerry. *MH & xmh E-mail for Users and Programmers*, O'Reilly & Associates, Sebastopol, CA, 1993, ISBN 1-56592-027-9.

Braun, Christoph. *UNIX System Security Essentials*, Addison-Wesley, New York, 1994, ISBN 0-201-42775-3.

Dulaney, Emmett. *UNIX Unleashed*, SAMS Publishing, Indianapolis, IN, 1994, ISBN 0-672-30402-3.

Hewlett-Packard, *HP-UX Reference* (Vol. 1), Hewlett-Packard, Fort Collins, CO, 1992, manual number B2355-90033.

HP-UX, AIX, IRX man pages

CompuServe UNIXFORUM Libraries

Appendix

An Overview of Available Editors

Editors allow you to look at data files and create scripts and source code. They vary in usability from none to extreme. If I had my druthers, I'druther not use vi, ex, or emacs. Unfortunately, however, these are the standard editors on most systems. If you are lucky, you will have an X-based editor, if so, ignore this appendix since the X-based editor will be easy to learn on the fly. If you have only ex, may God have mercy on you; if you have vi, you are slightly better off. I can see those vi bigots out there tossing this book down in disgust right now, but I just don't like vi. Sorry.

A LOOK AT VI

The **vi** editor was one of the first, if not the first, UNIX editor. In actuality, regardless of what its pundits would like you to believe, it is nothing more than a glorified line editor. You deal with text as lines or groups of lines, and each operation is governed by a line command. These line commands govern insert, update, delete, and movement. The vi editor has few modern features. It reminds me of the old ed editor on the PDP-11 series. Perhaps it's above the old editor, but not by much.

Those who take the time to master vi seem very loyal to it. Perhaps this loyalty is due more to being afraid that the next editor will be as difficult to learn or that they will have wasted all that time and effort just to move on to a real editor. Anyway, many great things have been done with vi, and it is still the default editor for many implementations of UNIX. One thing you can probably count on, if you have UNIX, you have vi (makes it sound like a disease, doesn't it?).

The vi Modes

The vi editor has two modes, command and text. Command mode is entered when you start vi. A file is edited by entering the following command:

```
$ vi filename
```

where **filename** is the file to edit.

To invoke vi in read-only mode, use the **-R** modifier:

```
$ vi -R filename
```

To invoke vi at a specified line:

$ vi +$—Start at the end of the file.

$ vi +n—where **n** is the line number.

$ vi +/pattern—where **pattern** is the pattern to search for; **vi** will open at the first occurrence.

If the file exists, it is opened and you are told the number of lines and characters. If the file doesn't exist, you are notified that it is a new file and you are placed at the top of it. If you want to always know what mode you are in, some versions will support the following command:

```
:set showmode on
```

which will display the mode at the bottom of the screen.

You start in command mode when you enter **vi**. If you exit command mode into text mode, you can get back to command mode by pressing the **Escape** key. The text mode is entered by one of the following commands: **a**, **i**, **o**, **O**, **R**, and **c**. These commands have the following meanings:

a   Append text after the cursor position.

A   Append at the end of the line.

i   Insert text before the cursor position.

I   Insert at the beginning of the line.

o   Open a new line below the cursor position.

O   Open a new line above the cursor position.

R   Write over existing text, beginning with the current cursor position until **escape** is pressed.

c   Either cw (change word) or c (change sentence) beginning at the cursor position.

Remember, to get back to command mode after you press any of these keys, press the **Escape** key. There are several other commands that must be terminated with escape; these are **r**, **J**, **u**, and **U**.

r   Replace the character under the cursor with next character typed.

J   Join the next line down to the line with cursor.

u   Undo last command.

U   Undo all changes to the current line.

e   Move to the end of the current word.

^g   Show the current line number.

^v	Don't pay attention to the next character.
(	Move forward one sentence.
)	Move back one sentence.
{	Move forward one paragraph.
}	Move back one paragraph.
!! command	Insert the results of the UNIX command specified here.
:! command	Invoke the specified UNIX command.
:ab a bcd	Create the abbreviation a for phrase bcd.
:ab	Show all current abbreviations.
:map a bcd	Map commands bcd into key a.
:map	Show all currently mapped keys.
:s/old/new	Substitute the first occurrence of old for new.
:s/old/new/g	Substitute all occurrences of old for new in this line.
:1,$s/old/new/g	Substitute all occurrences of old for new.
:e file	Edit the file specified without leaving vi.
:n	Move to the next file in the list, if vi is started with a file list as input.

The vi Cursor Movement Commands

The vi commands take effect from the current cursor location. You can't move the cursor outside of the existing text. The following commands control cursor movement: **j**, **k**, **h**, **L**, **Ctrl-d**, **Ctrl-u**, **Ctrl-b**, **Ctrl-f**, and **nG**.

j	Jump down one line.
k	Kick up one line.
h	Hop one space left.

L	Leap one space back (to the right).
Ctrl-d	Move down one-half page.
Ctrl-u	Move up one-half page.
Ctrl-f	Move forward one whole page.
Ctrl-b	Move back one full page.
nG	Move to the nth line in the file.

In most implementations, with a proper terminal definition the cursor movement arrow keys may also move the cursor.

The vi Text Deletion Commands

The commands to delete text in vi are **x**, **dw**, **dd**, **d)**, and **d}**.

x	Delete the character under the cursor.
dw	Delete from the cursor to the beginning of the next word.
dd	Delete the line containing the cursor.
d)	Delete the rest of the sentence.
d}	Delete the rest of the current paragraph.

Placing an integer in front of any of the above commands will repeat the action that many times.

The vi Search Commands

To search for a specific occurrence of a string, the following commands can be used: / and **n**.

/pattern	Search down for the pattern.
pattern	Search up for the pattern.
n	Repeat the last search operation.

The vi Text Movement Commands

To move text within a file, the following commands are used: **yy**, **p**, **P**, **"cY**, and **"cP**.

yy   Yank a copy of the line and put it in the buffer.
p   Put the last yanked or deleted item here (after the cursor).
P   Put the last yanked or deleted item here (before the cursor).
"cY   Yank a copy of this line and place it in the buffer denoted by the letter c where c is a–z.
"cP   Put the last line yanked into c here after the cursor (where c is a–z).

Saving and Exiting

The vi editor has several commands that are used to save (write), exit and save, and just get out of the editor. These commands are **:w**, **:q**, **:q!** (also known as emphatic quit), **:wq**, **ZZ**, **":n, kw file2"**, **":n, kw >> file2**. Each of these commands should be preceded by two presses of the **Escape** key. Some references will tell you a single escape, but I have found that in some cases on some systems once isn't enough. Two won't hurt, and the extra insurance is worth the added keystroke.

<esc><esc>:w   Write the current text into the file.
<esc><esc>:q   Quit if no changes were made (will tell you current changes not saved otherwise).
<esc><esc>:q!   Quit (emphatic). I don't care to keep the changes, I botched them.
<esc><esc>:wq   Write out the changes and quit; I think everything worked okay (I hope).
<esc><esc>ZZ   Write out the changes and quit; I think everything worked okay (I hope).

<esc><esc>:n, kw file2	Write lines n through k to another file specified by file2.
<esc><esc>:n, kw >> file2	Append lines n through k to another file specified by file2.

Some Miscellaneous Extras

There are certain commands that can make using vi easier. They allow wrap margin setting, keeping the screen current, and showing the mode at the bottom of the screen. These commands are listed below.

<esc>:set wm = n	Set the screen wrap margin at n characters.
<esc>:set redraw	Keep the screen current (otherwise, things can get confusing).
<esc>:set showmode on	Show the current editor mode at bottom of screen (a lifesaver).
<esc>:set nonumber	Turn off line numbering.
<esc>:set number	Turn on line numbering.

A LOOK AT EX

The ex editor is even more fun than the vi editor. It is a character/line editor on an even more basic scale than vi. If all you have is the ex editor, I feel sorry for you since this is really the pits as far as editors go.

You begin an ex session by entering the following command:

```
$ ex filename
```

where **filename** is the name of the file to edit (not that you would want to with ex).

The ex Editor Modes

The ex editor has two modes, just like the vi editor, and one mode that is similar to the vi mode, known as open or visual. The two common modes are command and insert. You start out in the command mode. To reenter it, start a new line with a period (.) and press **Enter** (I told you this was primitive). The command line prompt is a colon (:).

The insert mode is entered when you enter any of these commands in the command mode: **a**, **i**, or **c**.

a   Append text at the cursor position.

i   Insert on a new line.

c   Change starting here.

The open or visual mode is entered by entering either **o** or **vi**. To get back to command mode enter **Q**.

The ex Commands

The ex commands consist of addresses (character counts, line counts) and commands. The following are used to specify addresses:

n   The nth line in the current file.

n,k   The nth through the kth lines.

. (period)   The current line.

$ The last line.

+n   Go forward n lines.

−n   Go back n lines.

$−n,$ The last n+1 lines.

/pattern   Go forward to the first occurrence of the specified pattern.

The commands that use these addresses are

na	Append after line n.
n.kc	Change lines n–k to new text.
n.kcoj	Copy lines n–k to after line j.
n.kd	Delete lines n–k.
ni	Insert before line n.
n.kmj	Move lines n–k to after line j.
n.kp	Print lines n–k.
nr filename	Read file filename and insert at line n.
s/pattern1/pattern2/	Replace pattern1 with pattern2 (first occurrence only).
u	Doesn't really use addresses, but undoes the last command.

Searching in ex

The search in ex is identical to that in vi.

```
/pattern
```

where **pattern** is the string to search for.

Using the g (global) Operator

The **g**, or global, operator is used with the **s** (substitute) command to replace either all occurrences (if specified before the **s**) or just the occurrence in the current line (fi specified after).

g/ex /s/ex /g substitutes the second string for the first in the entire text.

Saving and Exiting

All good things must come to an end. So must ex sessions. How they come to an end depends on what command you issue.

w	Write the text to the current file.
q	Quit (like vi only if no changes pending since last w).
wq	Write out changes since last w.
q!	Quit (emphatic).
n,kw file2	Write lines n–k to the file specified.
n,kw >> file2	Append lines n–k to the file specified.

OTHER EDITORS

UNIX has several other editors available, such as emacs. However, you are only guaranteed to have vi or ex. I personally prefer a modeless, full-screen, X-based editor, since to insert you place the cursor and type; to delete you backspace or cut and paste using a mouse. X-based editing is the wave of the future. It makes vi, ex, and emacs look like museum pieces (which, compared to most other editors, they are.) If you have X-Windows, use the X-based editor provided and forget the rest (I like jot, which is available on HP-UX and IRIX). Since these vary system to system, I'm not going to cover them here.

Index